The Manual of
SOCCER COACHING

By
Roy Rees

U.S.A. National Youth Team Coach
Under 17

Published by:
REEDSWAIN INC
612 Pughtown Road
Spring City, Pennsylvania 19475
1-800-331-5191

Manual of Soccer Coaching

Copyright © 1987
Second Edition 1995
by REEDSWAIN, INC.
Spring City, Pennsylvania 19475

Printed by:
Port City Press
Collingswood, New Jersey 08108

Photographs by:
Phil Stephens · Dallas, Texas
Benjamin Cohen · Dallas, Texas

Illustrations by:
Tom Lee · Houston, Texas

Cover and Art Direction by:
Kimberly Bender

A special thanks to George R. Habgood

About the Author

After a career as a professional player, Roy Rees qualified as a Football Association (England) Coach and was invited to become one of that elite band of National Staff Coaches. In this role, he became involved in the training of senior coaches in England. He also became the coach for the British Universities select team, a position he held for sixteen years and he produced some outstanding talent.

Roy also coached Skelmersdale United, which became regarded as England's premier amateur team. After winning the Football Association Amateur Cup at Wembley in 1971, he took charge of Altringham Football Club, which at the time was struggling in the Northern Premier League, Under his guidance, Altringham emerged as the foremost semi-professional team in the country, whose exploits in the Football Association Cup are well-recorded. Altringham was successful in twice winning the Football Association Trophy at Wembley Stadium in London.

His duties as a Football Association National Staff Coach also included working on behalf of the Football Association in other countries as far apart as Iceland, Sudan, Iraq, Algeria and Nigeria.

From April, 1974 until December, 1982, Roy was the Director of Physical Education at the University College of North Wales, Bangor, and his main teaching field was in 'Child Development'. His academic background, coupled with his coaching exploits, gives him the best possible experience to write a book on soccer development.

Roy was Director of the Umbro Soccer Education Division from 1982-1985 and holds the U.S. Soccer Federations 'A' and National Coaching Licenses. He is a U.S. Soccer Federation National Staff Coach in charge of 'A' License coaching courses. He has coached both the U.S. Soccer Federation Under 16 and Under 17 teams with tremendous success.

As the National Under 17 Team Coach he took the U.S.A. team to an unprecedented four consecutive World Cups, a feat not equalled by any other country. In 1992 he lead the U.S. team to the CONCACAF Gold Medal in Cuba, the only U.S. team to win a major international tournament. His teams recorded victories over World powers Brazil, Argentina, Italy, Germany and Spain and were ranked 4th in the 1993 FIFA World Rankings.

Roy is currently the Director of Coaching for the Texan's Soccer Club, the USYSA Under 16 National Champions, and winners of the prestigious Dallas Cup.

He combines his unique background and knowledge of the game in this one volume. It will surely become the bible of soccer coaching.

Preface

There are very few original thinkers among soccer coaches. I do not claim to be one of them. My coaching knowledge has been earned the hard way through working with teams and from watching, listening and learning while in the company of a select hierarchy of world famous coaches.

I am particularly indebted to Allen Wade, former Director of Coaching for the English Football Association, who not only was my tutor at Loughborough University, but also gave me the opportunity to work for several years in the Football Association (England) Coaching Schools. During this period, I was also priviledged to be invited by the Football Association to coach national teams in Iraq, Iceland and Sudan, and help in their World Cup preparations.

I have also been inspired and stimulated by the thoughts of Charles Hughes, Assistant Director of Coaching for the Football Association. Although I do not agree with everything he puts forward about the game, he has nevertheless managed to provoke my ideas so that I have been able to establish a coaching philosophy based on proven educational ideals.

Now that I am settled in the United States, I have been honored to have had the opportunity of working with Karl-Heinz Heddergott, the former Director of Coaching for the U.S. Soccer Federation, as a National Staff Coach in charge of 'A' License courses. It has been refreshing to work with Karl and to gain an insight into German coaching methods.

I have also had the opportunity, during my period of office as Director of the Umbro Soccer Education Division, to work with youth teams throughout the length and breadth of the United States. I have been extremely impressed with the dedication and commitment of the coaches of these teams who, in most instances, have no previous experience of the game. These youth coaches eagerly grasp any crumb of information on how to work with their players and teams.

My experience as the U.S.A. National Youth Team Coach (under 16 group) also suggests that there is a large number of select team coaches, working with talented players, who are anxiously seeking advice on how to further develop their teams and players.

A review of U.S. soccer literature suggests that a book on coaching youth soccer is urgently required.

I dedicate this book to those thousands of youth coaches who will ensure the prosperity of the game in the United States.

CONTENTS

LEGEND

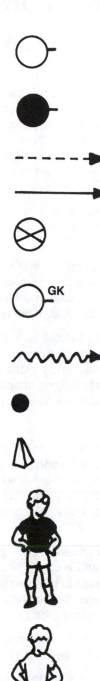

○— Defensive Player

●— Attacking Player

- - - -▶ Movement and Direction of Player

———▶ Path of the Ball

⊗ Coach

○GK GK/ Goal Keeper

∿∿∿▶ Dribbling Movement With the Ball

● A Soccer Ball

△ Cone

Attacking Player

Defensive Player

INTRODUCTION

The Game of Soccer

Soccer has been described as:

"A game played between two teams. When one team has the ball, its players try to score by dribbling it, running with it, kicking it, heading it, or passing it from one player to another without the use of arms or hands so that finally the ball is played through, past or over opposing players to score a goal. The team which does not have the ball tries to prevent shots towards the goal which it is defending by tackling for the ball, blocking shots, marking dangerous opponents, and by kicking, heading, dribbling or passing the ball away from danger areas near to goal. Only the goalkeeper in each team is allowed to control the ball with his arms or hands.

At the highest level, the game is played by eleven players in a team and there are seventeen rules which say how the game will be played. Younger players, however, learn to play the game by playing **much smaller-sided games with fewer and simpler rules.**"

From this simple description, it should be recognized that the first and most important principle in soccer is — BALL POSSESSION DETERMINES EVERYTHING. Once a team has lost the ball, its first consideration should be to regain it. This suggests that a team cannot be rigidly divided into forwards and defenders; immediately a team loses possession, all its players become defenders, while most of the team in possession become attackers.

The transition from offense to defense, and vice versa, throws up a series of unpredictable, undetermined situations to which each player must respond. His response will be based on his technical ability, his understanding of the game, his tactical knowledge, as well as his physical and psychological fitness. We can often observe a 'clash of wills' between two opposing players in which one is striving to achieve dominance over the other using abilities such as ball control and speed, and psychological qualities such as perseverance and mental toughness.

Coaching

Players learn through playing the game. In all practice or learning situations, every player should be exposed to the demands made by the game. Every player should be confronted by **enjoyable** challenges he is able to cope with. He should experience success in coping with these challenges and only then should he be exposed to more challenging and more stressful situations. Everyone can play, but not everyone is talented enough to learn advanced techniques and skills. More naturally gifted players need to be exposed to more challenging situations than the less gifted players.

The challenges facing a player in practice should be those challenges facing a player during the game. The game provides the **content** for the practice sessions and a coach should motivate his players to find adequate responses to a variety of challenges. Frequent exposure to the demands of the game will produce players who, with the coach's guidance, can find successful solutions to these problems. In this way, imaginative, creative and inventive players will be developed who play the game with flair and excitement.

But in order to set these challenges, a coach needs profound knowledge and insight into how the game is played. It is not necessary for a coach to have played at a high level, but it is necessary for him to **know the game**.

• Good coaches will be able to critically observe players' performance and assess their range of options in solving problems.

• Good coaches will challenge players individually by exposing them to match situations which include determined technical, tactical and psychological demands.

• Good coaches will be able to devise practices that will challenge their players to be creative, to make decisions and to solve problems.

• Good coaches will be able to open the eyes and minds of their players to read the game, to assess situations within a split-second and to make successful responses.

• Good coaches will understand the limitations of performance set by maturity levels and set tasks appropriate for each development stage.

• Good coaches will understand that coaching implies, not only teaching players how to play the game, but also how to educate human beings to behave themselves in provocative and stressful situations.

The Principles of Coaching

Soccer coaching, like coaching in most other team games, can be viewed as simply a matter of setting and solving problems. The coach who can set problems and also guide players towards successful solutions has an advantage. You don't need to have played pro-soccer to understand some of the simple principles that relate to soccer coaching.

These are:

1. Young players benefit most from practice involving as much contact with the ball as possible. They are inclined to be selfish. Don't worry, it's normal. Children do not understand the need for unselfishness, or for cooperation and team play, until they are about eleven or twelve years of age.

2. Children's interest is best maintained by offering them frequent, planned opportunities to play fun games in which each player will have the opportunity to pass, head, dribble and kick the ball **HIMSELF.** The larger the number of players in each tam, the fewer the opportunities to do so. THE SMALLER THE TEAMS, THE GREATER THE OPPORTUNITIES FOR INDIVIDUAL DEVELOPMENT.

3. Children under the age of 10 years should play a lot of three-a-side soccer and, at most, five-a-side. It could be argued that three-a-side is the real foundation of all soccer.

   It is not always necessary to have a designated goalkeeper but perhaps one handling player who should always be the one nearest to his own goal.

4. It is the responsibility of the coach to ensure that all his practices are understood, practiced and assessed.

5. The coach **must** evoke the imagination of players and challenge their ambitions. The coach should set standards that are just within their reach. At all times flair, imagination and individual creativity should be encouraged.

6. Young children respond to fun-related, competitively-structured game situations. They enjoy coming home first in relay races or belonging to a team that has accumulated the greatest number of points. Coaches should develop their own incentive schemes that spark the interest and imagination of players.

7. "An ounce of praise is worth a ton of blame." It is often amazing how a young player will respond to a coach if he is encouraged and his successes praised.

8. Finally, coaches must inculcate in the minds of children those qualities of fair play, honesty, integrity and fair-mindedness, which we hope they will translate to other social situations. Winning **is not** everything. It is also a valuable lesson to learn to lose. But do so with dignity.

It is much more important for a coach to consider the development of his players in terms of skill and character than it is to be concerned with meaningless winning records.

Presentation Hints for Coaches

1. Preparation: Pay attention to detail. Prepare your work thoroughly, bearing in mind the players' maturity and abilities, and the facilities and equipment at your disposal. Be prepared to adapt your plan dependent upon players' responses.

2. Warm-up: It is very important that warm-up sessions are well conducted as this is the time when the coach takes command and sets the tone. Start off as you intend to continue.

3. Action: Avoid lengthy and complicated verbal explanations. Get your players working as soon as possible.

4. Position: Select a position where you can see every player. Do not stand in the middle of the group. Observe from outside the activity.

   Players should not be asked to look into the sun at the coach; rather, the coach should face the sun.

5. Communication: Speak concisely and with authority. Do not begin to speak until all players are silent and attentive. Do not speak into a strong wind.

   If demonstrating yourself, do not speak while you are moving. A short explanation before and/or after is much better.

6. Demonstration: Only demonstrate when you are confident that you can perform well. Otherwise, choose a player who can perform efficiently. Direct players' attention to the most important points in the demonstration.

   Ask questions that will focus attention on the most important points in the demonstration: "Watch! Does he face forward or sideways?" Players then observe and answer, before dispersing to practice with the demonstration cue in mind. Question players and make them seek the solutions.

7. Involvement: Players learn by doing. Involve as many players as possible and try to ensure that each one has a specific and challenging role.

8. Development: Proceed from the simple to the difficult. Reduce the highest, most complex demands of the game to a level with which players can cope.

9. Realism: Make all practices as realistic as possible. Remember, you are coaching players and not soccer skills. Guide the players to successful responses to challenging situations.

10. Planning: The organization and planning of your practice session should be done in an orderly manner. The setting up and collection of equipment should be conducted with speed and precision. Remember to have an adequate supply of balls in order to avoid time-wasting, particularly during technical practices.

11. Reporting: After each session, produce a report on what was successful and what was unsuccessful considering your prior objectives.
    Keep a record of the progress of players and register all new ideas in your report book.

12. Evaluation: Assess your practice sessions by providing the answers to the following questions:
    Did the players improve? Did they have fun? Were they physically and psychologically challenged?

The Coaching Grid

The organization of practice sessions will be helped if you have a coaching grid to work in. A coaching grid is a playing space sub-divided into 10 yards X 10 yards squares. Ideally, the playing space should be at least 60 yards X 40 yards. One grid square (10 yards X 10 yards) provides a useful practice area for a small group of players — two, three or even four — depending upon their levels of skill. Single squares can be combined with others to form progressively larger playing areas for 2 vs. 2, 3 vs. 3, games. (Fig 1)

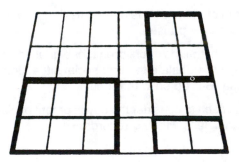

Fig. 1

CHAPTER ONE
THE DEVELOPMENT OF SOCCER SKILLS

It takes about 10-12 years to produce an accomplished soccer player. While most young players are introduced to the game about the age of six or seven years, it is unlikely that they will master many of the intricate skills requiring foot-eye coordination or fully understand the principles of play **before they are about sixteen years of age**.

The progress and development of the young player is dependent upon good coaching. If there were more good coaches there certainly would be a lot more good players. Through good coaching and practice a player learns what he can do with a soccer ball. The more a player knows he can do, the more he will try to do and the more he will succeed in doing.

Coaching is first and foremost getting players to practice, helping to bring out their skills. The only way a player can develop skills is to be taught to develop them, to make use of his natural ability by practicing in a stimulating and enjoyable environment.

In soccer, the coach cannot call the plays; rather he must prepare his players during practice to find successful solutions to the many problems that arise. **He does not provide the solution.** Instead, he should encourage his players to make decisions based on a clear understanding of the objectives of the game and the principles of play.

Coaches should also remember that age, sex and individual differences bring special requirements to soccer coaching. For instance, detailed instruction to eight year olds on overlapping or creating space for teammates can be a futile exercise and is not recommended.

Young children are not miniature adults. They are physiologically, mentally, emotionally and socially immature compared to an adult.

The chart below, adapted from the Fresno Department of Education's "Assessment of Developmental Status and Progress", presents a broad outline of the general physical and social behavior pattern of 6-16 year olds.

Age: 6 — 8 years. (Fig. 2)

Has one or two special friends. Is ambivalent about groups. Has short attention span. Requires constant motivation. Needs regular personal attention. Derives great pleasure from personal success. Inclined to be selfish. Specifies fears (injuries).

Fig. 2

Age: 8 — 10 years. (Fig. 3)

Is aggressive, independent, bossy (or timid). Highly critical of others. Winning and success become important. Helps others when needed. Is achievement — oriented. He needs objectives to strive for.

Fig. 3

Age: 10 — 12 years (Fig. 4)

Becomes intensely competitive. Has several friends. Accepts group criticism. Responsive to peer pressures. Sportsmanship becomes important. Will listen and ask pertinent questions. Time and schedules are important. Develops fine control over speed of movement. (ball control)

Age: 12 — 14 years (Fig. 5)

Fig. 4

Will invest maximum energy in skill acquisition. Listens critically for information. Has many friends (the gang age). Conforms to peer pressures. Acceleration in strength, size, musculature and energy. Tendency to awkwardness.

Fig. 5

Age: 14 — 16 years (Fig. 6)

Substantial improvement in coordination. Strives for uniqueness (reluctance to try new positions). Increased competitiveness. Speaks openly about feelings. Criticizes information (an inexperienced coach is better off working with younger players). Concerned with physique and fitness.

Fig. 6

Out of these basic profiles we can easily deduce that an eight year old, for example, is too immature to cope with the social relationships required in an 11-a-side game where he has to cooperate with 10 other players competing against eleven opponents.

Almost certainly young players under ten years of age should learn the game through playing small-sided games of between 5 and 9 a-side. The reasons are many:

1. There is more space on the field. This extra room gives players more time to make decisions.

2. Ball skills are more easily acquired, for more ball contacts are possible.

3. It is easier to observe and recognize situations of 2 versus 1 for example, than in an 11 a-side game, which tends to be crowded and chaotic. Fig. 7

4. Weakness in techniques are not hidden. An inability to head, trap, kick, dribble or tackle is soon spotted.

5. Smaller groups make for easier coaching. Corrections are more easily handled.

6. Stamina is increased. No one is out of the game.

Fig. 7

It is suggested that a "Syllabus of Soccer Training" detailed below should form the basis of player development from 6 - 19 years. On no account should a coach miss any of the developmental stages; neither should he attempt to accelerate the natural learning process by introducing concepts more appropriate for an older age group. Just as in math education where a student must learn the basics of addition, multiplication, subtraction and division before he can deal with problems in calculus, so in soccer education a player must learn the techniques of the game before he can hope to play as an accomplished team player.

SYLLABUS OF SOCCER TRAINING

A. THE AGE OF TECHNIQUE

The Development of the Individual Player

6 - 8 years — 5 - 6 a-side — **Techniques:** — Kicking, shooting, dribbling, control; G.K. — Catch and kick.

8 - 10 years — 7 - 9 a-side — **Techniques:** — heading, shielding, short passing, receiving, defending. G.K. — save, fall, throw.

Principles: — support in attack, cover in defense.

B. THE AGE OF SKILL

The Development of Combination Play

10 - 12 years — 11 a-side — **Techniques and Skills:** — long passing, interpassing, swerving, volleying, marking, tackling, communication, crossing and finishing.

Principles: — penetration in attack, delay in defense.

12 - 14 years — 11 a-side — **Techniques and Skills:** — Wall passes, spin-turns, forward runs, receiving and turning, tackling, marking and covering.

Principles: — width in attack, compactness in defense; mobility in attack, balance in defense; creativitity in attack, patience in defense.

C. THE AGE OF TACTICS

The Development of Team Play

10 - 16 years — 11 a-side — **Techniques and Skills:** — Overlaps, take-overs, creating space, set plays, lines of confrontation.

16 - 19 years — 11 a-side — Team organization, systems of play, tactics, reading the game, defensive systems, role of the sweeper, creating space for others, interchange of positions, off-side trap, set plays.

CHAPTER TWO
THE AGE OF TECHNIQUE

The Development of the Individual Player (6-10 years)

Just as in the construction industry where a superstructure cannot be erected without solid foundation, so in soccer a good player cannot be developed without satisfactory basic techniques.

Watch players aged 6-10 years in action and you will notice that they are attracted to the ball like a pin to a magnet. Everyone wants to get in on the act. (Fig. 8)

Fig. 8

Out of this simple observation and from our knowledge of physiological and personality profiles of 6-8 year olds (pp. 4-5), we can deduce that the priority techniques required at this age are:

A. Kicking (shooting, passing, crossing etc.)

B. Control

C. Dribbling

These techniques should be introduced through many 'fun games' and relay races. Team play should be reserved for 3, 4, 5 or 6-a-side games, with the coach emphasizing the use of good techniques and the basic principles of support.

KICKING

Fig. 9

It is vital that young players learn to kick the ball with power and accuracy with either foot. The more skilled the player, the more kicks (shots, passes, clearances or crosses) will reach their target. Accuracy is required, not only when the player can kick the ball undisturbed, but also when he is moving, has to receive the ball from an awkward angle, is challenged by an opponent or is close to side or goal lines. A good kicking technique is a player's most valuable asset. He can make use of his kicking ability in almost every phase of the game. The application of heading or dribbling, for example, is much more limited, as they can only be adopted under certain conditions.

'Kicks' can be described as passes, shots, clearances and crosses. It follows that their use is determined by the given tactical situation.

The basic action of kicking is composed of the following parts:

a) The approach

b) The backswing of the kicking foot

c) The contact of foot and ball

d) The follow-through

Separation of kicking into parts is, of course, artificial, since a kick is a continuous series of movements. However, it is important to deal with the components of the basic action of kicking, since, if we are familiar with them, it is easier to observe and correct faults — a basic requirement of good coaching.

There are three basic kicks which young players should master:

I. Using the inside of the foot

II. Using the instep

III. Using the outside of the foot.

I. Kicking with the inside of the foot

The inside of the foot is frequently used in kicking. This kick is the most effective for accurate short passing, because the largest possible foot surface comes in contact with the ball. The technique can be mastered fairly quickly, as the large, flat surface of the foot makes it relatively simple to perfect.

The actual kicking surface is that part of the foot bordered by the base of the big toe, the heel bone and the inner ankle.

Whether the ball is stationary or moving on the ground, the player should approach it in a straight line identical with the direction he wants the ball to go. The approach run should only be of three to four yards.

The non-kicking foot should be placed about 10 - 12 inches to the side of the ball and slightly behind the line of it. (Fig. 10)

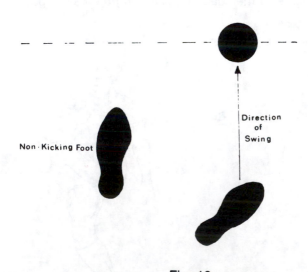

Direction
of
Swing

Non-Kicking Foot

Fig. 10

During the final approach stride the leg of the kicking foot should be turned outwards from as high as the hip. The knee should be slightly bent so that the sole of the foot is 2 - 3 inches from the ground (the center of the ball is about 5 inches from the ground). In this position, the leg should be swung slightly backwards.

The trunk is held upright and the ball is viewed out of the bottom part of the eyes. The arms are held near the body for balance.

The swing of the kicking foot starts at the hip joint and the knee and the ankle should be kept loose at the beginning of the swing. At the moment of actual contact with the ball, both the knee and the ankle joints should be tightened in order to provide a firm surface and force of impact. The swing forward should be controlled and is more of a push than a jab. By striking the ball at the mid-line or below the mid-line, the kicker can control the height of the kick. (Fig. 11)

Fig. 11

At the moment of contact with the ball, the upper part of the trunk should be inclined backwards very slightly from the hip of the non-kicking foot; this becomes more pronounced as the kicking foot follows through.

An age-old favorite supposedly designed to develop kicking (passing) is 'side-foot passing' with the ball stopped under the kicker. (Fig. 12)

NO!

THE BALL SHOULD BE SET UP IN FRONT OF THE KICKER.

Fig. 12

This practice should be avoided at all costs. It encourages players to look down which is contrary to our aim of developing awareness. It also allows opponents to read early the intent of the kicker with the result that the kick (pass) is often intercepted.

II. Kicking with the instep

The instep is the part of the foot extending from the base of the toes to the curve of the ankle; in other words, the part which is covered by the laced part of the shoe.

It is mechanically the most efficient method of kicking as the approach, the swing of the kicking foot, and the direction of the follow-through all converge in the direction of the kick.

A moving ball can usually be hit accurately with the full instep if it is moving in or from the intended direction of the kick. A ball coming from either side can only be kicked accurately by the full instep with the greatest of difficulty. For balls of this kind, the inside or outside of the foot is usually used.

The approach run to the ball is about 6 - 7 yards on a line identical with the intended direction of the ball. The first steps should be short, but the one before the kick is taken should be longer to allow ample time for taking up the correct position and for the backswing of the kicking foot.

The non-kicking foot should be placed about six inches alongside the ball and should point in the direction of the intended kick. Simultaneously, the other foot is swung backwards, again on an identical line to the intended direction of the kick.

The leg should be swing loosely from the hip. It should be bent at the knee and the foot is flung high as a result of the vigorous backswing of the thigh. The foot should be kept pointed slightly downwards.

The upper part of the body is almost upright and the eyes are kept on the ball. The arm corresponding to the non-kicking foot is swung forward, while the arm on the side of the kicking foot is behind the body to keep balance.

The forward swing is started at the hip. It pulls the thigh forward abruptly and the action of the quadriceps swings the foot forwards. Throughout the swing forward, the foot is kept down from the ankle and moves on the same plane as the ball will move after being kicked.

The knee is slightly bent at the moment of contact. If the ball is to be kept low, the knee should be bent over the ball (Fig. 13b). If the ball is to be kicked medium height or high, both knees should be behind the ball (Figs. 13a, 13c).

After the impact, the foot follows through in the direction of the ball's progress. The knee of the kicking leg straightens out and the leg swings on forward from the hip. Then the knee is slightly bent again.

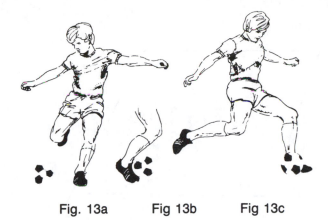

Fig. 13a   Fig 13b   Fig 13c

III. Kicking with the outside of the foot

The outside of the foot is the area bordered by the base of the small toe along the outer edge of the instep to almost the outside of the ankle.

The ball can be approached in two ways: straight on or with a slight turn. If the aim is to kick straight forward without any spin, the approach should be at a slight angle to the intended direction of flight. When the kick is taken with the right foot, the approach should be at a slight angle from the left and vice versa.

If the aim is to impart swerve on the ball, the approach run can be straight on. This approach makes it virtually impossible to turn the foot inwards far enough for the horizontal axis of the foot to be perpendicular to the direction of the kick. So the foot comes into contact with the ball slightly off-center, and the result is a swerved kick.

The approach run should be about 6 - 7 yards and the final stride should be a little longer than the others.

The non-kicking foot should be placed some 6 - 8 inches behind and to the side of the ball. The knee should be slightly bent.

When the approach is not straight-on, the distance between the ball and the non-kicking foot should be greater — 10-12 inches.

The arm of the non-kicking foot is stretched out beside the trunk or forwards, while the other is used for balance.

The leg should swing backwards as far as possible from the hip and the knee.

The swing forward starts at the hip. The foot should be turned inward as much as the ankle-joint will allow, and immediately prior to impact, the muscles and joints should be tightened. The foot should be kept down fully from the ankle and turned inwards.

After driving the ball forward, the kicking leg is straightened and swings across in front of the body from the hip. (Fig. 14)

Practices to Develop Good Kicking Techniques (6-8 years)

1. In pairs, one ball between two, two players to two grid squares. Keep the ball in your own area all the time. (Fig. 15)

Kick the ball to each other so that:

a) the ball rolls along the ground, or

b) the ball lifts off the ground, or

c) the ball spins.

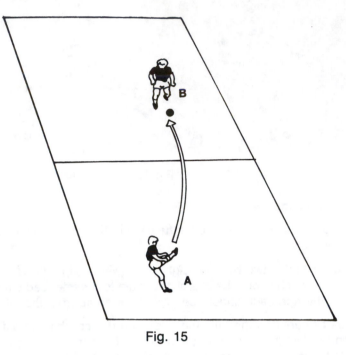

Fig. 15

Award points for the pair who first accumulate a certain number of successful kicks or the longest consecutive sequence of successful kicks.

Encourage the players to: — try kicking with inside of the foot, the instep and the outside of the foot.

The aim should be accuracy and they should concentrate on 'swinging the leg' and follow-through towards the target.

2. In pairs, one ball between two, two players stand in a grid square with one empty square between them. Kick the ball to your partner so that it doesn't touch the ground in the square which is empty. (Fig. 16)

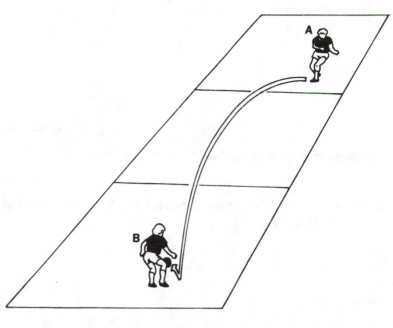

Fig. 16

Encourage: — striking the ball below the mid-line; swing through the ball towards your partner.

3. In pairs, one ball between two, two players stand in a grid square with two empty squares between them. A goal, 4 to 8 feet wide using corner flags or cones is set up on the mid-line. The player with the ball tries to shoot through the goal from any position in the end square. His partner repeats from the opposite end. (Fig. 17)

Award a point for every successful shot. The first player to accumulate ten points wins the game.

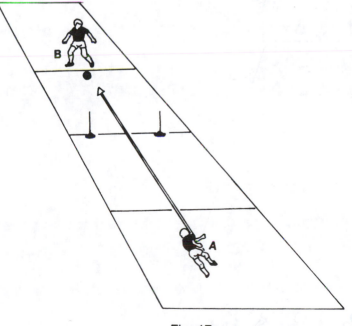

Fig. 17

Encourage: — getting up to the ball; striking with the instep; toe down.

4. In pairs, with one ball, standing outside and playing across one grid square. One player passes to his partner who must stop the ball with one touch and return the ball using a second touch only. Each player is allowed only two touches and must not enter inside the grid square. (Fig. 18)

Award a point for every ten consecutive passes.

Fig. 18

Encourage: — awareness of partner; setting up the ball in front; accuracy.

5. Working outside four squares (40 yards X 10 yards), two teams of players with a ball each try to knock down the largest number of cones. (Fig. 19)

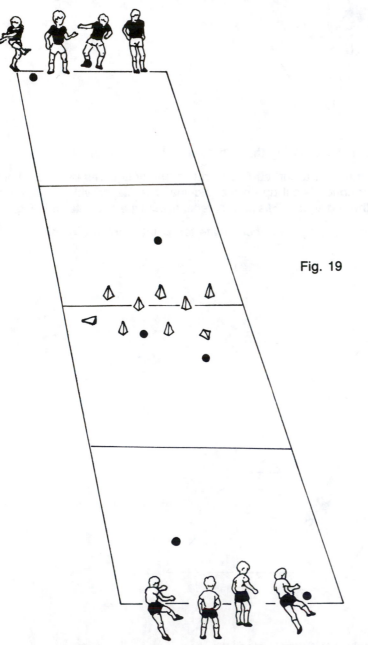

Fig. 19

Encourage: — the use of the low drive with the instep; get up to the ball; toe down.

6. Working in three grid squares (30 yards X 10 yards) with one ball between four players. Place a cone in the center of each of the end squares. Players kick the ball and try to knock down their opponents' cone. They must not guard their own cone. (Fig. 20)

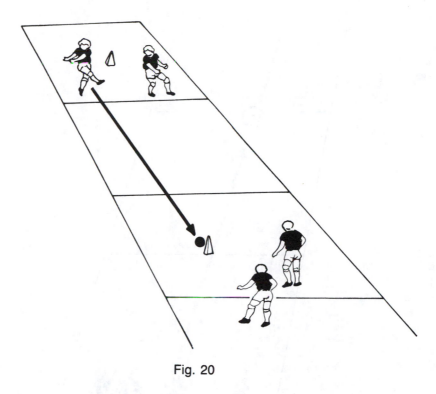

Fig. 20

Encourage the players to: — place their non-kicking foot close to the ball; swing their kicking foot through an imaginary line from the center of the ball to the center of the target cone; look at the ball at the moment of contact; keep toe down.

7. Two teams of four players with a ball each in four grid squares. From inside the end grids, the players kick their ball to try to move a heavy ball* placed on the center line into their opponents' end grid. All kicks must be taken from inside the end grid, but the players may go inside the middle grids to collect a ball. (Fig. 21)

*A medicine ball or a beach ball filled with water or a deflated basketball might be used.

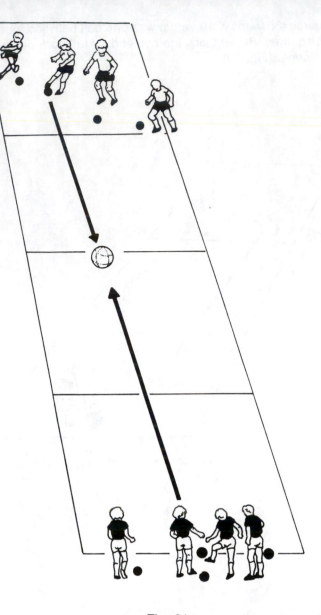

Fig. 21

Encourage: — the low drive using the instep; getting up to the ball; swing from the hips; toe down; follow-through towards the intended target; strike the ball near the mid-line.

8. Several pairs of players, with one ball between two, face each other about 20-30 yards apart down the length of a soccer field. One player kicks the ball as far as possible towards his partner who attempts to control (or stop) the ball. The partner then kicks the ball back, off the ground, from the position where the ball bounced or was controlled. The aim is to eventually drive the partner back so that the ball can be kicked over his goal line without bouncing. (Fig. 22)

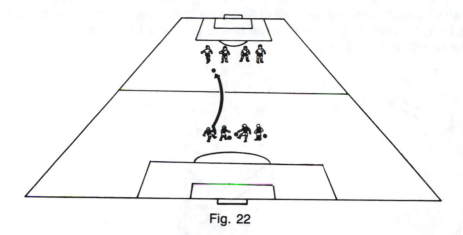

Fig. 22

Encourage: — the lofted drive; non-kicking foot to the side and behind the ball; swing from the hips; strike below the mid-line of the ball.

9. Several players standing with a ball each in their hands. Each player drops the ball in front of him and kicks it into goal in different ways — volley, half-volley, etc. — with the instep. (Fig. 23)

Fig. 23

When the players become proficient, they should move further away from the goal. Then they should practice the same kicks:

    a) while stepping forward two paces.

    b) while walking forward five paces.

    c) while running forward.

Encourage the players to: — drop the ball immediately in front of them; look down over the ball; get their kicking knee over the ball; toe down.

10. Two players facing each other at a distance of 8-10 yards, pass to each other through the legs of a third player who has his legs straddled. If an outside player fails to get the ball through the legs of the center player, he changes places with him. (Fig. 24)

Fig. 24

Encourage the players to: — 'push' the ball with the inside of the foot with 'gentle' accuracy; follow through towards the target.

11. A modified version of the above exercise, #1 pushes the ball through #2's legs to #3, then #1 and #2 change places. Meanwhile, #3 brings the ball under control and then pushes it back through #1's legs to #2, and changes places with #1, and so on. (Fig. 25)

Fig. 25

Encourage the players to: — control with one touch and pass quickly.

12. Several players form three or four columns with a captain (#1) facing each column at a distance of 6-10 yards. He pushes the ball to #2, heading the column, who returns the ball and runs along one side of the column and joins the end. Repeat with #3 and so on. The first column to return #2 to the head of the column wins the race. (Fig. 26)

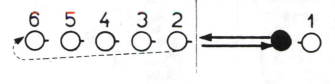

Fig. 26

Encourage the players to: — develop one-touch passing with accuracy.

13. Several players form a semi-circle, with one of them standing in the middle of the imaginary full circle. #1 starts by passing to #2, who returns the ball to him, and so on. As soon as the ball has reached the last man in the semi-circle, he does not return it, but dribbles it into the middle to replace #1, who has gone to the other end of the semi-circle. The passing goes on until #1 gets into the middle again. The team that wins is the one who gets #1 returned to the middle first. (Fig. 27)

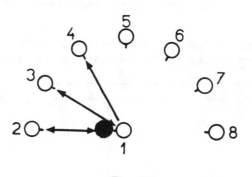

Fig. 27

Encourage the players to: — develop quick, one-touch passing using the inside of the foot.

14. Several players with a ball each move at right angles to a wall (or inclined bench). They kick the ball with the foot furthest from the wall, collect the rebound, and move on. (Fig. 28)

Fig. 28

Encourage the players to: — strike the ball low using the inside of the foot or instep.

15. A useful practice is to have a tennis ball or an indoor cloth soccer ball attached to a length of string. (Fig. 29)

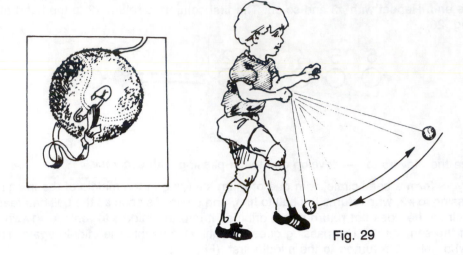

Fig. 29

This allows all the various kicks to be practiced, including volleys, half-volleys or balls on the ground.

16. Another useful practice is to hang soccer balls from the crossbar at various heights. Players can experiment with various methods of kicking and an imaginative coach can devise many fun games. (Fig. 30)

Fig. 30

17. Several players with a ball each dribble around a cone about 10 yards or so away from it. On a signal from the coach, they kick their ball to try to hit the cone. (Fig. 31)

Fig. 31

Encourage: — close control; immediate set up of the ball; get up to the ball; follow through towards the target.

18. From a cone placed about 10 yards from a wall, a player kicks the ball at the wall. He moves forward to collect the ball and dribbles it back to the starting position. Repeat several times. The player who completes the most actions in a given time is the winner. (Fig. 32)

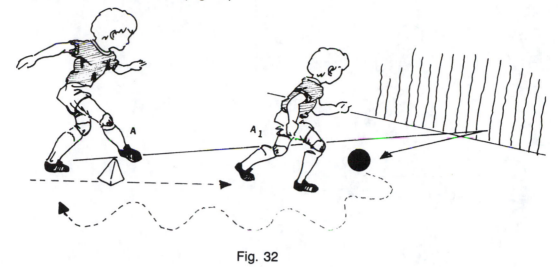

Fig. 32

Encourage: — hard, low, accurate kicks.

19. In fours, using four grid squares 40 yards X 10 yards. A rolls a ground pass into B's square. B runs forward to shoot through the goal 6 yards X 4 feet. He must do so first time without stopping the ball. Score a goal for every successful attempt. (Fig. 33)

Variation: For very weak players, allow them one controlling touch.

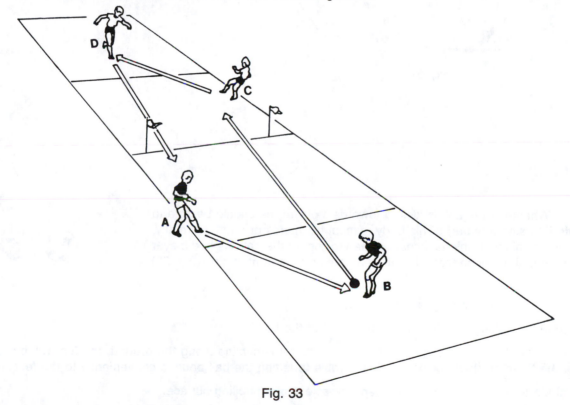

Fig. 33

Encourage the passer to: — roll the ball gently in front of B.

Encourage the shooter to: — stay deep and move forward to shoot; adjust his stride pattern so he can 'get up to the ball' with his non-kicking foot; keep his toe down; strike the ball with his laces.

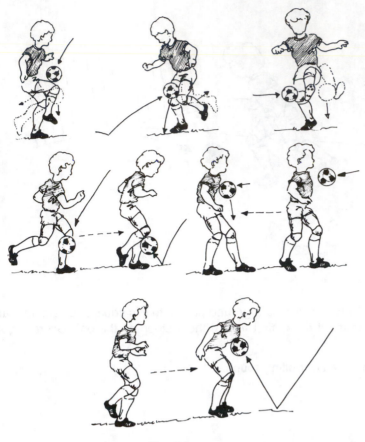

Fig. 34

Whenever the ball is kicked towards a player, he should be able to control it using any part of his body, except his hands or arms. Normally, he will use his feet, thighs, chest or head to control the ball. A good player will control the ball so that it is set up a yard or so in front of him. (Fig. 35)

Fig. 35

The requirements of good control are:

a) Move quickly into the line of the flight of the ball.

b) Select the controlling surface to be used. If it is coming along the ground, the foot will be used. If in the air, the thigh or chest (or head) is preferable to letting the ball bounce conveniently to the feet.

c) Go to meet the ball and present the selected controlling surface.

d) Be well-balanced to withstand a challenge, and withdraw the selected surface on contact.

Practices to Develop Control

1.   Three players with one ball in one grid square. Remaining within the square and keeping the ball inside the square all the time, practice:

a) continuous ground passing in one direction using two touches — one to control the ball, the second to kick it.

b) as above but change the direction of the passing flow and use the other foot.

c) as above but pass freely within the square and interchange position. (Fig. 36)

Fig. 36

2. Goals — 3 feet wide. Players on either side of goals, ten yards apart. Objective: To score 5 goals. Score by passing the ball through the goal to your partner. The ball is controlled, then passed back. (Fig. 37)

    Variations: Lengthen the distance; use alternate feet; pass without stopping the ball; pass from different angles.

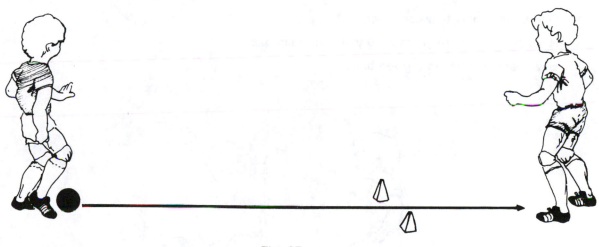

Fig. 37

    Encourage the players to: — get into the line of flight; offer a soft, controlling surface with either foot, in front of them; kick through the middle of the ball towards the intended target.

3. Players from all four sides outside a 5 yd. square serve the ball to a player in the center of the grid. This player must control the ball in the grid with one touch to score a point. After the ball is controlled, it is passed quickly back, then another ball comes from another direction. (Fig. 38)

Fig. 38

Encourage the receiver to: — get quickly into line of flight; be on balance ready to receive the ball; choose the appropriate controlling surface — foot, thigh, chest or head; withdraw the controlling surface just prior to contact; ensure the ball would come to rest no more than 3 yards away from him.

4.   Several pairs with one ball between two. The players try to keep the ball off the ground using their feet only, allowing maximum of two bounces between touches. Score a point for 10 consecutive, alternate touches. (Fig. 39)

Variations:

1.   One bounce only between touch.

2.   Restrict space to 10 yards X 10 yards for each pair.

3.   How many touches in a given time.

Fig. 39

Encourage the players to: — get into position early; lift the ball up in front of them using the instep as a platform; use the arms to balance.

5. Two players in a grid square with one ball. Free passing around the square but keep the ball in the air. The ball may not bounce more than twice before being played by the next player. Later allow one bounce only. (Fig. 40)

Fig. 40

Any part of the body, other than the hand or arm, can be used to pass the ball. Encourage the players to use different parts of their bodies as 'platforms' on which the ball is gently lifted.

Award points for the team which scores the highest number of consecutive passes.

6. In two grid squares, 6 players play 5 vs. 1 (or 4 vs. 2) Volley and Catch. Volley the ball from your hands so that it can be caught by one of your teammates before it bounces. The defender(s) try to intercept the ball. (Fig. 41)

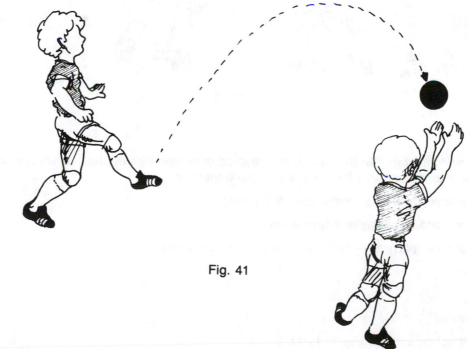

Fig. 41

7. In threes with one ball in three grid squares. Player A rolls the ball underhand along the ground to Player B who controls and turns in one movement to shoot at goal. C acts as a goalkeeper and the sequence can be reversed. (Fig. 42)

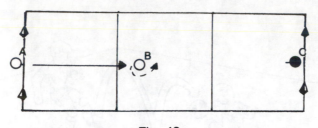

Fig. 42

Player B should attempt to experiment with methods of turning. The simplest and most obvious is to allow the ball to run through his legs or past him so that he could pivot and shoot.

This action is only possible, though, if the ball is moving towards him at a suitable speed. If it is moving too quickly, then he must take the pace off the ball by controlling it on the turn.

One suggested method is to offer the inside of one foot towards the ball and on contact withdraw the foot and pivot round at the same time. The objective being to set the ball up a yard or so in front of the player on the goal side. (Fig. 43)

Fig. 43

It should be remembered that this is only one method of turning with the ball. There are several; and each player should experiment until he finds one or more that suits him.

Practices To Improve Dribbling Technique (6-8 years)

The key factors in good dribbling techniques are:

1. Awareness of other players — both teammates and opposition.

2. Close Control.

3. Balance

4. Change of speed

5. Change of direction and the use of fakes.

All practices designed to develop 'dribbling' should include one or more of these key factors. If a practice develops habits that are contrary to the above, then it should **be eliminated from the program.**

An age-old favorite supposedly designed to develop dribbling is 'Dribbling throughCones'. **This practice should be avoided at all costs.** It encourages players to dribble with their heads down, which is contrary to the aim of developing awareness. (Fig. 44)

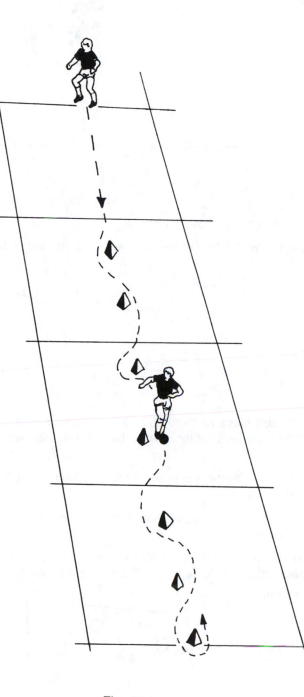

Fig. 44

1. In pairs, one ball between two, two players to two grid squares. Keep the ball in your own area all the time. Dribble the ball anywhere within the two grids, trying to prevent your partner from taking it away from you.

    a) How many times can you touch the ball with either foot before he takes it away from you?

    b) How long can you keep the ball by dribbling it with the same foot all the time?

    c) Running with the ball within your two grid squares, while your partner rests, how many different ways can you find of changing direction and stopping the ball? (Fig. 45)

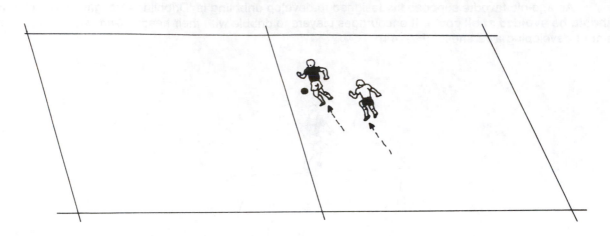

Fig. 45

Encourage: — awareness; close control.

2. Several pairs of players with one ball between two in a 10 yard X 10 yard grid.

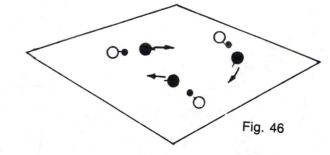

Fig. 46

The player without the ball leads and moves into the biggest space. The dribbler tries to stay close to him. On the command "Stop!", if the dribbler is within two yards of his partner, a point is scored. If not, the partner gets the point. (Fig. 46)

As a variation, the player without the ball should run backwards, or hop on one leg to prevent sprinting, as it is easier to run without the ball.

Encourage the dribbler to: — keep close control; keep his head up to watch his partner; look at the ball out of the bottom part of his eyes.

3. Three players, each with a ball. The remainder of the team has to avoid being hit by a ball kicked at close range. Tag only counts from the knee down. Players count their tags at the end of two minutes. (Fig. 47)

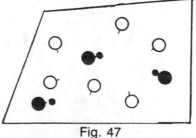

Fig. 47

Encourage the players to: — keep close control; keep their heads up; play the ball just in front of them; develop fakes and deceptions.

4. Four players with a ball each in one corner of a 10 yard X 10 yard grid. These four players dribble and try to tag the dodgers by kicking the ball to hit them below knee height from close range.

    Tagged players go to the base of the dribbler. The winner is the dribbler who has the most tagged players at his base after two minutes. Keep the balls in the grid. If a ball goes out, a player who has been tagged may return. (Fig. 48)

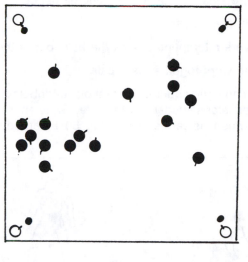

Fig. 48

Encourage the dribblers to: — keep close control; keep their heads up; play the ball just ahead of them; develop fakes and deceptions; develop changes of direction and speed.

5. Two players with one ball in one grid square. The player with the ball starts in one corner, with his partner in the middle of the square, and tries to dribble the ball to place his foot on the ball in any of the other three corners. (Fig. 49)

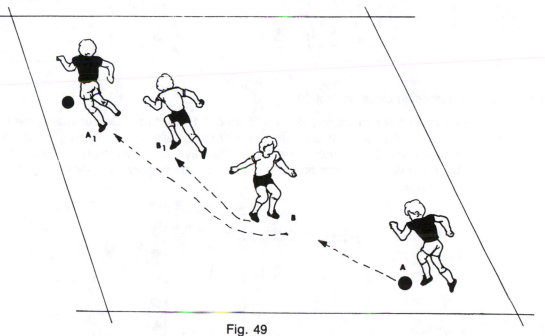

Fig. 49

Award the dribbler one point everytime he succeeds in getting into either of the adjacent corners with an additional bonus point if he gets into the furthest square. Rotate the players after five attempts.

Encourage: — the use of fakes and feints; change of direction.

30

6. One ball between two, several pairs in four grid squares. The player with the ball dribbles freely, keeping inside the four grid squares, while his partner follows behind (shadows) as closely as he can. The player with the ball uses changes of speed and direction to lose his shadow.

On a signal from the coach, the dribbling player puts his foot on the ball to stop it and leaves it for his shadow. The positions are now reversed and the practice continues.

Encourage: — close control; changes of speed and direction.

7. Several players with a ball, each dribble around in one grid square. One player without a ball tries to kick all the balls out of the square without making body contact with any dribbler.

Award points to the player who retains his ball for the longest period of time.

Encourage: — shielding the ball; awareness.

8. As above (7), but have two players attempting to kick the balls out of the grid square.

Encourage: — the two players to work together as a pair.

9. In pairs, one ball between two, in one grid square. The first player dribbles freely anywhere inside the square. His partner, whenever he chooses, stops suddenly with his feet wide apart. The player with the ball is allowed three touches to pass the ball between his partner's feet. (Fig. 50) Later reduce the number of touches allowed.

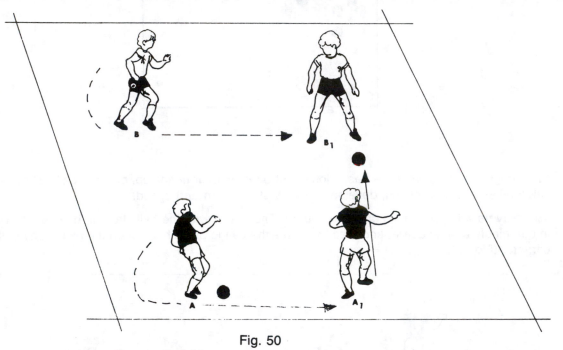

Fig. 50

Encourage: — awareness; close control.

10. Several players with a ball each stand outside a 10 yard X 10 yard grid. On command, they must play the ball forward so that they can control it and turn just over the 5 yard line of the grid to dribble back to their place. They are only allowed ONE touch of the ball on the way out. They then repeat over the 10 yard line. The first player back to his starting position with his foot on the ball wins the race. (Fig. 51)

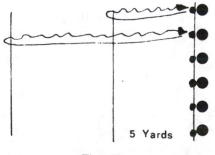

5 Yards

Fig. 51

Encourage the player to: — develop a touch on the ball appropriate to his running speed; make a relaxed, controlled strike of the ball at a point mid-way up the ball.

11. Two teams of players with a ball each stand facing each other. On the signal, all players dribble forward to cross over their opponents' end line, turn, and dribble back to the start line. The winning team will be the one that gets all its players 'home' first. Each player must end with his foot on the ball on his starting line. (Fig. 52)

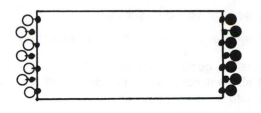

Fig. 52

Encourage the players to: — start slowly, look for a gap and accelerate forward; keep close control and be aware of opposing team closing in on them.

12. Several players with a ball each stand just outside a grid 20 yards X 10 yards. One player without a ball stands in the center of the grid. On the command, all the players with a ball dribble it, within the grid, to take it 'home' over the far end line. The player without the ball tries to kick as many balls as he can out of the grid over the side-lines. If a player 'loses' his ball, he is eliminated. Then reverse from the opposite end. (Fig. 53)

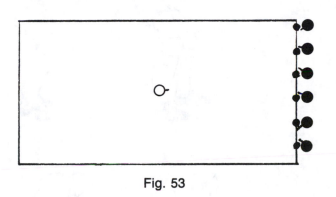

Fig. 53

Encourage the dribblers to: — keep close control; accelerate through any gaps; develop fakes and change of speed and direction.

Encourage the defender to: — take a boxer's stance.

The Development of Goalkeeping Technique (6-8 years)

The goalkeeper must develop a unique set of techniques quite different from those of outfield players, as he is the only player allowed to use his hands. He needs courage, agility and a safe pair of hands.

The golden rule of goalkeeping for young players is:

Get your body behind the ball (whenever possible) and pull it in securely to your chest as you catch it.

When saving chest high shots, the goalkeeper should get behind the line of flight of the ball and lean slightly forward so that the force of the shot will not push him backward off balance. He should reach out for the ball with both hands and pull it firmly into his chest. (Fig. 54)

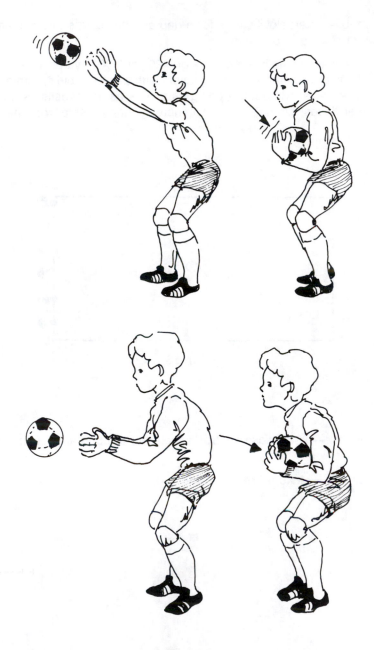

Fig. 54

On gathering ground shots, he should position himself with one knee on the ground, the other pointing slightly across the path of the ball, so that the hands are backed up by the legs. The goalkeeper should ensure that no gap is left between the legs through which the ball could squeeze through if mishandled. (Fig. 55)

The hands should reach out for the ball so that the ball can roll up the forearms to be clasped into the chest. If challenged by an opponent, the goalkeeper should roll onto his side and avoid going backwards over the line into goal.

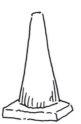

Fig. 55

Some Practices to Improve Goalkeeping Technique (6-8 years)

1. Several goalkeepers, in pairs, on their knees facing each other about 6 - 8 yards apart. One rolls the ball gently, slightly wide, so that the other has to make a small, safe dive.

    Encourage the goalkeepers to: — fall on their sides; keep their eyes on the ball; get their hands behind the ball.

2. Several goalkeepers, in pairs, crouching facing each other about 6 - 8 yards apart. One rolls the ball gently, slightly wide, so that the other has to fall sideways to make a safe dive.

    Encourage the goalkeepers to: — keep their chest towards the ball; keep their eyes on the ball; fall on their sides.

3. Two goalkeepers in one grid square with goals 4 yards wide. Roll the balls at one another. Score a point if:

    1. Goal is scored.

    2. Ball is fumbled. (Fig. 56)

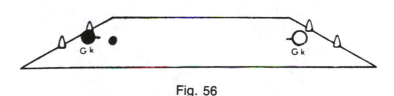

Fig. 56

Encourage the goalkeepers to: — get behind the line of the ball; make sure both hands are together and behind the ball.

4. Several pairs of players with a ball each stand facing each other about 5 yards apart. Simultaneously they throw the balls into the air, then move to catch their partner's ball. The distance between the players can gradually be increased.

Fig. 57

Encourage the goalkeeper to: — choose a direct route to the ball through the crowded group of players; catch the ball while his feet are off the ground; make the letter 'W' with his hands and get them behind the ball. (Fig. 57)

5. Two players in one grid area pass or dribble the ball. A third player — the goalkeeper — tries to win the ball by diving on it or knocking it out of the grid area. (Fig. 58)

Fig. 58

Encourage the goalkeeper to: — narrow the angles; 'spread' himself; get back onto his feet quickly.

Practices to Improve Kicking (8-10 years)

1. In fours, using four grid squares (40 yards X 10 yards) and from outside the grid. Player A rolls a ground pass into Player B's square. Player B runs forward to shoot through the goal 8 - 10 feet wide (use corner flags or cones). He must do so in no more than two touches, one to control and one to shoot. He may shoot first time if he wishes. The sequence is repeated by Player C and D from the other end. (Fig. 59)

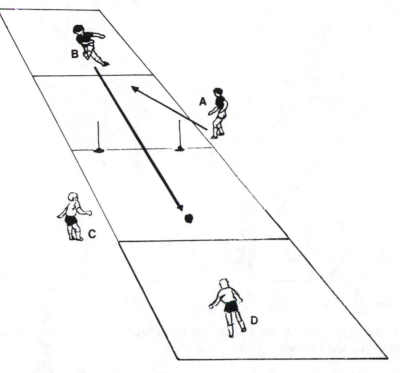

Fig. 59

Encourage the kicker to: — get up to the ball; keep his toe down; swing through the ball towards the target.

2. In pairs working across and outside one square, Player A passes to Player B and then moves to a new position along the line. Player B in two (or one) touches, tries to play a ground pass to A's feet. (Fig. 60)

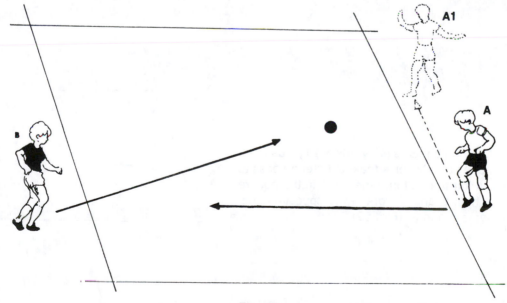

Fig. 60

Remember that the ball should be set up on the first touch. As soon as Player B has anticipated the line of A's pass, he should glance up to note A's new position.

Encourage: — awareness of partner; accuracy of pass; follow through towards partner.

3. Working in four squares (40 yards X 10 yards) in groups of three with one ball. Player A stands outside the area and takes a throw-in so that the ball bounces in B's square. B must control the ball on the first bounce or in the air, taking no more than two touches, and shoot accurately through the goal. C can repeat from the other end. A can serve for both players. (Fig. 61)

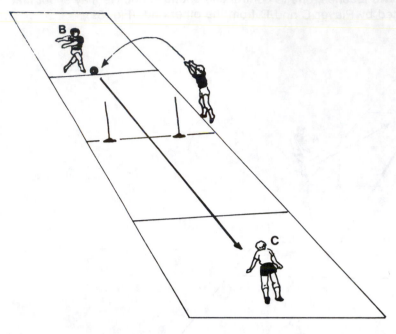

Fig. 61

Encourage the kicker to: — set up the ball on his first touch; to go for accuracy first, then power; keep his toe down.

4. Working in four grid squares (40 yards X 10 yards), four players with one ball. Player A makes a ground pass to B who tries to loft the ball into the hoop in the square furthest from him. C and D work in the opposite direction in the same manner. (Fig. 62)

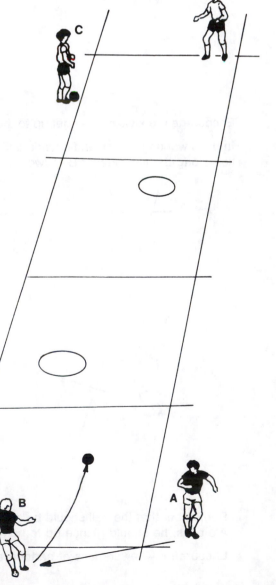

Fig. 62

37

Encourage the players to: — position themselves 'side on' to the target hoop. They should focus their eyes on the contact point on the ball and NOT at the target; swing the kicking leg from the hip; strike the ball below the mid-line.

5. Working in three grid squares (30 yards X 10 yards) with one ball. Starting in the center square, Player A makes a ground pass to Player B in the end square.

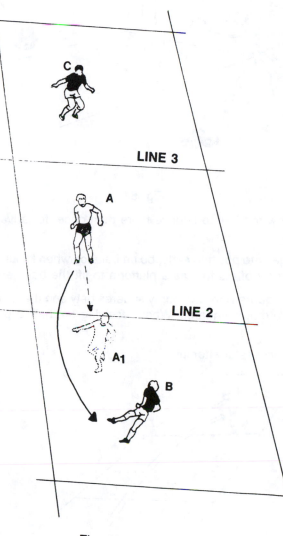

Fig. 63

When the ball crosses line 2, Player A may move forward to try to block B's attempt to loft the ball over his head to C in the furthest square. The practice is then repeated, A passing to C from behind line 3. (Fig. 63)

Encourage the kicker to: — adjust his position as the ball rolls towards him so that a first-time lofted kick is possible.

6. Several players with a ball each stand outside a line 5 yards from a wall on which is marked a line 1 yard high. Each player tries to keep the ball in play by continuously kicking it against the wall above the 1 yard line and allowing it to bounce once only. No player may play the ball inside the 5 yard line. (Fig. 64)

Score: 1 point for 5 consecutive kicks.
2 points for 10 consecutive kicks, etc.

Fig. 64

Variation: For beginners, allow the ball to bounce more than once; for advanced players, ask them to play it on the volley.

Encourage the kicker to: — get into position early; be on balance when kicking the ball; use his arms to maintain balance; use any large part of his foot as a platform to lift the ball gently.

7. A and B each stand in a grid square with two empty squares between them. The players kick the ball to each other so that it clears the two empty squares. When receiving the ball, a player must not leave his square to collect the pass. (Fig. 65)

Score: One point for each successful attempt.

Fig. 65

Encourage the kicker to: — swing the kicking leg from the hip; approach the ball slightly sideways-on; hit the ball with the inside line of the laces.

Encourage the receiver to: — get early into the line of flight of the ball; be on balance when receiving the ball; offer a soft surface to cushion the ball; set the ball up in front of him.

39

8. Player A rolls the ball to C who kicks it to B, clearing the shaded area. B, receiving the ball, must control it using any part of his body with no more that 2 touches inside his square. The practice continues with B rolling the ball to D and so on. (Fig. 66)

   Score 1 point for every successful kick or control.

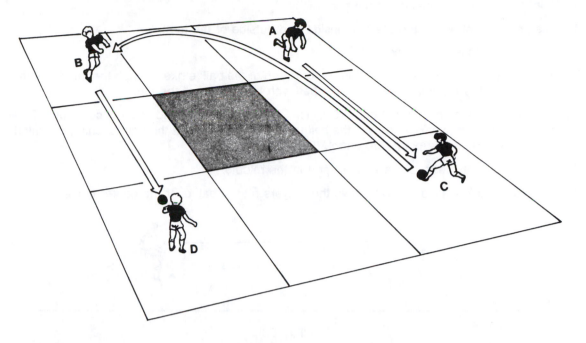

Fig. 66

Encourage the kicker to: — swing his leg gently from the hip; hit the ball below its mid-line; point the opposite arm to his kicking foot towards the intended target.

Encourage the receiver to: — get early into the receiving position; select an appropriate controlling surface; be on balance by using his arms; offer a soft withdrawing surface to the ball.

9. Mark out a goal 4 feet X 1 foot on a wall. From a distance of 5 - 10 yards, kick the ball against the goal. The objective is to hit the goal with consecutive passes. Missing requires a restart. (Fig. 67)

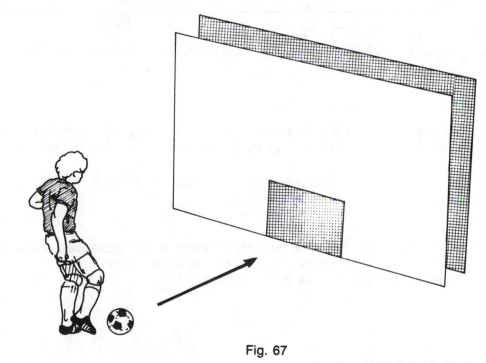

Fig. 67

Variations:

1. Increase the distance.

2. Count the number of passes in a given time.

3. Count the longest sequence of passes.

4. Pass and control with alternate feet (inside and outside of the foot).

5. One touch passes without control.

Encourage the players to: — get into the line of return of the ball; strike through the middle of the ball; swing the leg towards the intended target; hit the ball with large parts of the foot.

10. Two players with one ball in three grid areas. The players in the end grids cannot come out of their own grid. To score a point, a player has to pass the ball to a teammate without the ball touching the middle grid. The receiving player gets one point for control. (Fig. 68)

If you have good success, place another grid in the middle.

If you have a marked field for play, have the players hit the ball over the center circle.

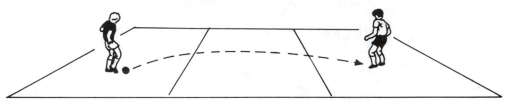

Fig. 68

Encourage the players to: — get early to the landing position and be on balance to control the ball; offer a soft surface so the ball is set up for the return pass.

11. Three players in an area 10 yards X 40 yards. The middle player moves only in the two middle grids and may try to intercept the long pass by players at either end grid. (Fig. 69)

Fig. 69

Encourage the end players to: — get early into a receiving position; offer a soft receiving surface; set the ball up for a quick pass; kick through the ball at a point below the mid-line; swing the leg from the hip.

12. Standing behind B and beyond the end line of the grid, A throws the ball to bounce in the end square. B must control the ball with one touch in that square and shoot to score through cones one yard apart. The sequence can be repeated by C and D at the other end. (Fig. 70)

41

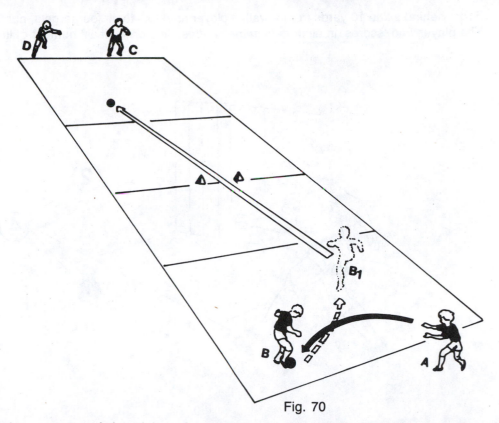

Fig. 70

Encourage the kicker to: — move early into the receiving position; be in a position sideways — on to the target; control the ball so that it would come to rest no more than 3 yards from him; swing the leg from the hip; hit the ball with the instep, toe down; get up to the ball, looking down at it at the moment of contact.

13. A and B stand in the end squares. The ball must be kicked to clear the empty squares and the left foot and right foot must be used alternately. A and B must remain in their squares all the time. Players must control the ball with one touch. (Fig. 71)

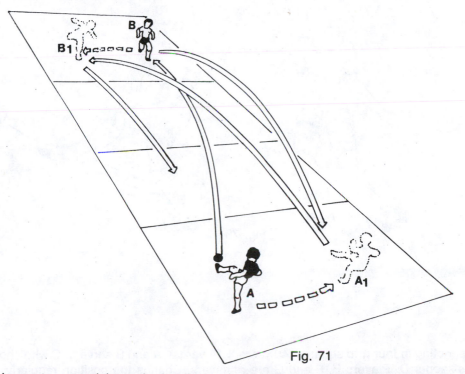

Fig. 71

Encourage the players to: — anticipate the landing area; choose an appropriate controlling surface; offer a soft receiving surface to the ball; control the ball so that it comes to rest just in front of them; strike the ball at a point below the mid-line; kick with a relaxed swing from the hip; make contact between foot and ball at a point along the inside of the laces just above the big toe; use the arms to maintain balance.

14. From behind a line 10 yards from a wall, a player attempts to hit four targets, numbered 1 — 4 in sequence. The player who 'scores' in all targets in the shortest time or the least number of kicks is the winner. (Fig. 72)

Fig. 72

Encourage: — the swing of the kicking leg from the hip; contact with the inside line of the instep; non-kicking foot pointing towards the target; use of arms for balance; follow-through towards the target; eyes on the ball. (Fig. 73)

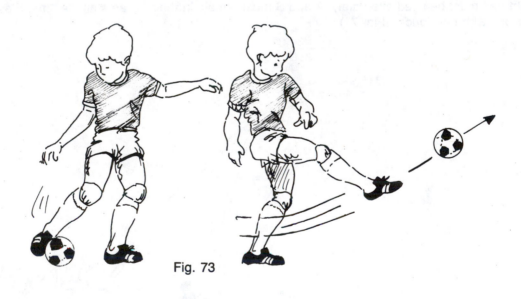

Fig. 73

15. Target shooting in four grid squares (40 yards X 10 yards). A and B serve to C who shoots first time to score past goalkeeper D. Players E, F and G are retrievers. Change the position regularly. (Fig. 74)

43

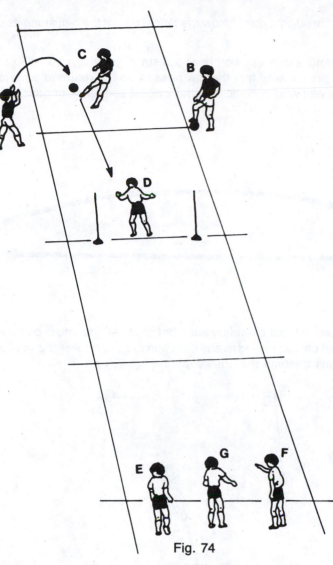

Fig. 74

Encourage: — getting up to the ball; knee over the ball; toe down.

16. In fours with one ball working in four grid squares (20 yards X 20 yards). A rolls a ground pass to B who kicks a lofted pass across to C. C controls the ball and pushes a ground pass to D who kicks a lofted pass to A and so on. (Fig. 75)

Encourage players to: — kick **through** a point below the fattest part of the ball along its vertical mid-line towards the target player.

17. Two players with one ball stand facing each other at a distance of about 10 - 15 yards. They pass the ball with the inside of the foot in such a way that the low pass of one is returned as a lob by the other. After a while, they reverse roles. The pair who accumulates the longest sequence of passes wins the game. (Fig. 76)

Fig. 76

18. 2 Vs 2 Vs 2. The game is played without boundary lines but shots at goal must be taken from inside the grid squares in front of goal. The ball can be played in any direction around or over the goal and play is continuous. The first pair to score two goals become the goalkeepers. (Fig. 77)

Fig. 77

Encourage the players to: — accept every opportunity to shoot and insist on low shots which hit the target.

Volleying

The technique of kicking the ball when it is in the air (volleying) is seldom performed as well as kicking a rolling ball. Yet it should not be neglected, as the opportunity for volleying comes frequently in a game.

There are two main types of volley kicks:

1. where the ball is dropping and is struck about knee height;

2. where the ball is bouncing and is struck about waist height.

Some practices to improve both types of volleys are:

1. Several players with a ball each face a goal at a distance of about 5 yards. Each player throws his ball about 10 feet in the air to bounce immediately in front of him. As the ball comes down from the bounce, it is volleyed into goal. (Fig. 78a)

   Players should note that the flight path of their kick will depend on which part of the swing of the foot that the ball is hit. The further in front of the body the ball is struck, the more likely it is to rise. (Fig. 78b)

Fig. 78a   Fig. 78b

2. A variation of the above practices is where players stand sideways-on to the goal. The ball should be thrown up in front of them (towards the side line) so that the players have the opportunity of falling away from the ball, thus getting their kicking legs as high as possible. (Fig. 79)

Fig. 79

46

3. Several players in two groups. The players in Group A with a ball each pass the ball square across the face of the goal for one of Group B to shoot at goal. After each shot, the player in Group B retrieves the ball and joins the end of line A. After each pass, the player in Group A joins the end of line B. (Fig. 80)

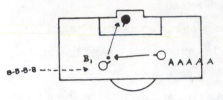

Fig. 80

Encourage the shooter to: — get up to the ball (if need be, even in front of the line of flight); point the leading shoulder towards the goal; kick slightly 'around the corner' with a full leg swing from the hip; get the arms out wide to keep balance. (Fig. 81)

Fig. 81

Practices to Improve Touch and Control (8 - 10 years)

1. In pairs, one ball between two, one player serves by hand. The other kicks it back so his partner can catch it. Ten attempts, then change. Passes must be returned accurately.

   More advanced players: "two-touch" juggle, returning with a side-foot volley. (Fig. 82)

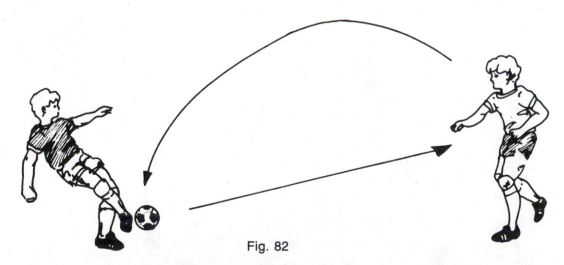

Fig. 82

Encourage the players to: — move early to the flight of the ball; be on balance when receiving the ball; offer large, firm surface to the ball.

2. Working in one grid square with one ball between four players, player A throws the ball with a two-handed under arm action to B, C and D in turn. Each player controls the ball with one touch and passes it back to A with his second touch. The players change positions until each has completed his turn as the server. The two teams compete against each other to finish first in their team starting positions. (Fig. 83)

Fig. 83

3. In pairs with one ball in one grid square. One player volleys the ball in the air to land in the square; the other player lets it bounce once or twice and then volleys it up in the air. The pair that accumulates the longest sequence of consecutive volleys wins. (Fig. 84)

Fig. 84

4. Several players, with a ball each, control the ball with either foot, thigh, chest or head, allowing the ball to bounce on the ground between each touch. Each player must use a different body surface after each bounce. The player who accumulates the longest sequence of touches wins. (Fig 85)

48

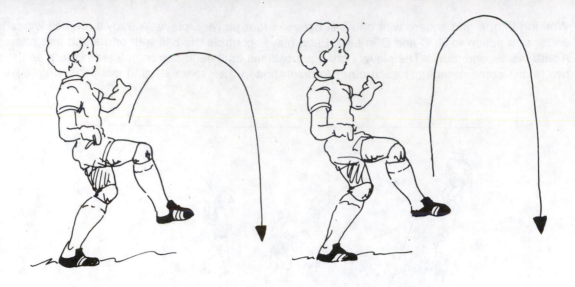

Fig. 85

5. Several players with one ball form a rough circle. They lob the ball using the instep in an attempt to keep it in the air as long as possible. The ball may bounce once only before it is played by a second player. (Fig. 86)

The team which accumulates the longest sequence wins the game.

Fig. 86

Encourage the players to: — move into the line of flight of the ball; use the arms to balance; lift the ball upwards with the 'platform' of the instep.

6. Two players with one ball in one grid square. Standing with his feet apart, A throws to B who controls the ball with one touch before it touches the ground. B must pass the ball back to A so that the ball passes cleanly between A's feet. (Fig. 87)

Fig. 87

Encourage the receiver to: — think of the controlling surface as a hard pillow which will absorb the pace of the ball.

7. In fours, or any number greater than four, throw, control, pass. A throws to B who controls with his chest, thigh, instep or head. After each player throws the ball or controls and passes it, he runs to the end of the opposite team. (Fig. 88)

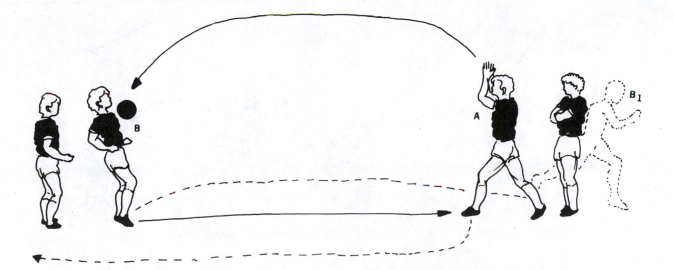

Fig. 88

8. Several pairs with one ball between two. The player with the ball drops it out of his hands, lets it bounce, then volleys it up for his partner to catch it. Score a point for every successful attempt. (Fig. 89)

Fig. 89

Encourage the player kicking the ball to: — use his instep as a platform to lift the ball.

9. In fours, A and B face C and D, standing no less than 5 yards away. C has his back to A and B, but faces D some 8-10 yards away. D throws to C using a controlled throw-in. C controls the ball and with one more touch, he must turn and pass to A or B five yards away. A and B return pass to C who controls and turns to pass the ball back to D once again using a maximum of 2 touches to do so. (Fig. 90) Score: 10 in succession.

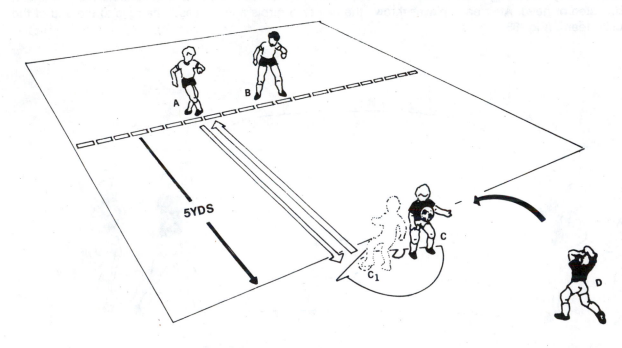

Fig. 90

More advanced players should pivot and turn with one touch in one movement.

Encourage the receiver to: — get early into position; be on balance when receiving the ball; choose an appropriate controlling surface; receive the ball slightly sideways—on to A and B; knock the ball about 2 yards diagonally behind him.

51

10. In a 10 yard grid square, A throws to B, standing not less than 5 yards away, who controls the ball before it touches the ground. Using no more touches, B must pass the ball back to A so that the ball passes cleanly between two skittles 1 yard apart. (Fig. 91)

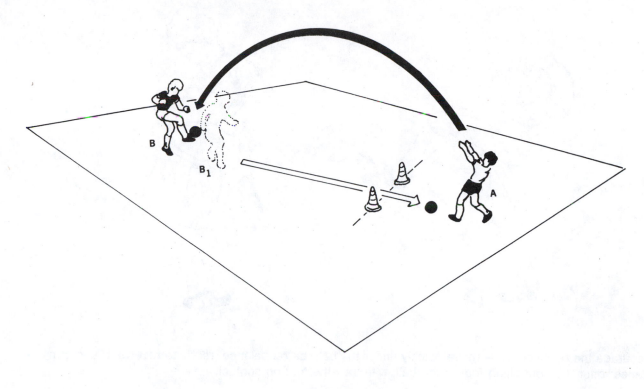

Fig. 91

Encourage the receiver to: — move quickly to the landing area; be on balance to receive the ball; choose an appropriate controlling surface; offer a soft receiving surface to the ball; set the ball up in front for a return pass.

11. In threes with one ball. Player A throws the ball underhand to Player B 6 - 8 yards away, who controls it and turns in one movement to pass to Player C a further 6 - 8 yards away. Repeat 5 - 6 times, then change positions. (Fig. 92)

Fig. 92

Encourage the receiver to: — get quickly into position; be on balance when effecting the turn; use the hips and shoulders to turn; offer a soft, withdrawing surface to the ball.

12. Several pairs with one ball between two. The player with the ball throws it high into the air and his partner tries to catch it on his instep so that the ball is set up a yard or so in front of him. (Fig. 93)

Fig. 93

Encourage the receiver to: — move quickly under the ball; be on balance, ready to receive it; use arms to balance; offer the controlling foot to the ball; withdraw the foot on contact.

Practices to Improve Dribbling Technique (8 - 10 years)

1. Two players with one ball in two grid squares. There are two target corners and when Player A takes his foot off the ball, B may begin his challenge to prevent A from getting into either of the T corners. (Fig. 94)

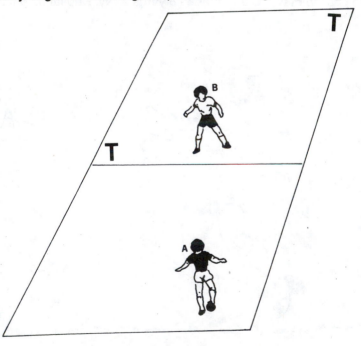

Fig. 94

Encourage the dribbler to: — pretend (feint) to attack one T corner and turn or accelerate quickly to attack the other. It is important that Player B learns to 'close down' Player A without selling himself by rushing in.

2. Two players with one ball in one grid square. Player A, with the ball, tries to turn past B to cross the line behind him. (Fig. 95)

Fig. 95

Encourage: — awareness; changes of speed and direction.

3. In two squares, one player starts in one square with the ball while his partner waits in the other square. The player with the ball tries to dribble the ball into his partner's square and over the goal line behind him. His partner tries to kick the ball over the sidelines of the grid squares. (Fig. 96)

Fig. 96

Encourage: — change of speed; change of direction.

4. Two players with one ball in one grid square. The player with the ball starts on the line and tries to dribble past his partner to place his foot on top of the ball in either of the target corners (T). (Fig. 97)

Change over after every three attempts.

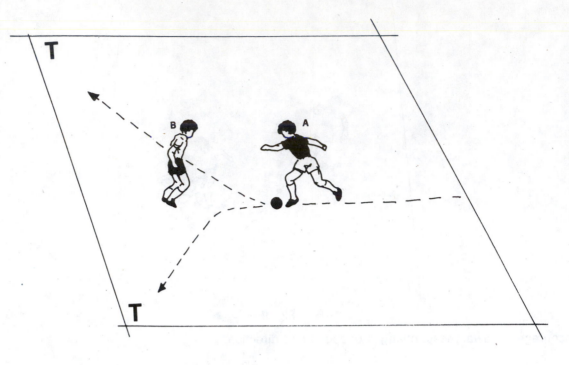

Fig. 97

Encourage: — the use of fakes and feints; change of direction.

5. Three players — one server, one attacker and one defender — with one ball in two grid squares. The server plays the ball to the attacker on the mid-line; the defender is outside the far line. As soon as the attacker touches the ball, the game is live and the defender may come in to win the ball. To score, the attacker must stop the ball in either end corner by placing his foot on top of it. (Fig. 98)

Fig. 98

Encourage the server to: — give quick, accurate service.

Encourage the attacker to: — look behind him as the ball is served; turn quickly in one movement; attack the defender by dribbling at a corner; develop fakes and feints.

Encourage the defender to: — force the attacker to go to his weaker side; adopt a boxer's stance; close down early.

6. Several players in pairs facing each other on the end line of a 20 yard X 10 yard grid with one ball between two. The player without the ball walks toward his partner who retreats by dragging the ball back with the sole of the foot. On reaching the end line, the players reverse roles and the first pair back to the start wins the race. (Fig. 99)

Fig. 99

Encourage the ball player to: — keep good balance at controlled speed; keep the ball just in front of him.

7. In pairs with one ball; the player with the ball runs with it at his feet, keeping it on the side away from his partner. If the partner overtakes him, he turns away from the partner and goes the other way, playing the ball with the other foot. The partner may steal the ball, provided there is no body contact. (Fig. 100)

Fig. 100

Encourage the dribbler to: — keep close control; be aware of his partner's position; run with the ball outside his body line; always turn away from his partner.

8. Three players with one ball in a triangular area marked by three cones, 10 yards apart. The player with the ball always plays against the other two and tries to kick the ball to knock over any of the 3 cones. (Fig. 101)

Fig. 101

Encourage the dribbler to: — attack the unguarded cone; develop fakes and disguises; keep close control; protect the ball by shielding it from the nearest challenger; develop a quick turn with acceleration.

9. Two players with one ball in one grid square. The player with the ball starts in one corner and dribbles to an agreed target, corner T. His partner starts outside a neutral corner and remains there until the dribbler moves out of his corner. The partner tries to prevent the dribbler from putting his foot on the ball when stopping it in corner T. (Fig. 102)

Fig. 102

Encourage: — close control; change of speed.

10. 1 Vs 1 game in a 10 yard X 10 yard grid. One player passes the ball to his partner. When the ball is controlled, the passer moves in to the challenge. Each player defends and attacks two corners. A goal is scored when the ball is stopped in a corner. When the ball is out of bounds, play is restarted with a pass. (Fig. 103)

Fig. 103

Encourage: — change of speed and direction; fakes.

11. Several players with a ball each dribble in the center circle. On the command of 'TURN' from the coach, they change direction and accelerate out of the turn. (Fig. 104)

Fig. 104

Variation: On the command, the players may decide to fake a turn, but then carry on in the same direction.

Encourage the players to: — get over the ball during the turn (or fake); experiment by using different parts of the foot to effect the turn (sole, inside, outside); accelerate out of the turn; step over the ball with either foot.

Practices to Improve Goalkeeping (8-10 years)

1. Three goals set up about 10 — 15 yards apart with a goalkeeper in each goal. Each goalkeeper may throw the ball into either opponent's goal. (Fig. 105)

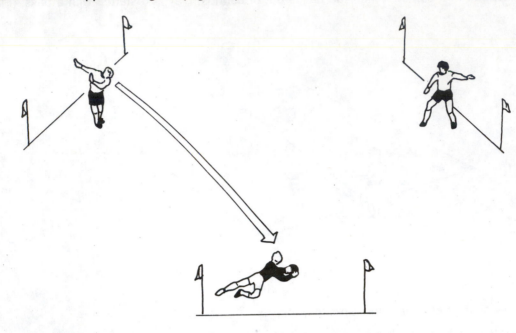

Fig. 105

Variations:

1. Goalkeepers to volley or half-volley the ball out of their hands.

2. For four goalkeepers, set up four goals in a square with each goal facing the center of the area.

Encourage the goalkeepers to: — get his angle and 'set' position right; get into the line of the flight of the ball; hold rather than parry the ball.

2. Two players against one plus goalkeeper in a space about 20 yards X 15 yards with small goals. The pair with the ball attacks the opponents' goal. The defending team plays one in goal, the other out. As soon as a goal is scored or the defenders win the ball or the ball goes out of play, the pairs reverse roles. (Fig. 106)

Fig. 106

Encourage the goalkeeper to: — communicate with his fellow defender; 'spread' himself at the feet of attackers; hold on to the ball.

3. Five players with one ball in a grid area 20 yards X 5 yards. A goal is set up across the mid-line defended by one of the players in the role of goalkeeper. The two end players either pass or head the ball to each other for a first-time shot at goal. The first pair to score a given number of goals wins the game. (Fig. 107)

Fig. 107

Encourage the goalkeeper to: — study the play in front of him and anticipate the shot; get in the ready position; where possible, get his body behind the ball; get both hands behind the ball.

4. Two goals facing each other, 10 yards apart. Goalkeepers take turns throwing the ball, trying to score in the opponent's goal. (Fig. 108)

Fig. 108

Variations:

1. One player on each sideline waiting to follow-up with a shot and score if the goalkeeper fails to hold the ball or clear it to safety.

2. A volley or half-volley from the hands but with the goals further apart.

Encourage the goalkeeper to: — adopt a good 'ready' stance; get into the line of flight and get his body behind the ball; get his hands behind the ball; fall on his side and not on his front.

5. Two goals 5 yards wide are set up 10 — 12 yards apart. From behind each goal, the player with the ball tries to score through his partner's goal. The first player to score a given number of goals wins the game. (Fig. 109)

Fig. 109

Encourage the goalkeeper to: — adopt a good balanced stance with his hands in the ready position; fall sideways so that his chest is towards the ball; get his hands behind every shot except those hit into his chest or midriff; clasp the ball tightly once he gets it.

6. Several pairs of players with a ball each stand facing each other about 5 yards apart. Simultaneously, they throw the balls into the air, then move to catch their partner's ball. The distance between players can gradually be increased.

Encourage the goalkeeper to: — choose a direct route to the ball through the crowded group of players; catch the ball while his feet are off the ground; make the letter W with his hands and get them behind the ball.

7. A goalkeeper in goal (without a net) and with two players, one in front and the other behind, 10 yards away. The two players take it in turns to throw the ball hard at the goalkeeper, aiming for the middle of the goal. (Fig. 110)

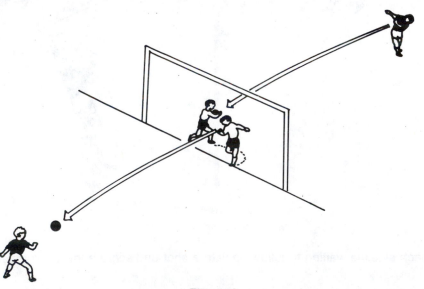

Fig. 110

Encourage the goalkeeper to: — adopt a balanced 'ready' stance; pull the ball into his tummy; get into the line of the flight of the ball.

8. A goalkeeper plus one defender versus three attackers. The attackers are not allowed into the shaded area; that belongs to the goalkeeper. Three saves = one goal. The attackers shoot to score. (Fig. 111)

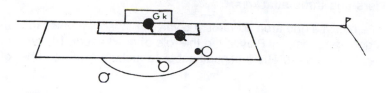

Fig. 111

Encourage the goalkeeper to: — adjust his position to guard against shots from different angles; get behind the line of the ball; try to get at least two body surfaces behind the ball for low shots; get his hands behind the ball for all shots other than those directly into the midriff or chest.

9. A server lobs a high ball into the goal area and follows it in; and the goalkeeper has to jump and catch or punch the ball. (Fig. 112)

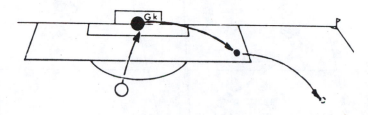

Fig. 112

It should be stressed that the ball is punched only when it cannot be caught. Punching situations occur when the goalkeeper cannot get an easy run at the ball. (Fig. 113)

Fig. 113

Award points:

3 points — Catch or punch high and wide landing outside the penalty area on the first bounce.

2 points — Punch high and wide landing outside penalty area on the second bounce.

1 point — Punch a high clear

A minus point — ball punched down.

Encourage the goalkeeper to: — get a run to the ball from a one-footed take-off; get two fists to the ball; punch the ball on a point below the mid-line to send it high and wide.

Variation:

1. Add one defender and one attacker.

2. Add two defenders and two attackers

3. Add three defenders and three attackers.

10. Three players with one ball in a grid area 30 yards X 5 yards. Player 1 dribbles forward and shoots from inside the middle area at a goal defended by Player 2 in the role of goalkeeper. Player 2 then dribbles forward and repeats against Player 3 and so on. The first goalkeeper to make a given number of 'saves' wins. (Fig. 114)

Fig. 114

Encourage the goalkeeper to: — get set for the shot; where possible, get his body behind the ball; get his hands behind the ball, except at chest and midriff heights; clasp the ball tightly.

11. In pairs, with a ball, facing a wall. The player with the ball kicks the ball high against the wall so that his partner can catch the rebound. Count the number of successful attempts. (Fig. 115)

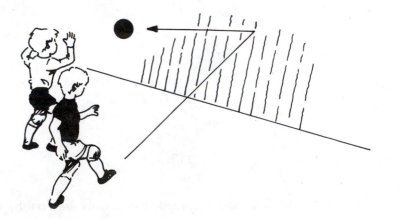

Fig. 115

Variations:

1. Set a goal 5 yards wide behind the partner. The kicker tries to get the rebound through the goal.

2. Allow high and low kicks.

3. Increase or decrease the distance between the goalkeeper and the wall.

Encourage the goalkeeper to: — get into the set position; get both hands behind the ball; fall on his side; clasp the ball tightly. (Fig. 116)

Fig. 116

12. In threes with one ball in a 20 yard X 5 yard grid. The two end players try to kick the ball to each other from behind the end lines through the goal defended by the goalkeeper. Change position after every three goals. (Fig. 117)

Fig. 117

Encourage the goalkeeper to: — study the kicker and anticipate the shot; be in the 'ready' position; get his body behind the ball (if possible); get both hands behind the ball; fall on his side.

Practices to Introduce Passing (8-10 years)

1. 3 Vs 1 in one grid square, play "Keep Ball". The three players with the ball attempt to make as many uninterrupted passes as possible before the player in the middle touches the ball or causes it to leave the grid. The player responsible for losing the ball goes into the middle. (Fig. 118)

Fig. 118

Encourage the players to: — **get into position** early to receive a pass (by forming wide triangles); on receiving the ball, **set it up** on the first touch away from the player in the middle; try to **disguise** your passing intentions.

Look at the passing opportunities of player 3 in Fig. 119 A. He cannot be seen by player 1, thus simplifying the defender's job. A pass may only be made to player 2.

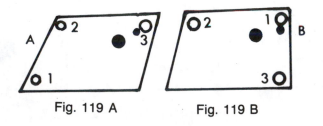

Fig. 119 A   Fig. 119 B

In Fig. 119 B, player 3 has now become an easy target for player 1. Two passing options are now open. If this is repeated over and over again, players can expect real success in game situations.

2. In threes, two players with one ball try to dribble it through a goal, 5 yards wide marked by two cones and defended by a third player. There are no boundary lines and the attacking players may dribble through the goal from either side. (Fig. 120)

Fig. 120

Encourage the defensive player to: — keep the play in front of him; force the offensive players to either pass or dribble; take up a defensive stance which allows him to retreat at speed.

Encourage the ball player to: — attack quickly; force the defender to retreat; keep the ball, the defender and his support player in view; decide whether to pass or dribble dependent on the defender's actions.

Encourage the support player to: — move alongside the ball-player where he can be seen; leave space in front of him to receive a possible pass; accelerate on to any pass.

3. 2 Vs 1 over two grid squares. A and B try to dribble or interpass past C to cross the end line in control and stop with a foot placed on top of the ball. (Fig. 121)

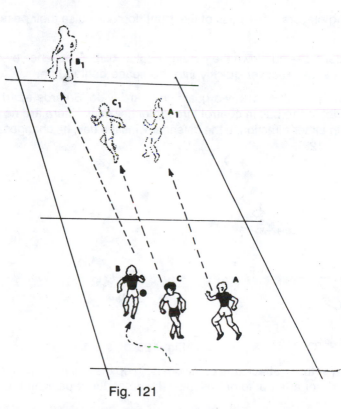

Fig. 121

Encourage A and B to: — attack the space behind C; use the full width of the grid; pass off the front foot; get into a position to receive the ball so that they can run forward with it at speed.

4. 2 Vs 1 in two grid squares. A and B must get past C and over the end line with the ball in control by using interpassing movements only. Ignore the offside rule. C must make an initial challenge for the ball in his opponents' square. (Fig. 122)

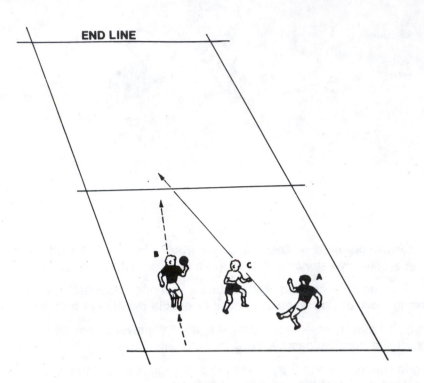

Fig. 122

Encourage the passing players to: — pass of the 'front' foot; disguise their passes; run into the space behind the defender.

Encourage the defender to: — cut down the passing angles; display patience by not lunging into tackles; adopt a stance from which he can recover quickly into the space behind him.

5. One pair of players with a ball attack two goals one yard wide, 5 yards apart, defended by a third player. The pair attempt to dribble the ball in control through either goal. There are no boundary lines and they may play through the goal in either direction. If the defender wins the ball, he changes places with the player responsible for losing it. (Fig. 123)

Fig. 123

Encourage the ball-player to: — attack one of the goals; keep the ball just ahead of him; know the exact whereabouts of his partner; either attempt to dribble past the defender or pass off the front foot; develop fakes and dummies.

Encourage the defender to: — take up a position which forces the ball player to do what he (the defender) dictates; develop fake challenges; take up a stance which allows him to go diagonally backwards at speed.

6. Three players and a goalkeeper guard a 6 yard goal and play against three other players guarding a 3 yard goal in an area 40 yards X 30 yards. (Fig. 124)

Fig. 124

Encourage the players to: — seek good passing angles whereby they get a clear line between them and the ball. (Fig. 125)

Fig. 125

7. Two teams, each split in half, facing one another, ten yards apart. Goals three feet wide. Players pass through the goal then run forward to the end of the opposite line. If a pass misses the goal then the player has to repeat. First team to finish wins the game. (Fig. 126)

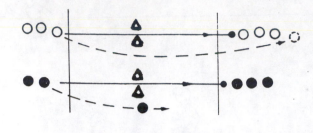

Fig. 126

Encourage the players to: — set the ball up when they receive it; kick through the middle of the ball towards the intended target.

8. Two teams five players each. Two players are at the extreme ends of each team, 25 yards apart, each with a ball. The player in the middle receives a pass, controls and returns the ball, then runs to the other end player to do the same. Player #2 and #3 then follows sequence. The post players must count the number of passes they receive in a specified period of time. (Fig. 127)

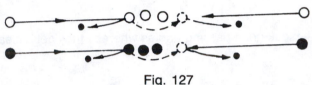

Fig. 127

Variation: One player only in the middle. Continue for only 30 seconds at a time, then switch with a post player. Or, use only left foot, or alternate feet. A good conditioner if you lengthen the distance between the post players.

Encourage all players to: — control the ball by setting it up in front of them; strive for accuracy of pass by kicking through the middle of the ball towards the intended target.

9. 2 Vs 2 in four grid squares (20 yards X 20 yards). There is no need for goalkeepers, although one player in each team can be allowed to handle the ball near his own goal. (Fig. 128)

Fig. 128

Encourage the players to: a) if your partner has the ball and can kick (pass) it forward unchallenged toward your opponent's goal, then run past opponents to meet his pass and try to score;

b) if your partner cannot pass the ball forward easily, then move into a part of the playing area where he can pass to you (if he wants to).

69

Practices to Introduce Heading (8-10 years)

1. In pairs, working in one square with one ball. One player holds the ball against his forhead, at the same time nodding the ball out of his hands towards his partner. (Fig. 130)

Fig. 129

Remember that the ball should be struck with the flat part of the forehead above the eyebrows. The player should nod through the fattest part of the ball towards his partner. (Fig. 129)

Develop this practice by asking players to adopt a lunging position with one foot forwards and the other backwards so that they can swing their bodies to add power to the nodding (heading) movement.

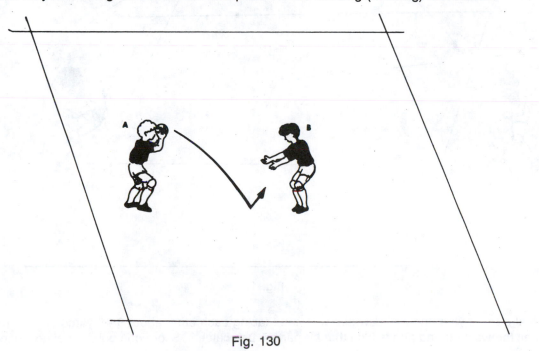

Fig. 130

2. In threes, standing about 2 yards apart in line. One player holds the ball in his hands and nods it over the middle player to the third player. The ball must pass cleanly over the second (middle) player and must be caught by the third player before it touches the ground.

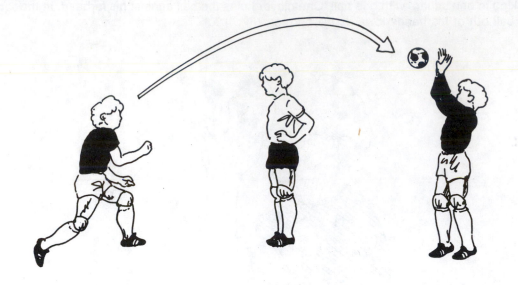

Fig. 131

3. Working outside one grid square and playing across it, two players with one ball. A throws to B who heads the ball back so that A can control it and pass it back to B within 2 touches, one to control and one to pass back. (Fig. 132)

Award a point for every five consecutive successes.

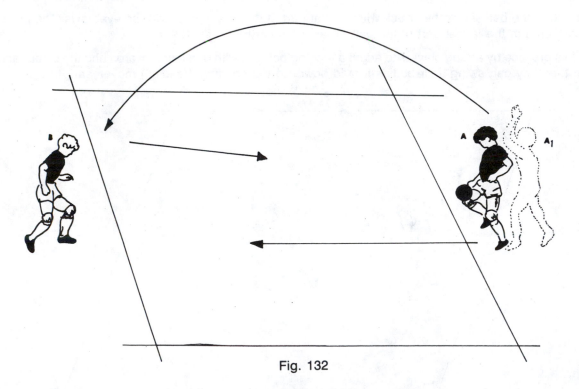

Fig. 132

4. Several players with one ball between two stand facing each other about 6 - 8 yards apart. The player with the ball throws it up and heads it so that his partner can catch it. Score one point for every successful catch. (Fig. 133)

Fig. 133

Variation: Head for distance. Partner repeats the practice from the position where he caught the ball or where it bounced.

Encourage the player to: — 'strike' the ball with his head; use his legs, trunk and neck to generate power; hit the ball with the forehead.

5. From behind a mark on the ground 3 yards from a wall, head the ball to hit the wall above the 4 feet mark. Catch the rebound before it bounces. Score 1 point for every successful attempt. (Fig. 134)

Fig. 134

Encourage the players to: — strike the ball with their forehead; hit the ball about its mid-line; use legs, trunk and neck to generate power.

6. In pairs, in a 10 yards X 10 yards grid, the goals are 6 yards wide, 2 feet high, players 8 yards apart. Players remain on their own goal-line while serving. Gentle service by hand to partner, who tries to head a goal. The serving player becomes a goalkeeper. Alternate with each attempt. Time: 3 minutes. (Fig. 135)

Fig. 135

Encourage the heading player to: — hit the ball with his head; direct it downwards by getting his head above the ball; keep his eye on the ball; strike the ball with his forehead; use his neck muscles to generate power.

7. Two players with one ball. The player with the ball throws it to his partner and runs into position to receive a headed pass from his partner. He controls the ball and shoots for goal set up in front of a wall 10 yards away. (Fig. 136)

Fig. 136

Encourage the heading player to: — move to meet the ball; direct the ball softly downwards by slightly 'sinking' at the knees on contact.

8. In pairs, play 'throw, head and catch' at a distance of 3 - 5 yards. Count the number of successful attempts. (Fig. 137)

Fig. 137

Encourage the heading player to: — meet the ball with his head; thrust his body towards the ball; hit it with his forehead with his eyes open.

9. In pairs with one ball. The goalkeeper throws the ball to his partner about 5 yards away, who tries to head back through the goal 5 yards wide. (Fig. 138)

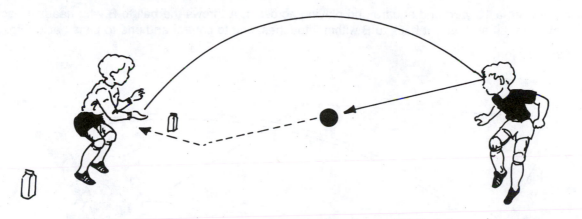

Fig. 138

Encourage the heading player to: — move to meet the ball; hit it with his forehead, with his eyes open, using his legs, trunk and neck to generate power; direct the ball downwards towards the goal line.

10. Two players with one ball stand 15 — 20 yards apart facing each other. The player with the ball throws it up and heads it as far as he can; his partner lets it bounce and marks the spot. The partner then repeats the action in the other direction. Each player tries to force his partner back over a marked line.

Fig. 139

Encourage the player to: — hit the ball with his forehead; use his legs, trunk and neck to generate power; keep his eyes on the ball; throw his arms back and his chest out at moment of impact. (Fig. 139)

11. Standing outside a 10 yard grid square and playing across it, A throws the ball to B who heads it back so that A can control it and pass it back to B within 2 touches, one to control and one to pass back. (Fig. 140)

Score: 5 in succession.

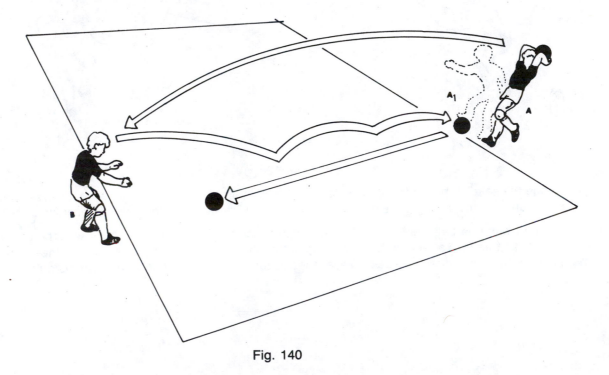

Fig. 140

Encourage the heading player to: — move to meet the ball; hit it with his head just above the eyebrows; head the ball down towards A's feet; keep his eyes on the ball throughout; use his arms to maintain a balanced position.

Practices to Introduce Defending 8-10 years)

1. A passes to B, the attacker, who tries to reach the end line behind A. As soon as B touches the ball, C comes to 'help' A, not by tackling, but by covering A. If A's defensive approach and position are correct (see page 119), it will help C to recognize where he needs to support A. (Fig. 141)

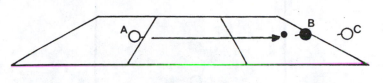

Fig. 141

Encourage A to: — move forward into a jockeying position; adopt a boxer's stance; force B to go away from his preferred route.

Encourage C to: — take direct line of recovery to support A; communicate with A once he is in a covering position.

2. 1 Vs 1 in 3 grid squares 30 yards X 10 yards. Player A with the ball starts from the end line and as soon as he enters the first square, player B moves forward from the other end line. Player B tries to kick the ball over the side lines of the middle square, while Player A tries to dribble over end line B. (Fig. 142)

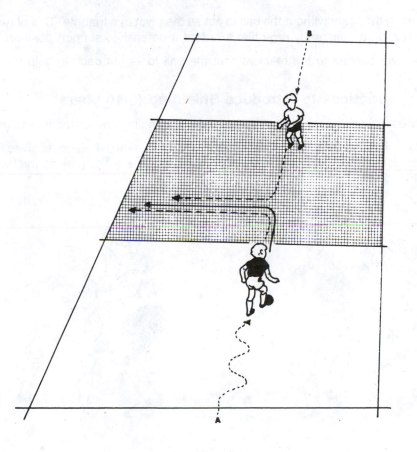

Fig. 142

Encourage the defender to: — close quickly on Player A without "selling" — he should take a challenging position on A as he is about to enter the middle square and take up a stance which allows him to move forward or back at speed (i.e. a boxer's stance); force Player A to go to his weaker side (usually this will be onto his left foot); develop fake challenges.

3. 3 Vs 3 plus goalkeepers in an area 30 yards X 20 yards. (Fig. 143)

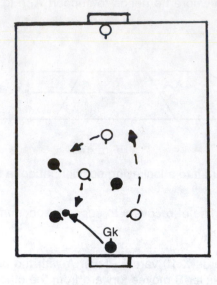

Fig. 143

Encourage one player in the team without the ball to act as the pivot in a triangle. This player should be nominated and the coach should constantly urge him to adopt a defensive, support position.

Encourage the other two players in the team without the ball to — get back to help the cover player.

Practices to Introduce Shielding (8-10 years)

Many of the practices included in the section concerned with dribbling are appropriate for improving shielding.

Probably any 1 Vs 1 situation in which the ball player is tightly marked when he receives the ball will require him to shield the ball. He does this by turning sideways-on to his opponent and playing the ball with the foot furthest away from him. (Fig. 144)

Fig. 144

If the opponent tries to challenge for the ball across the face of the ball player, the latter should hold off the challenge by making a solid base through 'sinking' at the knees and hips and using his arms to widen the screen. In no way, however, should the ball player be allowed to push the opponent away. (Fig. 145)

Fig. 145   Fig. 146

If the opponent tries to go round behind the ball player to challenge for the ball, then the ball carrier should pivot quickly to play the ball with the other foot while still keeping sideways-on to the opponent. (Fig. 146)

The Introduction of Team Play — Understanding The Game

The basic factors in a player's performance are:

1. Individual skill and technique.
2. Understanding the game.
3. Physical and psychological fitness.

These factors are inter-dependent and no player should miss an opportunity to improve himself in all three aspects of the game. In the past, coaching was largely concentrated on improving players' technique, but it is now recognized that however technically efficient a player may be, failure to apply his technique in the right situation at the correct time will render him much less effective.

The basic problem for the soccer coach is the development of understanding and skill learning. He must be able to present the 11-a-side game in such a way that all young players at all levels of ability understand the problems inherent in the game. The basis for this learning is the principles of the game, and whatever system of play or tactical consideration is used, the players in a successful team must obey these principles. The principles of the game are not new; they have certainly applied since 1925 when the present offside law was introduced, and there is no reason to suspect that they will ever change, unless there are radical changes in the laws of the game.

The first and most important principle in soccer is that ball possession determines everything. Once a team has lost the ball, its first consideration should be to regain it. This suggests that a team cannot be rigidly divided into forwards and defenders; immediately a team loses possession, all its players become defenders, while most of the team in possession become attackers. There are times, however, when a team may risk losing possession, especially if there is an opportunity to shoot a goal, and the closer the play is to the opponents' goal, the more a team is justified in taking such a risk. Conversely, the nearer the play is to a team's own goal, the fewer should be the risks taken.

As a general rule, the field of play can be divided into three areas. (Fig. 147)

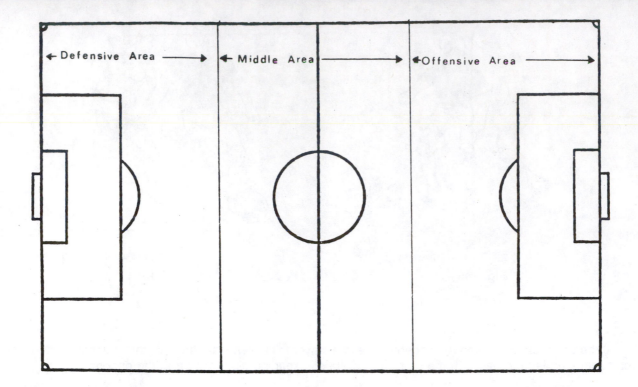

Fig. 147

The defensive area is the one in which defenders take no risks of losing ball possession, as lost possession could well result in the opposition scoring. SAFETY is the first essential of a good defender, and the player who takes risks in the defending area may well pay dearly for any mistake that he makes.

The offensive area is the one in which attacking players can feel justified in taking risks. In this area, the player who can "take on" one or two defenders will be most effective. A player with this ability will create havoc against any defensive system and his ability will be most useful in this area of the field. Similarly, a team may be justified in taking risks with long penetrative passes into this area, especially if the defenders have been drawn into square positions and there is space behind them for the forwards to run into.

This question of space behind a defense leads us to consider the area which offers attacking players the greatest opportunity of scoring. Without being too rigid, a reasonable guide for young players is that all shots from 20 yards or less present a scoring threat to the defending side, and the finer the angle of the shot, the less likely it is to score. We might then decide that an attacking player in possession in the shaded area in Fig. 148 presents a real threat to the defending side, and experience has shown that the great majority of goals are scored from within this area.

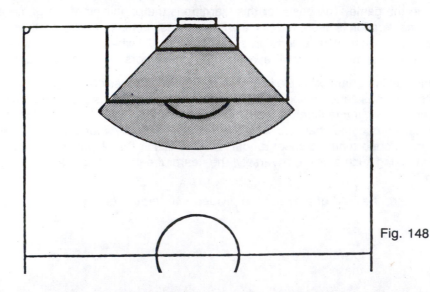

Fig. 148

Experience has also shown that a high percentage of goals originate from an attacking player collecting the ball unchallenged in the space in front of the defense (Fig. 149)

Fig. 149

Here the Black 8 has the ball and is moving towards the White goal. Sooner or later, one of the defending players must come out to challenge him and the Black 8 then has the opportunity of passing the ball into the space left unguarded, or otherwise, he may attempt to beat the challenging defender. In either case, the action taken by the Black 8 will cause the defenders considerable trouble and could well lead to a forward receiving the ball in the shaded danger area.

The importance of the space behind and in front of defending players should by and large, determine systems of play and tactics adopted by teams. Defending players should aim at preventing any forward from getting clear possession in the area in front of the opposing defense and playing it into the area behind the defenders, while attacking players should try to get the ball into the danger area to a player who can get a shot at goal. Out of these important considerations we arrive at the first two principles of the game — Support in Attack, and Cover in Defense.

Support in Attack

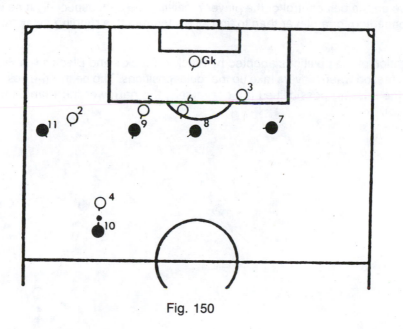

Fig. 150

In Fig. 150, the Black forwards have taken up flat positions and have thus considerably reduced the Black 10's passing possibilities. In these flat positions, the forwards are not threatening either of the danger areas, unless the Black 10 beats the White 4. In order to increase the attacking possibilities, the forwards should aim at giving SUPPORT in the positions which they have adopted.

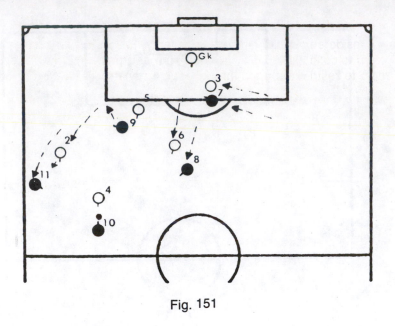

Fig. 151

In Fig. 151, both the Black 11 and the Black 8 have moved toward the Black 10. This immediately increases the Black 10's passing possibilities, for he can now pass quite easily to either of these players. The movement of the Black 11 and Black 8 also poses serious problems for the White 2 and White 6, for they must now decide whether to follow their immediate opponents and leave a space unguarded behind them, or allow the Black 11 or Black 8 to collect the ball unchallenged in the danger area in front of the defense. If they decide to follow the Black 11 or Black 8, the Black 9 and Black 7 can then move into the space left unguarded to receive a through pass from the Black 10.

This example indicates that if some players move toward the ball-player, while others move away from him, then the passing possibilities for the attacking side and the problems confronting the defending side will be increased enormously. Most young players tend to run away from the ball-player, while few move toward him. It is extremely difficult to pass accurately to a player running away and, even if the pass is accurate, considerable demands will be made on the ball control of the player receiving the ball, especially if he is being marked. There is nothing more disconcerting for a player than to find all his team-mates running away from him when he wishes to pass.

Closer examination of the positions adopted by Black 7, Black 8 and Black 11 in Fig. 152 shows that passing possibilities are increased when players take up triangular positions. The nearer the positions form an equilateral triangle, the greater the passing possibilities (a); conversely, the narrower the triangle becomes, the fewer the passing possibilities (b).

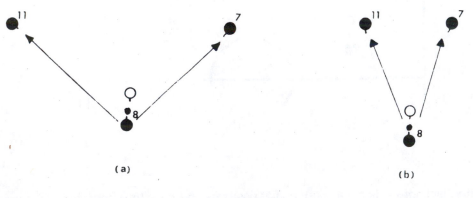

Fig. 152

Cover in Defense

Basically, the same considerations apply to cover in defense. Defenders are concerned with restricting possibilities for attacking players to collect the ball in front of them and playing it into the space behind them. The defense, therefore, attempts to restrict the gaps through which penetrative passes can be made.

In Fig. 153, the three defenders are lying square and a through pass which beats one of them beats all three. Neither are they covering one another, nor, more important still, do they cover the space behind them.

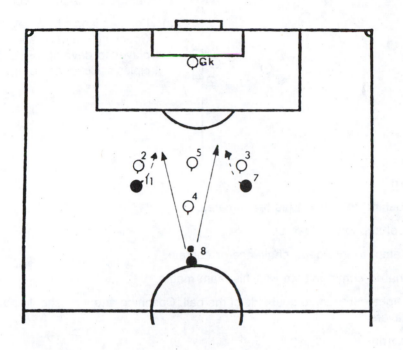

Fig. 153

In Fig. 154, the White 5 has moved back to cover the space into which the Black 8 might wish to pass the ball. The defenders' positions will allow Black 8 to pass to either Black 11 or Black 7, but defenders are not beaten by this pass.

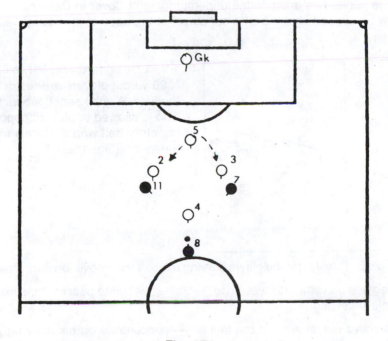

Fig. 154

Defensive structures are, therefore, similar to attacking structures in that they are basically triangular in formation. Again, the shape of the triangle is important; the flatter it is, the less the cover for the defenders, and the nearer the defenders are to their own goal, the tighter the triangular formation becomes.

Practices to Introduce Team Play (8-10 years)

The problem for any coach is how to convey the understanding of the game, implicit in the principles of Support in Attack and Cover in Defense, to his players aged 8-10 years. Obviously, this is very difficult, if not impossible, through the 11-a-side game. The prudent coach would therefore be well-advised to base his team practices on small-sided games.

1.

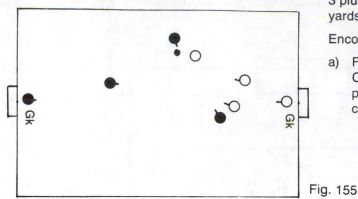

Fig. 155

3 plus goalkeeper vs 3 plus goalkeeper in a space 30 yards X 20 yards. (Fig. 155)

Encourage the team without the ball to:

a) Form a triangle by always keeping one player back. Coaching attention should be focused on this one player to develop his understanding of the principles of Cover and Delay in defense (pp. 118-121).

He should learn:

1) How close behind to support his team mates.

2) What angle of support to take up.

3) When to attempt to intercept, challenge or contain.

4) How and what to communicate with his team mates.

b) Make a tight-knit triangle goal-side of the ball. Coaching attention should now be focused on the two other players.

They should learn:

1) What to do when the ball is lost.

2) How and where to recover into defensive positions.

3) How to mark and cover after they have retreated into defensive positions.

Variation: When one player has grasped the understanding of Cover in Defense, the team of three without the ball should now be asked to have a different player at the apex of the triangle each time the ball is lost.

Other variations: 4 Vs 3, 4 Vs 4, 5 Vs 4, 5 Vs 5, etc.

2.

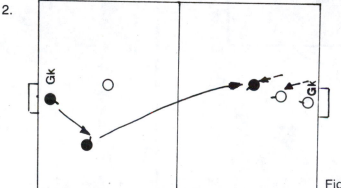

Fig. 156

1 Vs 1 plus goalkeeper in two halves of a field 40 yards X 20 yards; players are restricted to their own half of the field. A goalkeeper serves the ball to his defender who is allowed to play it unopposed to the attacker in the other half who is closely marked by the opposing defender. (Fig. 156)

Variation: 2 Vs 2, 3 Vs 3, 4 Vs 4, etc: the player serving the ball may move forward into the other half to support.

Encourage the defensive player in possession to: — deliver accurate passes; time his passes to coincide with the movement of his receiving player.

Encourage the defensive player without the ball to: — concentrate on his marking position so that he can:

1) Intercept, or

2) Challenge, or,

3) Contain.

3. Two attacking players with a ball try to beat two defenders to take the ball under control over the end line. The defenders are restricted to their own grid square. (Fig. 157)

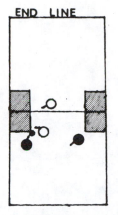

Encourage the challenging defender to: — force the play towards either corner of his grid square (shaded area). He should adopt a defensive position that restricts the attackers' possibilities to either dribble or pass.

Encourage the covering defender to: — read the play so that he meets the point of any attack in one of the shaded areas in his grid square: to communicate with his challenging defender.

Fig. 157

4. Two attacking players with a ball try to beat two defensive players to take the ball under control over the end line. As soon as the play commences, a third defensive player makes a recovery run to make a defensive unit of three players. (Fig. 158)

Encourage the offensive player to: — attack at speed; commit the nearest defender; ensure that the player without the ball is always in a good receiving position.

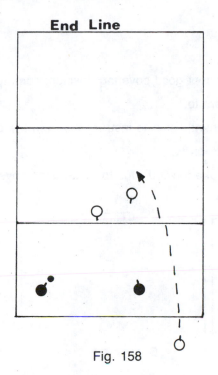

Fig. 158

Encourage the two defensive players to: — cover each other; restrict the attackers' options by retreating and containing.

Encourage the third defensive player to: — get back into a covering position by taking the shortest route; communicate with his fellow defenders; form part of a defensive triangle having retreated into a covering position.

5. Conditioned, 5-a-side games in a 40 yd. x 30 yd. area.

   1. Maximum of 3 consecutive touches on the ball by any one player. Later reduce this to 2 touches.

   2. Two passes before a shot on goal can be made.

   3. Pass must be accompanied by shout of 'man-on' or 'turn', where appropriate.

6. 3 plus GK versus 3 plus GK in an area 30 yds x 20 yds, with miniature goals. An extra player (circled in Fig. 159) always plays with the defending team.

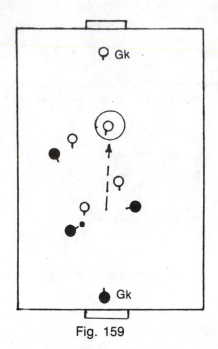

Fig. 159

Encourage the free player to:

Recover into covering position; adopt good covering position; communicate with his co-defenders.

Encourage the challenging players to:

Pressurize their immediate opponent; listen to instructions from the covering players.

Encourage the players in possession to:

Adopt good support positions; make forward runs to destroy the covering defense; take up good receiving positions.

7.

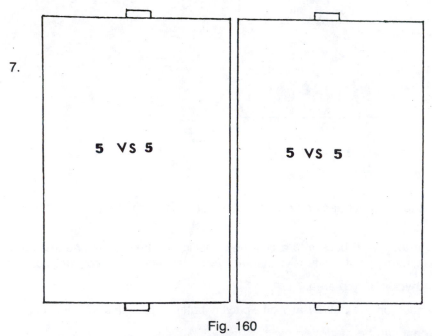

Two games of 5-a-side on adjacent areas 30 yds. x 20 yds. The coach can organize tournaments on an inter-group basis — knock out, league, round-robin etc. (Fig. 160)

Fig. 160

Almost certainly such competitions should form the basis whereby players of this age learn to understand the basic principles of team play.

The coach should encourage all players to recognize and understand the need for support in attack and cover in defense during these small-sided games.

CHAPTER THREE

THE AGE OF SKILL —
The Development of Combination Play
(10-14 years)

Practices to Improve Kicking (10-12 years)

1. Working across and outside two grid squares, two pairs of players with one ball. Player B makes a ground pass to A, who gives a controlled return ground pass. B hits a lofted pass over the two squares to C. C controls the ball and plays a short pass to D, who gives a return ground pass. C hits a lofted pass to B, who controls and so on. Change positions frequently. (Fig. 161)

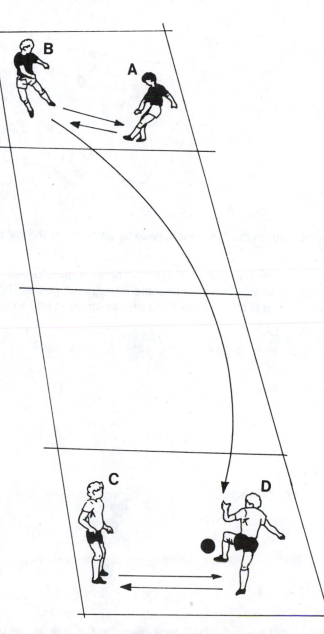

Fig. 161

Encourage: — relaxed swing of the leg from the hip; contact the ball with the inside line of the instep.

2. Working outside and through four grid squares (40 yards X 10 yards), two pairs of players with one ball. Player A, standing behind B and beyond the end line of the grid, throws the ball to bounce in the end square. B must control the ball in that square and shoot to score in 2 touches or fewer. The sequence is repeated by C and D at the other end. Award a goal for every successful attempt. (Fig. 162)

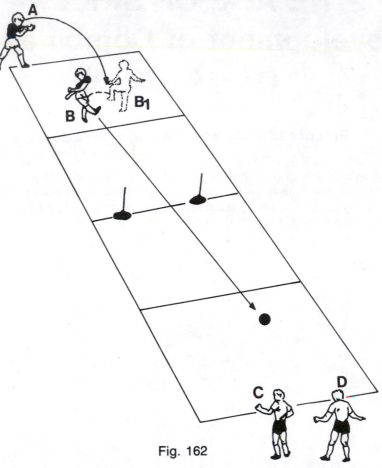

Fig. 162

Encourage: — setting the ball up on the first touch; relaxed swing from the hips; contact with the inside line of the instep.

3. Standing behind B and beyond the end line of the grid, A plays a ground pass into the end square. B runs forward into the end square and shoots first time to score through the posts. The sequence may be repeated by C and D at the other end. A and B change positions and so on. First pair to score a given number of goals wins. (Fig. 163)

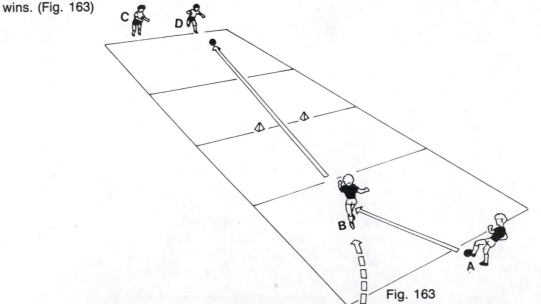

Fig. 163

Encourage the players to: — get up to the ball; look down on the ball at the point of contact; keep the toe down; swing the leg from the hip; approach the ball slightly sideways-on; use their arms to keep balance.

87

4. A server behind the goal throws several balls in rapid succession to his partner who starts from the penalty spot. He runs on to the ball to either volley or half-volley the ball into the net. Count **2** points for every volley into the net, 1 point for every half-volley into the net. (Fig. 164)

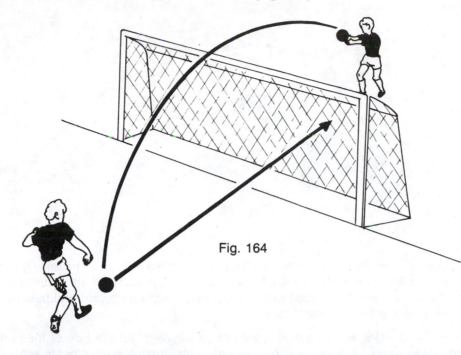

Fig. 164

Encourage the shooter to: — go for each ball; anticipate the flight of the ball and quickly get into position; keep the toe down; get as close to the ball as he can; hit the ball at the lowest part of his leg swing.

5. In threes in four grid squares 40 yards X 10 yards. Player A throws the ball so that it bounces in B's square. B takes a shot from inside the end square allowing the ball to bounce once only. A then repeats and serves to C. The first player to score 5 goals wins. Losing player changes place with A. (Fig. 165)

Fig. 165

Encourage the kicker to: — get early into position; strike the ball above the mid-line; get the knee above the ball.

6. In threes with one ball. The server throws the ball with a two-handed underarm service to the second player who either lets the ball bounce or volleys it immediately over his head for the third player to control. Count one point for every successful attempt. (Fig. 166)

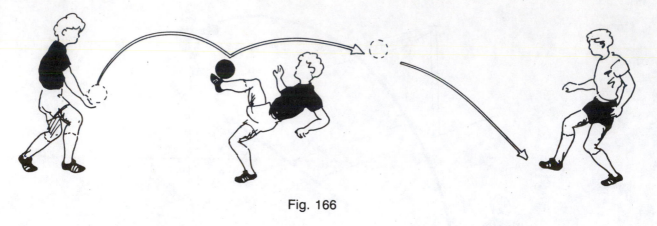

Fig. 166

Encourage the kicker to: — move early into the landing position of the ball; be on balance on one foot immediately prior to contact; strike the ball about chest height; curl his trunk and look at the ball; overbalance backwards during the kicking action; hit the ball with the full instep with an upward and backward swing of the leg; fall gently, breaking the fall with hands and arms.

7. Six players, working in 3 pairs, set up a goal (cones or corner flags) on the side of the penalty area. One pair becomes the goalkeepers while the remaining two pairs play against each other to score. When one pair scores 3 goals, the other pair goes into goal and the goalkeepers come out for the game to continue. (Fig 167) The first pair to win 5 games wins the series. Several games can be played simultaneously in a 60 yards x 40 yards area.

Fig. 167

Encourage the players to: — shoot whenever they think they can score; put accuracy before power.

8. Several players with a ball each stand about 10 — 15 yards from the goal. Throw the ball in the air towards the side lines let it bounce and volley it into goal.

   Variation: Volley it before it bounces.

   Encourage the players to: — fall away from the ball; point a shoulder towards the target; get the knee above the ball; swing the leg in a horizontal plane.

9. Several players, with one ball, form a circle about 20 yards in diameter. One player takes up a position in the center of the circle and the ball is kicked over his head to a player on the opposite side of the circle, who returns it after one bounce, to the opposite side of the circle.

   If the kick is intercepted, the center player changes places with the player who made the kick. The center player must attempt the interception from the center of the circle (Fig. 168).

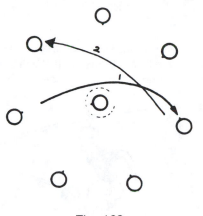

Fig. 168

Encourage the players to: — use the inside of the instep; take a relaxed swing of the kicking leg from the hip; strike the ball below the mid-line.

10. Several players form three columns to make a star formation with about 10 yards separating the head of each column. A-1 should pass the ball to B-1 and then run to the end of column B to join it. B-1 passes to C-1 and joins column C. C-1 passes the ball to A-2 and joins column A, and so on. (Fig. 169)

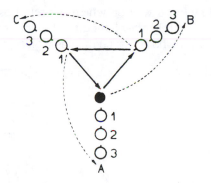

Fig. 169

Encourage the players to: — set the ball up on the first touch, pass with the second; be on balance to receive the ball; push through towards the target.

11. As above, but this time the players do not join the column to which they have passed the ball, but run to the back of the third column. (Fig. 170)

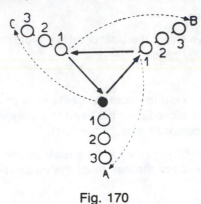

Fig. 170

12. Three players with one ball form a line with about six yards between each player. Player #2 pushes or lobs the ball to #3 and runs to change places with him. #3 passes the ball to #1 and runs to replace him. #1 passes to #2, who has already replaced #3 and runs to change places with #2, and so on. (Fig. 171)

Fig. 171

Encourage the players to: — play two touch — control and pass. When they become experienced, then low, first-time passes can be made.

As this exercise is difficult and physically demanding, frequent breaks should be introduced.

13. Two players with one ball stand facing a wall on which a circle has been drawn, at a distance of about 5 yards. They return the rebound alternately after letting the ball bounce once, counting a point for each successful ball hit into the circle. The player who first accumulates a given number of points wins the game. (Fig. 172)

Fig. 172

Encourage the players to: — move into the line of the rebound; be on balance for the kick; follow through towards the target.

14. Two corner posts are stuck into the ground 3 - 5 feet inside the goalposts. Several players take part in a penalty kick competition. Each player in rotation attempts to score in the space between either corner post and goal post. If a player misses, he is eliminated from the competition. (Fig. 173) Encourage the players to — use the instep and outside of the foot.

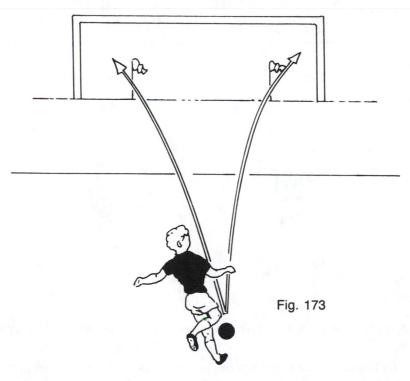

Fig. 173

15. Four players standing behind a goal throw the ball over the crossbar into the penalty area. Another four players stand facing the goal some 10 yards from the goal line; they allow the ball to bounce once, then they half-volley it into the net. As a variation, they can volley the ball either before or after the first bounce, or half-volley it at the first bounce. (Fig. 174)

Fig. 174

Encourage the players to: — anticipate the flight and bounce of the ball and quickly get into position; knee over the ball; toe down.

16. The ball is placed 20 - 25 yards from goal. Two corner flags are set up to form an imitation wall. The player has to bend the ball past the wall into the opposite corner of the net. (Fig. 175)

Fig. 175

Encourage the players to: — experiment with different methods of swerving the ball, using inside of the instep and outside of the foot.

17. One player with a ball sends a low cross into the penalty area. His partner shoots it into goal first time. At a later stage, the wide player can send over a variety of crosses while making the kick on the run. (Fig. 176)

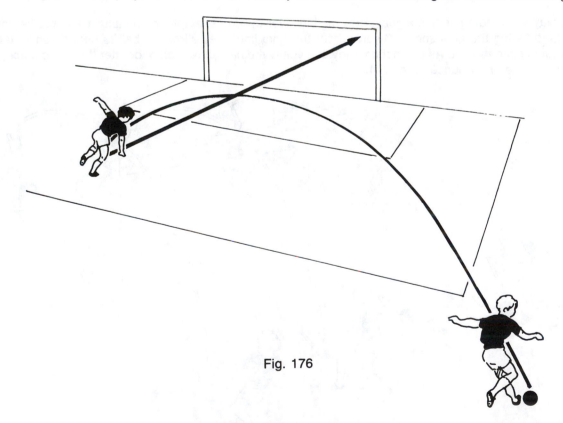

Fig. 176

Encourage the wide player to: — cross the ball in front of the shooter into a space about 10 - 12 yards from goal.

Encourage the shooter to: — anticipate the direction and height of the cross by watching the movements of the wide player; move into position early; keep his shot low.

18. A player takes up a position just outside the penalty area. His partner who is standing behind him throws or kicks the ball ahead of him. The player runs onto the ball and shoots for goal. At first, he should practice shooting a rolling ball, but later he should use half-volleys after one or two bounces, and then volleys. (Fig. 177)

Fig. 177

Encourage the shooter to: — move quickly into position; relax; strike the ball with a short backswing and follow through; keep the ball low.

19. A ball is thrown in an arc over the crossbar towards a player who is standing near the penalty line. A corner flag is placed on the 6 yard line between the player and the goal. He should try to lob the ball, kicking it as it bounces over the obstacle into goal. (Fig. 178)

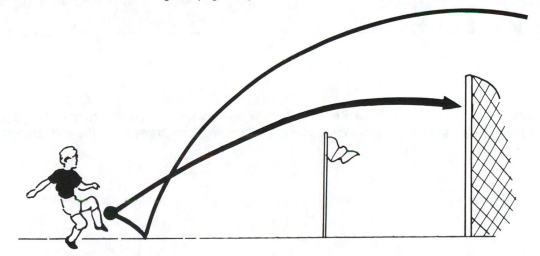

Fig. 178

20. This practice can be varied when a goalkeeper stands in the goal and, after throwing the ball in an arc, he moves forward 3 or 4 yards. The player has to lift the ball over the goalkeeper and into the net. (Fig. 179)

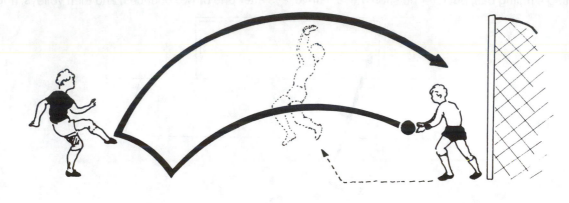

Fig. 179

Encourage the player to: — move quickly to the bounce of the ball and strike it gently with a relaxed upward swing of the leg.

21. Two players stand at a distance of 12 - 15 yards with a third player half-way between them. One of the end players throws a lob to the one in the middle, who makes an overhead kick with the instep to the third player, from a standing position or with the body falling backwards. Then he does a half-turn to do the same the other way around. (Fig. 180)

Fig. 180

Encourage the player to: — get quickly into position; be well balanced in going into the falling back position; strike the ball with a gentle, relaxed swing; use the full instep; keep his eyes on the ball; break his fall with his hands.

Practices to Improve Touch and Control (10-12 years)

1. In pairs, outside the penalty area. Player A, facing the goal, throws to B, who is standing 18 - 20 yards from the goal with his back towards it. B controls the ball, turns and shoots into the goal so that the ball hits the back of the net before hitting the ground. (Fig. 181)

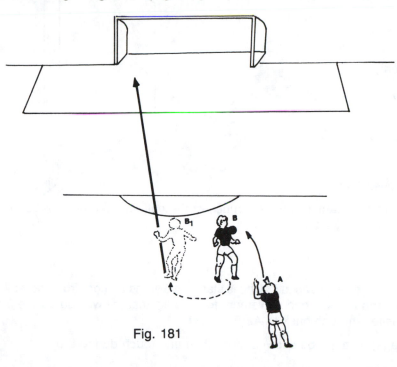

Fig. 181

Encourage Player B to: — control and turn in one movement; get early into the line of flight and choose the appropriate controlling surface; set the ball up on the turn.

2. A rope is fixed 1 yard high between two uprights mid-way along a 10 yard X 10 yard grid. Two players play foot-tennis, where the ball may bounce no more than twice before being returned. (Fig. 182)

Variations:

1. No more than one bounce.

2. No bounces.

3. Introduce two more players.

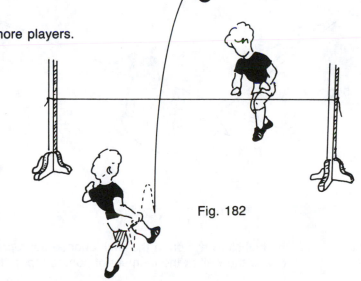

Fig. 182

Encourage the players to: — get quickly into position to play the ball back; lift the ball gently using the foot as a platform.

3. Continuous volleying against a wall allowing the ball to bounce once only. Count the number of successive volleys. Restart if the ball bounces twice or misses the wall. (Fig. 183)

Variations:

1. Side-foot volley only.

2. Instep volley only.

3. Alternate feet.

4. Weaker foot only.

5. No bounces.

6. How many in a given time.

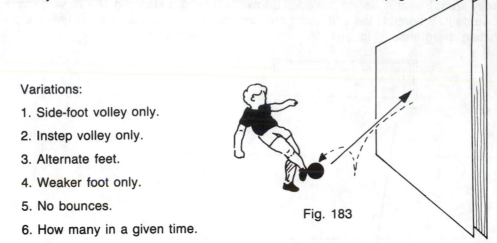

Fig. 183

Encourage the player to: — anticipate the bounce of the ball and get into position early; use his foot as a platform to lift the ball gently against the wall.

4. In pairs facing a wall, Player A throws to B, who is standing 5 yards or more from the wall with his back towards it. B controls the ball and turns in one movement to pass against the wall below the 2 feet mark. B controls the rebound and passes the ball back to A. (Fig. 184)

In the beginning stage, B might be allowed more than one touch during the turn.

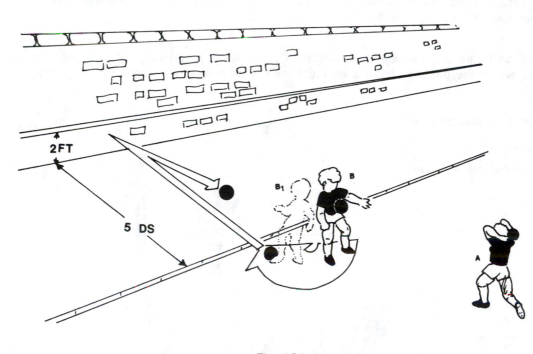

2FT

5 DS

Fig. 184

Encourage the receiver to: — take the ball sideways-on to the wall; choose appropriate controlling surface — foot, thigh, chest or head; pivot to face the wall at the moment of contact; 'pop the ball up' on the turn.

97

5. Several players form a circle. They keep the ball up using the instep, allowing it to bounce once only. No player can play the ball twice in succession. (Fig. 185)

Variations:

1. Have the players play the ball in numbered succession.

2. Play the ball without any bounces.

3. Eliminate any player who loses control.

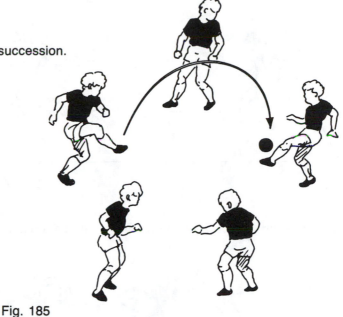

Fig. 185

Encourage the players to: — lift the ball gently inside the circle of players; use the full instep as a platform; balance on one foot, using arms for balance; get early into position under the ball.

6. One player inside a grid square 10 yards X 10 yards tries to prevent the ball from being played over his head by two other players standing just outside the grid square. If he intercepts the ball, he changes position with whoever was responsible for lost control. The ball may only bounce twice before being returned. (Fig. 186)

Fig. 186

Variation:

Reduce the number of bounces.

Encourage the outside player to: — get into position early; balance himself for the return; use the foot as a platform to lift the ball gently; use arms to balance.

7. In threes in three grid squares 30 yards X 10 yards. Player A passes to Player B who receives and turns in one movement to pass the ball to C. Repeat several times, then change positions. (Fig. 187)

Fig. 187

One method of receiving and turning would be: (Fig. 188)

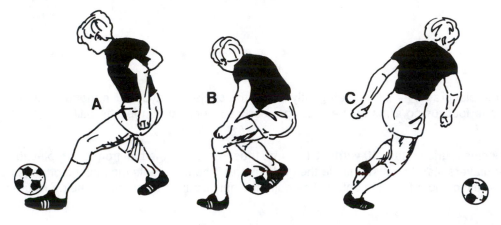

Fig. 188

A. Go to meet the ball and plant your left foot alongside the ball as if to make an inside of the foot pass. Lean back, pushing against the left foot.

B. Allow the ball to get under your body and meet it with the outside of the right foot., withdrawing and rolling the foot around in the opposite direction at the moment of contact to take the pace off the ball. Move your weight back, pivot from the shoulders and hips, and put your weight onto your right foot.

C. Pivot your right foot and stride towards the ball which should be about 2 yards in front of you.

Another method would be:

Take the ball through your legs with the inside of your right foot. Pivot on your left foot over your left shoulder, keeping the ball within playing distance. (Fig. 189)

Fig. 189

Practices to Improve Dribbling (10-12 years)

1. 2 Vs 2 in four grid squares (40 yards X 10 yards), Dribble and Shoot. The goalkeeper must roll the ball out to his partner. (Fig. 190)

Fig. 190

Encourage the players to: — shoot at every opportunity; fake or feint to get the defender out of the line of a possible shot.

2. 2 Vs 2 in a six grid square area. Place three cones in a 15 - 20 yard triangle. The players in possession attempt to kick the ball to knock down any of the three cones. First team to score 3 goals wins the game. (Fig. 191)

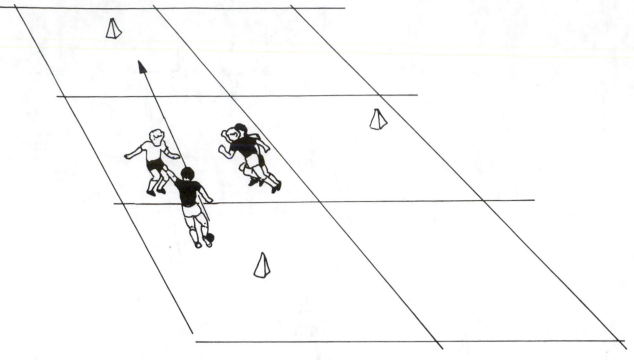

Fig. 191

Encourage the players on the following points: —

a) when you have the ball:

    1. use **change of speed and direction** to dribble past your opponent.

    2. **disguise** your intentions to attack a particular cone with fakes and feints.

    3. get into position so that your partner can pass to you (if he wants to).

b) when your opponents have the ball:

    1. **deny** them a clear route to the nearest cone.

    2. **mark** your opponent closely.

    3. **get behind** your partner (cover) in case he is beaten.

3. 1 Vs 1 in 2 grid squares with a third player resting (#3). The player with the ball (#1) dribbles it into his opponent's square (#2) and tries to beat him to place his foot on the ball on the end line. If #1 'scores', he dribbles the ball back again and tries to beat #3 and so on. If #2 or #3 wins the ball, he takes over as the dribbler. (Fig. 192)

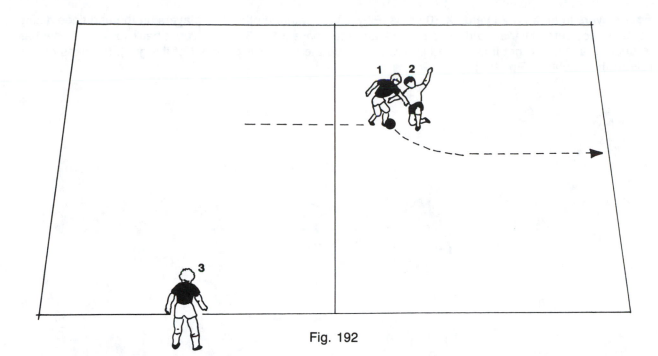

Fig. 192

Encourage the dribbler to: — 'attack' the defender; develop fakes and feints; change speed and direction.

Encourage the defender to: — close down the dribbler; force the dribbler to the sides; develop the boxer's stance.

4. Three players with one ball in an area about 30 yards square with three 5 yard circles (or squares) marked at distances about 20 yards from each other. Each player has a 'home' circle. (Fig. 193)

    The practice is started by a throw into the middle and all three players try to get the ball and dribble it into their home circle, the other two trying to stop the one with the ball. In other words, it is a rapidly changing 1 Vs 2 situation. If the ball goes out of play area, or after a 'goal' is scored, restart with a throw into the middle.

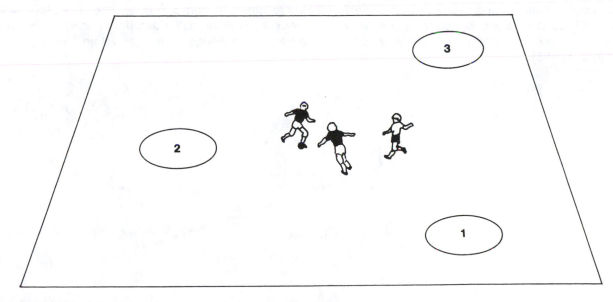

Fig. 193

Encourage the dribbler to develop: — quick control and dribbling bursts; fakes and feints.

Encourage the defenders to: — work as a pair by close marking and covering.

5. Four players in an area 20 yards X 10 yards. Play 1 Vs 1 with the other two players on the end lines acting as pass receivers. #1 tries to dribble past #2 and then pass it to #3, who gives it back to #1. #1 now has to beat #2 again and get it to #4 and so on. If #2 wins the ball (or it goes out of the grid), he takes on the role of the dribbler. (Fig. 194)

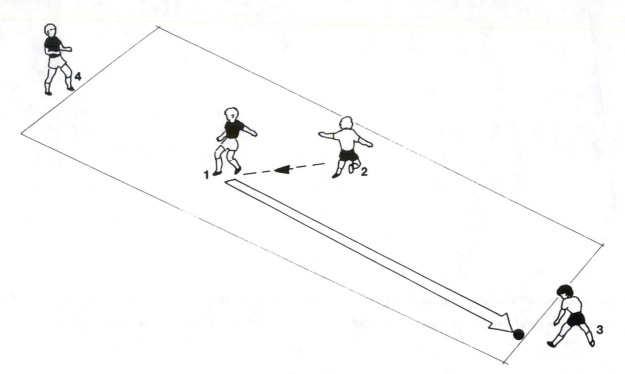

Fig. 194

Encourage the dribbler to: — make runs to receive the ball from the end players; develop receiving positions where he can see the ball and the defender; turn and attack the defender.

Encourage the defender to: — close down and deny the dribbler the opportunity to turn.

6. Two players stand facing each other on a line 15 - 20 yards long, with cones at either end. The player with the ball tries to fake out his partner and knock over either cone with the ball. Each player stays on his own side of the line. The defender is only allowed to cross the line to challenge for the ball within 1 yard of each cone. (Fig. 195)

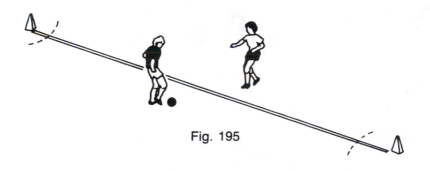

Fig. 195

Encourage the dribbler to: — develop quick turns; develop fake turns; accelerate whenever an opportunity arises to change direction; play the ball with the foot furthest away from the defender.

7. 1 Vs 1 in a grid square 10 yards X 10 yards. Players take turns in attacking the opponent's end line, trying to take the ball over it under control. Score a point for every successful attempt.

    Encourage the dribbler to: — develop fakes and feints.

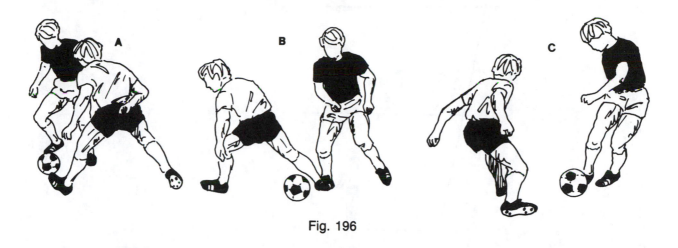

Fig. 196

The dribbler threatens to go to the left of the defender, but at the last possible moment, the dribbler cuts back and beats the defender by either: pushing the ball through his legs (the nutmeg) Fig. 196b or by pulling the ball back sharply and taking it past the defender's right side. (Fig. 196c)

8. Working in four squares (40 yards X 10 yards) in groups of four with one ball. Player A passes to B standing in the second square. As soon as the ball enters the second square, C, starting from the third square, challenges for or tries to intercept the ball. On receiving the ball, B turns and tries to pass to D in the far end square. Play can then be reversed to start from D's end. (Fig. 197)

    Change the middle players after every five attempts. Award a point for every successful attempt.

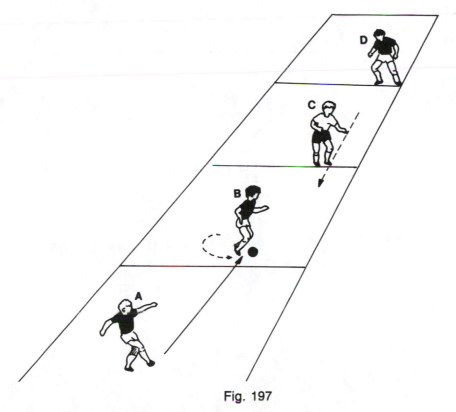

Fig. 197

Encourage B to: — receive the pass half-turned towards D.

9. Working in four grid squares (40 yards X 10 yards) with one ball between four players. Starting behind the end line, A dribbles into the first square. As soon as he enters this square, B may move forward to challenge.. If A beats B, he can move into the second square and, again, as soon as he enters the square, C may move forward into the square to challenge. A tries to 'climb the ladder' until he reaches the far end line without losing the ball and without the ball leaving the channel of squares. (Fig. 198)

Fig. 198

Practices to Improve Passing (10-12 years)

1. Two teams of 3-a-side play around and outside a circle 5 yards radius with a cone in the center. A shot which misses counts as a goal to the defending team. The first team to score 3 goals wins. (Fig. 199)

Fig. 199

Encourage the players on the following points: —

a) when you have the ball:

   1. shoot whenever you think there is an unblocked line from your foot through the ball to the goal (cone);

   2. to get a shot in, pass to a teammate (or dribble) past an opponent quickly and shoot early.

b) when your opponents have the ball:

   1. mark your opponent closely on a line between him and the cone.

2. 7 Vs 4 in a small (40 yards x 30 yards) field, with goals 5 yards wide. The team with 7 players tries to score in the opponents' goal or make 5 consecutive passes. The team with four players tries to score in the opponents' goal.

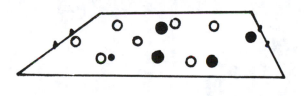

Fig. 200

Variation: With improvement, increase the number of passes required to score a goal.

Encourage the team of four players to: — pressurize the player with the ball; to play together, one or two challenging, the others covering.

Encourage the team of seven players to: — shoot whenever the opportunity arises; create passing angles by getting a clear line between themselves and the ball; be prepared, not only to go forward but also sideways and backwards.

3. 3 vs 3 in nine grid squares (30 yards x 30 yards). Again, no goalkeeper is needed, but perhaps one handling player (Fig. 201)

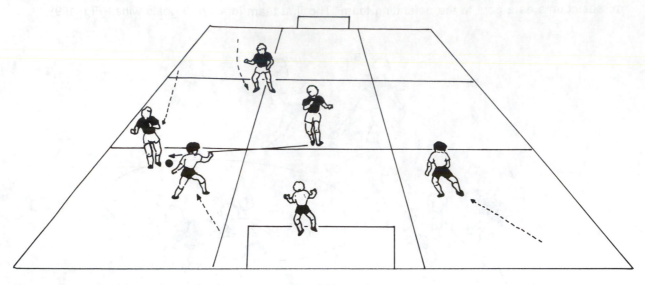

Fig. 201

Encourage the players on the following points: —

a) When dribbling past an opponent, try to do it so that you can then shoot, or so that you can pass to your team mates.

b) Try to find positions where your partners can pass the ball to you easily (if they want to) and where you can also shoot, dribble or pass — if and when you get the ball.

c) If your two team mates are moving forward with the ball either by interpassing or dribbling, then support them from behind.

d) shoot whenever you have the opportunity and when you think you can score.

e) If your team loses the ball, either challenge (tackle) the opponent who has the ball or get behind (cover) a team mate who is challenging for the ball. Prevent opponents from shooting by getting into position to block their shots.

4. Three goals one yard apart are set out in a triangle 10 - 12 yards apart. 2 Vs 2 trying to score a goal through any of the goals. There are no boundary lines and goals may be scored from either side of each goal. (Fig. 202)

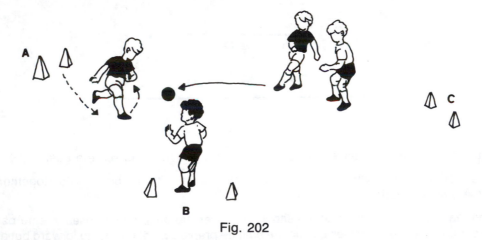

Fig. 202

Encourage the attackers to: — attack any goal at speed; develop fakes and quick changes of direction; shield the ball and not take too many risks; take up receiving positions where they have a clear line to the ball all the time; keep close control on the side away from the nearest defender.

Encourage the defenders to: — work as a pair; force the attackers to play outside the triangle; force the attackers to go to the furthest goal.

5. Two players with one ball about 25-30 yards from goal. Player A dribbles the ball, passes it to B, and immediately runs forward to receive a return pass and make a first-time shot into goal. (Fig. 203)

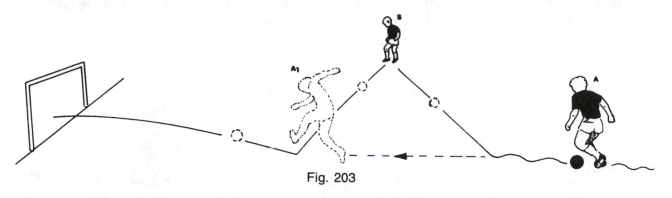

Fig. 203

Encourage Player A to: — dribble at controlled speed; pass the ball off his front foot with accuracy; accelerate to receive the return pass; adjust his stride pattern to get into a shooting position.

Encourage Player B to: — receive the ball facing sideways-on; make a quick return pass directly into the path of Player A.

6. 6 Vs 2 in an area 40 yards x 40 yards. Attackers must make 5 consecutive passes without the defenders touching the ball for a score. If they get the ball the defenders must make one pass to score. (Fig. 204)

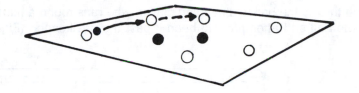

Fig. 204

Variation: Make the area smaller (30 yards x 30 yards), with 6 vs 1. The defender must kick the ball out of the area to score.

Encourage the team of six players to: — get a clear line of sight between themselves and the ball; ask for the ball whenever they think they are in a good position.

Encourage the ball player to: — keep his head up, control the ball in front of him, and play it SIMPLY AND QUICKLY.

Encourage the defenders to: — work together as a pair, one challenging, the other covering.

7. 3 Vs 1 in an area around and outside a circle 5 yards in radius with a cone in the center. The three players interpass in order to get a clear shot at the cone. The defender attempts to stay between the ball and the cone all of the time.

Practices to Improve Heading (10-12 years)

1. In threes in a 10 yard X 10 yard grid. "A" serves to "B", who tries to head the ball over "A" to "C". If he succeeds, it's a goal. "A" may intercept with hands. Three interceptions = one goal. (Fig. 205)

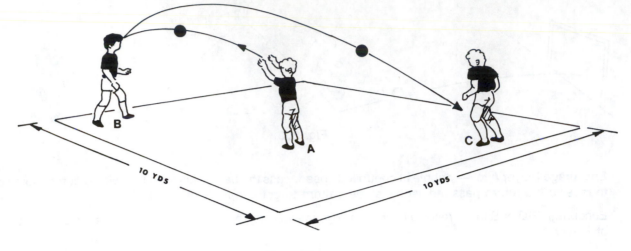

Fig. 205

Encourage the heading player to: — attack the ball by hitting it with his head; use legs, trunk and neck to generate power; hit the ball at a point below the mid-line; keep his eyes on the ball throughout; strike the ball with the forehead.

2. A 'server' on the goal line throws the ball to a heading player, who runs round a marker on the penalty spot before running to meet the ball and attempting to head it past the goalkeeper. (Fig. 206)

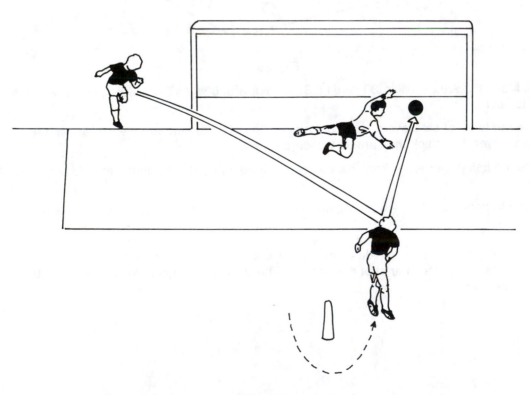

Fig. 206

Encourage the heading player to: — 'hit' the ball with his forehead; attack the ball; head the ball downward.

3. Six players in any clear space. One player makes alternate headers to the others in turn. The sequence is 1-2-1-3-1-4 and so on. (Fig. 207)

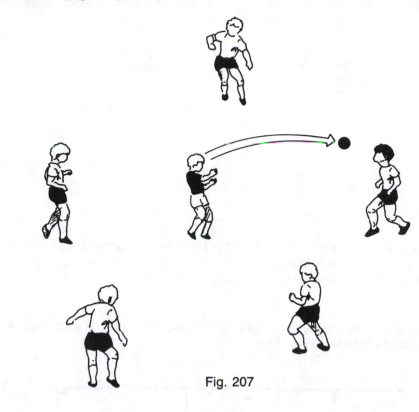

Fig. 207

4. Two pairs, A and B play against C and D. Goals 8 yards X 2 feet. "A" serves by hand with a lobbed center and "B" moves into goal area to head. "C" is the goalkeeper and "D" the defender, who runs in 2-3 yards behind "B". Each player has 10 tries. The team with the most goals wins. (Fig. 208)

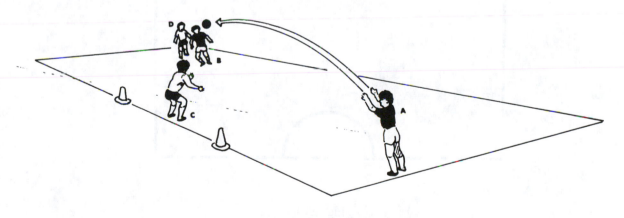

Fig. 208

Encourage the heading player to: — attack the ball by hitting it with his head; use his neck muscles for power; strike the ball at a point just above the mid-line so that the ball is directed downwards; keep his eyes on the ball.

Practices to Improve Goalkeeping (10-12 years)

1. A server with a supply of balls simulates crosses by throwing them into the goal area. (Fig. 209)

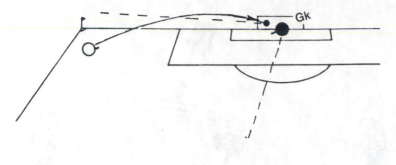

Fig. 209

Encourage the goalkeeper to: — start from a central position so that he can cover either post; be just off the goal line with an angle of vision that allows him to have a wide view of the play; try to intercept high balls at the highest point; try to intercept low balls as early as possible.

2. A server with a supply of balls simulates crosses by throwing them into the goal area. A goalkeeper and a defender play against one attacker. (Fig. 210)

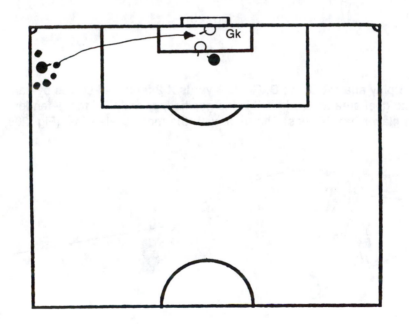

Fig. 210

Encourage the goalkeeper to: — make early decisions of whether to come for the ball or stay on his line; communicate with his defender. "Keeper" means the goalkeeper is coming for the ball and the defender gets out of the way. "Away" means the goalkeeper stays on his line and the defender should clear the ball as it is too far to come out and safely reach the ball.

3. Two players against one plus goalkeeper in a space about 20 yards X 15 yards with small goals. The pair with the ball attacks the opponent's goal. The defending team plays one in goal, the other out. As soon as a goal is scored or the defenders win the ball or the ball goes out of play, the other pair attacks. (Fig. 211)

Fig. 211

Encourage the goalkeeper to: — communicate with his fellow defender; 'spread' himself at the feet of the attacker; hold on to the ball.

4. Two goalkeepers in two goals on the same line about 15 - 20 yards apart. The goalkeepers throw crosses for each other. (Fig. 212)

Fig. 212

Variations: Goalkeepers volley or half-volley the ball out of their hands.

Encourage the goalkeepers to: — adopt a good starting position on the goal line; take-off to catch the ball at the highest point; get both hands behind the ball.

Practices to Improve Tackling (10-12 years)

1. Two players in a grid square 10 yards X 10 yards with one ball. One player pushes the ball ahead and runs after it while his partner closes in and executes a sliding tackle to knock the ball over the side line. In the beginning stages, the defender should be given a definite advantage in reaching the ball first and no body contact should be allowed. (Fig. 213)

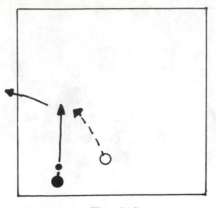

Fig. 213

Encourage the defender to: — go down on his side while breaking the fall with his hand; to reach for the ball with his foot and hit it with the instep (or even the toe). (Fig. 214)

Fig. 214

As a development, players should strive to keep possession rather than merely kick the ball out of play. The defender should raise his foot slightly off the ground and hook it round the ball to form a block. The dribbler's momentum might carry him on over the blocked ball, allowing the defender time to regain his feet with the ball under control. (Fig. 215)

Fig. 215

113

2. Two players stand facing each other on either side of a line on which a ball is placed. On the signal, they both go for the ball by executing a block tackle. (Fig. 216)

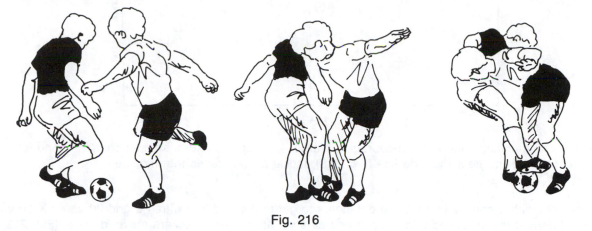

Fig. 216

Variation: Make each player:

    1. Take one step towards the ball.

    2. Start from 3 strides away.

Encourage the players to: — sink at the hips and knees to form a solid base; push hard through the contact foot.

Practices to Develop Communication (10-12 years)

At this age, players should be learning how to combine with each other to beat small groups of opponents. An important consideration in developing combination play is how they communicate with each other.

There are two methods of communication:

a) Verbal communication

b) Body language.

Each method is of vital importance to a developing soccer player.

Verbal communication is used by players in:

1. Defensive support positions

2. Defensive recovery positions

3. Advising receiving players of situations behind them

4. Overlapping runs (pp. 189-191)

5. Retaining the shape of the team

Body language is used by players to:

1. Catch the eye of team mates with or without the ball.

1. One player with a ball tries to beat two defenders to get to the end line through a grid 20 yards X 10 yards. The defenders are restricted to their individual squares. (Fig. 217)

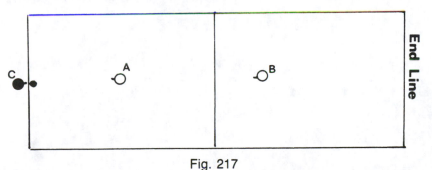

Fig. 217

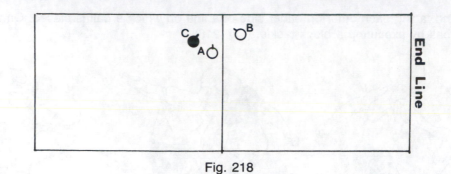

Fig. 218

Get B to communicate with A by encouraging him to: — adopt a boxer's stance; contain C and force him to cross the mid-line near the side line (Fig. 218); tackle as C crosses the mid-line.

2. Two players with a ball try to beat two defenders to get to the end line within a grid 20 yards X 10 yards. A third defender is introduced into the practice as soon as the two attackers move forward. (Fig. 219)

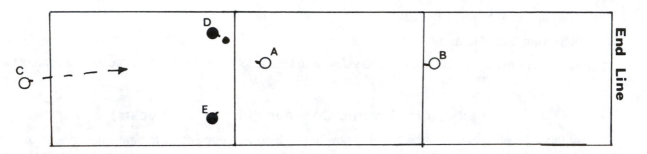

Fig. 219

Get B to communicate with A by encouraging him to: — adopt a boxer's stance; contain and fall back in the face of the attack; to force the play to one side.

Get B to communicate with C by encouraging him to: — recover quickly into a covering position. (Fig. 220)

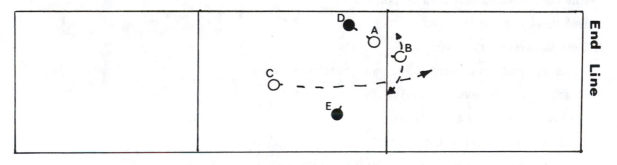

Fig. 220

It is important that C should not recover into a position too deep behind B. He should get back far enough to become part of a tight defensive triangle.

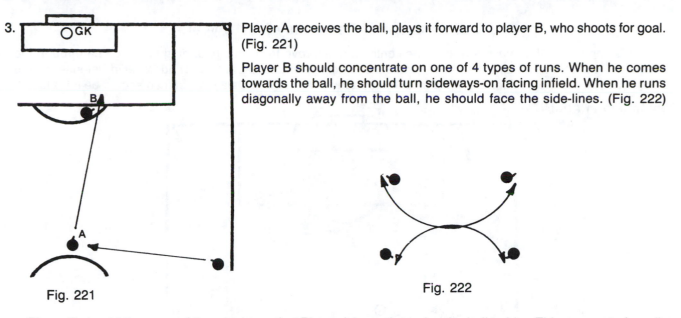

3.

Player A receives the ball, plays it forward to player B, who shoots for goal. (Fig. 221)

Player B should concentrate on one of 4 types of runs. When he comes towards the ball, he should turn sideways-on facing infield. When he runs diagonally away from the ball, he should face the side-lines. (Fig. 222)

Fig. 221

Fig. 222

Player B should time one of these runs so that Player A is ready to play the ball to him. This moment of readiness is usually when his head comes up just after controlling the ball. Player A must read the body language of Player B to give him the ball on the exact spot, with the exact speed of pass that the run dictates.

4.   As above, but introduce a defender. (Fig. 223)

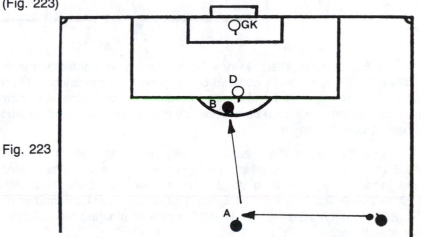

Fig. 223

Encourage A and B to: —read each other's intentions; for A to inform B if he can turn on a ball when he has run towards A, and D has not followed closely. (Fig. 224)

If D has tracked B tightly, then the shout should be 'MAN ON'.

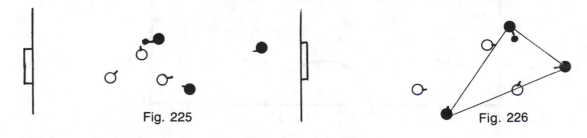

Fig. 224

5.   One of the most important considerations for young players is to retain the shape of their team. The basis for learning this shape is 3-a-side, as the game is essentially about triangular formations (pp. 81-83).

Encourage defenders to: — develop compact, triangular units when the ball is lost. (Fig. 225)

Fig. 225

Fig. 226

Encourage offensive units to: — develop larger triangular units so that space is created between defensive players. (Fig. 226)

The Development of Team Play (10-12 years)

It is imperative that players of this age continue to improve their understanding of the game through the principles of play. Small-sided games to reinforce the principles of Support in Attack and Cover in Defense should be continued, while the additional principles of Penetration in Attack and Delay in Defense should be introduced.

Penetration in Attack

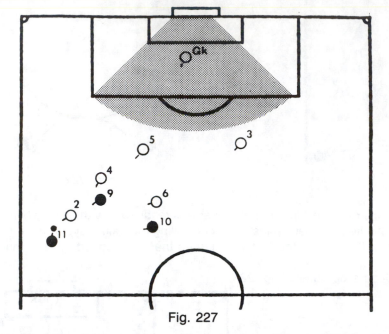

Fig. 227

In Fig. 227, the Black 11 has the ball and is confronted by the White 2. He has the option of either trying to beat the White 2 who is covered by the White 4, or passing to Black 10. In either case, little will have been achieved in terms of penetration, as the attack is still a long way from getting the ball into the danger area. A speculative center will also be covered by the White 5 and White 3 who are restricting the space into which the attacking players may move.

In this situation, the attacking players should not allow the defense the luxury of a covering defender, and the Black 9 should move toward the "sweeper" and stay as far upfield as the laws of the game will allow him. This immediately poses problems for the defense, especially if the White 4 has been detailed to mark the Black 9. Does the White 4 go with the Black 9 or does he take up another role? If he does go with the Black 9, as in Fig. 228, then it means that the Black 9 is now committing two defenders and reduces the problem for the other forwards to that of 1 Vs 1 or 2 Vs 2.

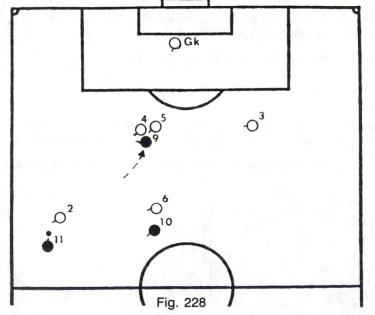

Fig. 228

If the White 4 does not go with the Black 9 and stays to cover the White 2 and White 6, then it might be possible for the Black 11 or Black 10 to play a quick one-two with the Black 9 (Fig. 229).

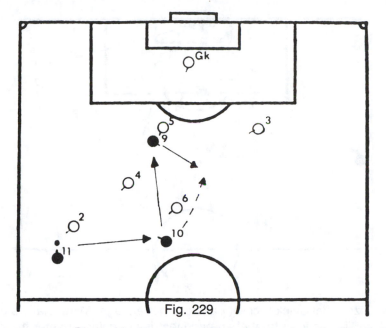

Fig. 229

Here the Black 11 passes to Black 10 who pushes the ball through to the Black 9 who lays it off for the Black 10 following up. It is essential here that the Black 9 shows himself as a target for the Black 10's pass and that the Black 10 follows up after he has made the pass. Too often, the ball is played towards the danger area but attackers do not follow up to receive return passes. Alternatively, if the Black 9 has good ball control and can turn quickly, he may turn with the ball and take on the White 5, or if the White 5 lays off, he may have a shot-at-goal.

Perhaps the greatest lesson for any team wishing to achieve penetration in attack is that they must have players in front positions as far forward as the laws of the game will allow them to go. The ball can then be played forward to these front players either to shoot at goal, dribble past defenders, or lay off for supporting players. Too often, teams are forced to play square because they haven't got forwards willing to take on the responsibility of playing in these forward positions. They all want to make the goals rather than score them. This feeling is perfectly understandable as defenses are bound to mark tightly near their own penalty box, and perhaps one of the chief qualities of a forward playing in these front positions is that he displays great courage. He must be prepared to withstand keen tackling in this area, often with his back to his opponents' goal, and once he starts to look for the ball out on the wings or come back into mid-field for it, his team will be forced to play square, as there will be nobody to play the ball forward to.

Delay in Defense

If penetration is a major objective in attack, delay must obviously be a principle of defense. Once a team has lost possession, its first task is to get its defense organized so that it is not vulnerable to a quick thrust by the opposition. The forwards and the mid-field players should ensure that the opposition take a long time in building up their attacks so that the defense can be quickly organized.

It is obvious that the deeper inside the opponents' half these delaying tactics are used, the longer will be the time that the defense will have to get organized. It is, therefore, vital that all forwards realize the importance of tackling back. Whenever possession is lost, the forward nearest to the defender must become the "delay" man by confronting the defender in possession. He must, if he can, dispossess the defender, but it should be remembered that a wild challenge which allows the defender to beat him is enough to expose other members of the defending side. Delaying forwards should, therefore, never allow themselves to be beaten by making wild challenges.

Delay in defense should begin the moment the ball is lost to the opposition. The opponent in possession must be put under pressure as quickly as possible. So the player nearest to him sets about an immediate challenge, while his teammates make their recovery runs into their defensive positions. The challenging player must make a quick recovery from an attacking position and get between his opponent and his goal. This swift recovery takes extra effort, especially if the challenging player is a forward. (Fig. 230)

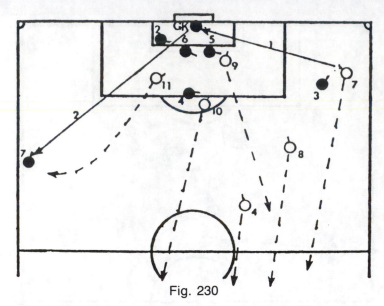

Fig. 230

It should be emphasized that quick recovery alone is not enough. Many players confront their opponent — but fail to pressurize him. To stand in front of an opponent is not going to deter him from making a pass or from trying to run through. He must get close enough to his opponent so that he can just about touch him with an outstretched hand.

Stance is also very important. If the challenging player stands chest on to the attacker, he is exposed to dummies and feints. The attacker has momentum on his side, and can dictate the outcome of the confrontation. The challenging player should adopt a stance not unlike that of a boxer — shoulder facing his opponent — so that he is better positioned and better balanced to turn quickly, and move either forward or backward. (Fig. 231)

Fig. 231

Fig. 232

The angle of approach at which a challenging player confronts an opponent is critical. The angle should be such that it denies the possibility of playing the ball forward and forces him away from possible passing angles upfield or even crossfield. (Fig. 232)

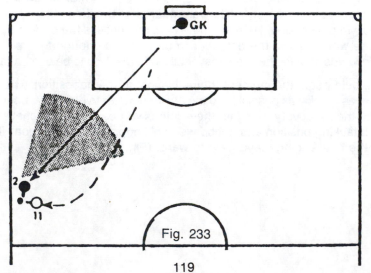

Fig. 233

In Fig. 233, White 11 has made a recovery run to close down Black 2. Note that White 11 is facing the side line, i.e. he is in the boxer's stance but his angle of approach on the Black 2 does not allow the latter to cut infield. Black 2's safe passing angles are restricted to the shaded area behind him.

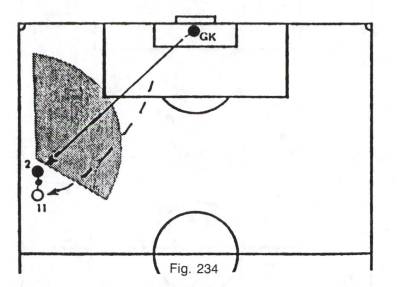

Fig. 234

In Fig. 234, White 11 has recovered to a position on a line immediately facing Black 2. This allows Black 2 a far greater safe passing range as shown by the shaded area.

Having developed a good stance — one that allows him to go forward or backward easily — the challenging player adopts an aggressive attitude. When an opponent realizes that he will come under pressure the moment he receives the ball, no matter where he is standing, he is going to be keen to play the ball hurriedly. Pressure = anxiety, and anxiety leads to errors.

Controlled pressure is vastly different from the hasty, lunging efforts that concede free kicks. Having recovered, closed down and confronted his opponent, applying controlled pressure, the challenger watches closely for the moment when his opponent drops his head to look at the ball. This now means that the opponent cannot see other options available to him. At this point, the challenging player should use body feints and dummies on the player with the ball. Too often, it is accepted that forwards sell dummies to defenders — so why not get the upper hand by posing the opponent problems with a few faked lunges. Very often, the opponent loses control of the ball and the challenging player can win the ball back, either with a firm tackle or preferably by stealing it.

Assuming the opponent in possession retains the ball, the challenger's next priority is to force him to turn away from his intended path. If he is forced to turn sideways, he can either risk a back pass or opt for a square, cross-field pass. Either pass gives the recovering team the chance to consolidate their defensive positions and also draws the sting out of the attack.

Forcing an opponent to turn backward toward his own goal is even better. Now he is not only facing the wrong way, but his colleagues have probably raced into attacking positions and left gaps. Now is the time to become relentless. The opponent must not be allowed to turn. To win the ball now gives the challenging player the best possible kind of possession.

Not only must forwards be instructed to get "goal side" of their opponents when they have lost possession, but mid-field players and defenders must realize the value of slowing up the opposition's attacks. A team which falls back in front of an opposing attack invariably slows it down and in this way the attack is delayed and valuable time gained for defensive reorganization.

In Fig. 235, the White 8 and White 10 have lost possession deep in the opponents' half of the field and the ball has been played quickly to the Black 10. The White defense is out-numbered 6-5 and it is the task of the White 4 to delay the Black attackers until the White 7, 8 and 10 can recover into defensive positions.

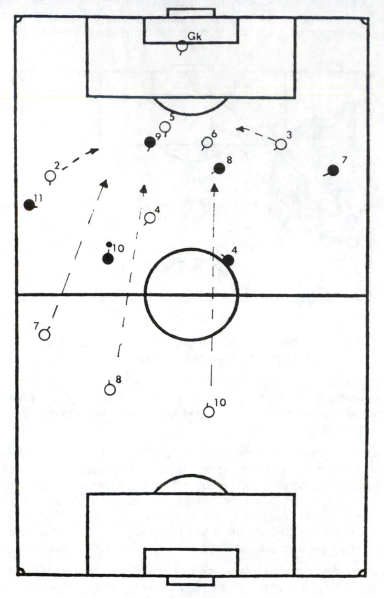

Fig. 235

In Fig. 235, White 4 has taken up a position between the Black 10 and Black 4 and is "inviting" the Black 10 to pass either to the Black 11 or the Black 4. In either case, the White 4 will be achieving his aim of gaining time; as in the first case, a pass made to the Black 11 will be a pass made away from the danger area, and an early square pass to the Black 4 will achieve little as the White 4 has time to move to his left to block the Black 4's approach to goal.

Clearly, the attackers will want to achieve penetration as quickly as possible while they still retain a numerical advantage and the Black 10 must commit the White 4 so that he can then push the ball to the Black 4 who can in turn "attack" the defense. Basically, the Black 10 and Black 4 against the White 4 is a 2 Vs 1 situation and the attackers must expoilt this as quickly as possible, while the defender aims at delaying the attackers so that his teammates may have time to get back to reduce the numerical disadvantage. As soon as the White 4 sees that the Black 10 is bringing the ball at him, he must try to slow down the Black 10 by falling back. It is really remarkable how such a simple tactic as this will result in the dribbler slowing down, expecially at the youth level. When the dribbler has slowed down, the White 4 can then decide to tackle, but on no account should he lose the ball. If he attempts to tackle and fails to win the ball before the White 7, 8 and 10 have got back, then his defense will be out-numbered to the extent of 6-4. It is imperative, therefore, that any defender placed in a similar situation to the White 4 should never attempt to tackle unless he is absolutely sure that he is going to win the ball. It is far better to fall back to just outside shooting distance where opposing forwards, despite holding numerical advantage, will have less space to work in. It should be remembered that defenders should not fall back into their own penalty area to delay the opposing forwards. They must make a stand when the opposing forwards arrive with the ball within shooting distance of their goal. Their task of making a good tackle will be made easier, however, if they have managed to slow down the opposing forwards just outside shooting distance.

121

Practices to Develop Team Play (10-12 years)

1.

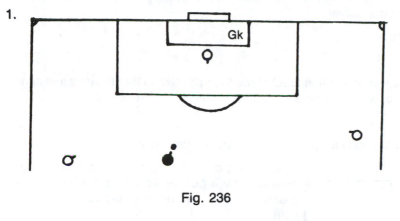

Fig. 236

The Black attacker attempts to score a goal before either of the White defenders can block his shot. (Fig. 236)

Encourage the attacker to: — attack at speed; develop an awareness of the position of the defenders.

2.

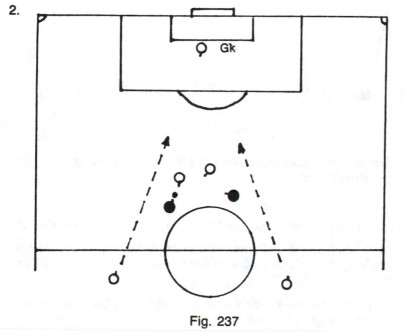

Fig. 237

The two Black attackers are confronted by two White defenders and a goalkeeper. Two additional defenders join the play as soon as the attackers make two touches on the ball. (Fig. 237)

Encourage the attackers to: — penetrate quickly either by dribbling or passing.

Encourage the challenging defenders to: — delay the attack by not committing to reckless tackles; communicate with each other and the recovering defenders.

Encourage the recovering defenders to: — take the shortest recovery line to a covering position; communicate with the challenging defenders.

Encourage the goalkeeper to: — adopt a position in which he cannot be beaten by a long shot over his head, and where he is ready to dash out to intercept a through pass; communicate with his fellow defenders.

3.

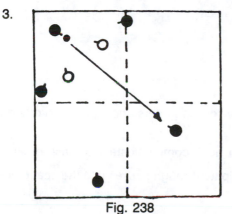

Fig. 238

Five Vs Two in four grid squares. The five try to accumulate the highest possible number of consecutive passes. (Fig. 238)

Variations:

1. Maximum of 3 touch, 2 touch or 1 touch per player.

2. Bonus attack if a pass splits the defense.

Encourage the attackers to: —

Take up good receiving positions; set the ball-up on the first touch; time their passes so that the defense cannot close down any attackers; give accurate, weighted passes; play the ball off the front foot.

Encourage the defenders to: —

Work as a pair; close down passing angles as quickly as possible; pressurize attackers into making mistakes.

4.

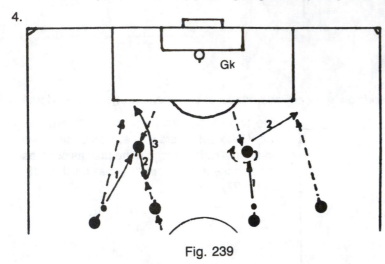

Interpassing between 3 players to attack a goal defended by a goalkeeper. Two possible interpassing moves are shown in the diagram. (Fig. 239)

Fig. 239

Players should be encouraged to devise their own interpassing moves while the action is taking place. On no account should the moves be pre-planned and then drilled.

Encourage the passing players to: —

Pass accurately and firmly to the receiver; time their passes dependent on the movements of the receiver.

Encourage the receiving players to: — move into position just before the passer is ready to release the ball; be in a relaxed, balanced position when receiving the ball; be aware of what is happening all-round him; make an early decision of what to do with the ball.

Encourage the overlapping players to: — make their runs dependent on the options available to the receiving player; anticipate the receiving player's intended course of action.

5.

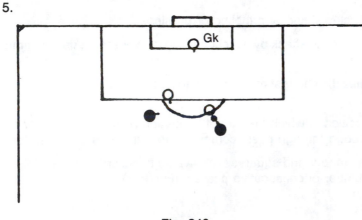

Two Vs Two in front of goal defended by a goalkeeper. The two attacking players must play one of the following options — spin turn, takeover, through pass, 1-2, or immediate shot. (Fig. 240)

Fig. 240

Encourage the attackers to: — seek to make options happen; develop an understanding of each other's play through body language.

Encourage the defenders to: — work hard to prevent any shot at goal; communicate with each other.

Encourage the goalkeeper to: — be on guard for long shots; anticipate through passes into the space behind the defense.

6.

A player with the ball plays it to a midfield target player and follows up for a lay-off pass. He then immediately plays the ball into a striker and follows up for a lay-off pass attempting a first time shot. Allow receiving players to spin on the ball provided they know what is behind them. (Fig. 241)

Fig. 241

Encourage the receiving players to: — move to meet the ball at a slightly sideways-on position; be aware of the situation behind them; lay the ball off gently into the stride path of the running player; spin quickly with the ball in a tight circle and play the ball forward accurately.

Encourge the passing players to: make accurate, well-weighted passes off the front foot; time their runs so that they can move onto the lay-off passes; shoot accurately.

7.

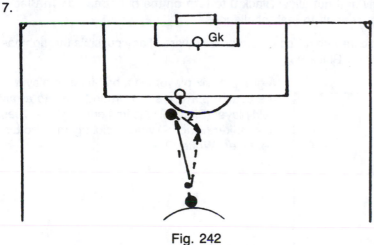

A midfield player plays the ball forward to a striker who is marked by a defender. The striker has the options of

Fig. 242

a) trying to beat the defender

b) letting the ball run through into the space behind the defender

c) shooting on the turn

d) laying the ball off to the midfield player who must attempt a first time shot. (Fig. 242)

Encourage the midfielder to: — communicate with his striker — 'Man-on' or 'Turn'; play an accurate, well-weighted pass — exactly to where the striker demands; follow-up for a possible lay-off pass.

Encourage the striker to: — develop an awareness of the defender's position; indicate by his movement exactly where he wants to receive the pass.

8.

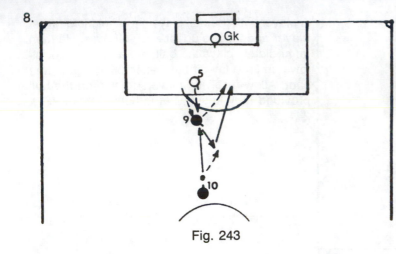

Fig. 243

Black 10 plays the ball to Black 9 who has 'come-off' his defender. Black 9 has the option of turning with the ball to either shoot or attempt to dribble past White 5, or to lay the ball off to Black 10 who then plays a through pass for Black 9 to run onto. (Fig. 243)

Encourage the Black 10 to: — pass accurately and firmly to Black 9; to instruct Black 9 on a possible course of action — 'Man on' or 'Turn'; to move into a support position for a possible lay-off; be on balance to play the through pass; bend the through pass into Black 9's stride path.

Encourage the Black 9 to: — develop an awareness of White 5's position through the use of eyes and touch; time his runs towards and away from Black 10 when the latter is in a position to play the ball; develop a repertoire of fakes, feints and dummies; turn quickly in a tight circle if the opportunity arises; develop a range of tricks in which to beat the defender in a tight circle; shoot accurately.

Encourage the White 5 to: — mark tightly and not allow Black 9 to turn on the ball; track down Black 9 on any forward runs; exercise patience and not commit to rash challenges.

Encourage the goalkeeper to: — communicate with his co-defender; be aware of any possible through pass into the penalty area; anticipate any snap shots by Black 9.

9.

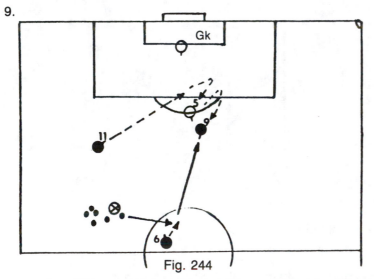

Fig. 244

A group of six players in a half-field. A player (or the coach) plays a short ground pass to a midfield player (Black 6) who immediately hits a pass to a striker (Black 9) who is closely marked by a defender (White 5).

An additional attacker (Black 11) is positioned to make forward runs onto any pass or flick-on by Black 9. (Fig. 244)

Encourage the midfield player to: — make an approach whereby he can easily move onto the coach's pass and play a first time pass to the striker; read the striker's body language and play the ball at the right speed to the required spot; commmunicate with Black 9 — 'Man-on' or 'Turn'.

Encourage the striker to: — time his run just prior to Black 6's head coming up; come off the defender with a full awareness of the latter's position; get into a line between the ball and his opponent; be on balance when receiving the ball, develop a repertoire of tricks — feints, dummies, fakes etc.

Encourage Black 11 to: — read Black 9's body language and anticipate his next action; react to this prediction and run into position; delay his forward run so as not to get into an offside position.

Encourage the defender to: — get to the ball first; clear the ball high, wide and far; beware of penetrative passes; obey the instructions of his goalkeeper.

Encourage the goalkeeper to: — be aware of penetrative passes into the penalty area; communicate with his defender.

125

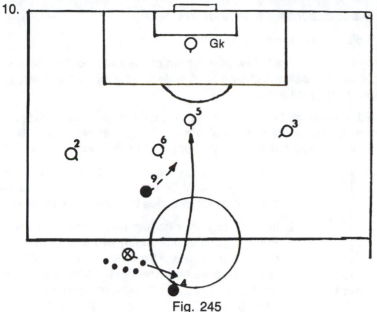

10.

The coach plays a short ground pass to a player who hits a long, first-time pass deep into the opponents' half of the field. The two central defenders (White 5 plus 6) must decide on one of several options before they are closed down by Black 9.

Fig. 245

1) Make a first-time clearance

2) Let the ball run through and play it back to the goalkeeper.

3) Control it and play it forward, or pass it to a co-defender.

4) Make a first-time pass to a co-defender. (Fig. 245)

Encourage the central defenders to: — read Black 4's approach to the ball and anticipate the length and height of his kick; get into line of flight early; communicate with each other verbally and through the use of body language; be aware of Black 9's challenge; make an early decision on the course of action to be taken.

Encourage the full backs (White 2 and White 3) to: — adjust their positions dependent upon Black 4's kick; anticipate the central defenders' action and take up an appropriate position; be on balance when receiving a pass from the central defenders; set the ball up on their first touch.

Encourage the goalkeeper to: — anticipate kicks over the top of the central defenders; communicate with the central defenders for back passes.

11.

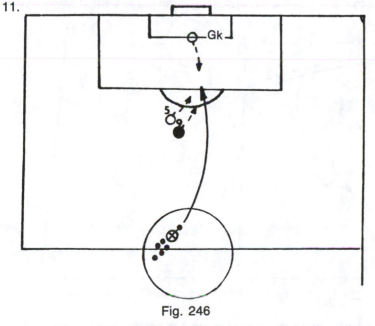

A midfield player (or the coach) plays the ball past, or over the top, of a defender (White 5) into the penalty area. An attacker (Black 9) follows up to try to score. The defender and his goalkeeper try to clear the ball through one of the following options:

Fig. 246

1) The defender intercepts the ball and clears it away high, wide and far.

2) The central defender shepherds the ball back to his goalkeeper.

3) The central defender passes the ball back to his goalkeeper.

4) The goalkeeper comes out to catch the ball or punch it high, wide and far.

5) The attacker gets the ball and White 5 dispossesses him. (Fig. 246)

Encourage the central defender to: — make an early prediction of the path of the ball; get into position early; track down any forward runs by the striker; attack the ball and clear it high, wide and far; obey his goalkeeper; develop a deft touch in passing the ball back to the goalkeeper.

Encourage the goalkeeper to: — anticipate the length and direction of the kick; get into position early; communicate with his defender; be in a comfortable, balanced position to receive back passes; attack any balls he can get to first; catch (and hold tight) whenever possible; punch the ball high, wide and far if closely challenged.

12.

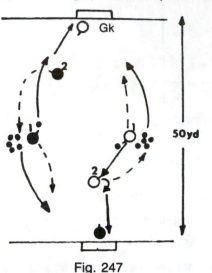

Black 1 plays the ball to Black 2 who should control and shoot. At the same time White 1 plays the ball to White 2 who tries to score at the other end.

Immediately after he has taken his shot at goal, Black 2 sprints to a supply of balls and passes one of them forward for Black 1 to shoot at goal at the opposite end. The Whites compete against the Blacks to score the most goals in a specified time. (Fig. 247)

Fig. 247

Encourage the shooting player to: — take up a position whereby he can run onto the ball or turn quickly; develop tight control on the turn; concentrate on accuracy before power.

Encourage the passing player to: — read the receiver's body language and play the ball to where he indicates; pass the ball accurately at the right speed.

Practices to Improve Touch and Control (12-14 years)

1. Two players in each grid, the middle pair tries to get the ball by intercepting it (all players must stay in their own grid). (Fig. 248)

Fig. 248

Encourage the end players to: — control the ball with their first touch; set the ball up for their partner to chip it over the heads of the middle pair.

2. Six players (the providers) form a circle about 30 yards in diameter, three with a soccer ball and three without, with two players (the receivers) in the middle. The receivers, who operate independently without getting in each other's way, each call to a different provider for the ball, which must be driven in firmly to them. The receiver controls the ball and then passes it to a provider without a ball (but not the one he received it from). (Fig. 249)

The practice can be developed to receivers playing two-touch (one to control the ball, one to pass it).

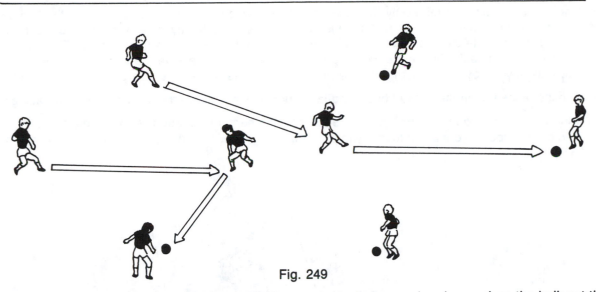

Fig. 249

Encourage the receivers to: — move toward the pass; be on balance when he receives the ball; set the ball up on the first touch; look up immediately to find a free player.

3. Several players with a ball each face a wall from a distance of about 5 yards. They keep the ball off the ground by continuously kicking it against the wall. Count the longest sequence of passes.

Variations: a) Allow the ball to bounce twice
   b) Allow the ball to bounce once only
   c) Half-volleys
   d) Volleys
   e) Ground passes

Encourage them to: — get early into the line of the flight of the ball; be on balance; offer a solid platform for ball contact.

4. Several players with one ball between two face each other about 10 yards apart. They keep the ball off the ground by passing it back and forth to each other, feet only, one touch to control, next touch to pass. Count the longest sequence of passes. (Fig. 250)

Encourage them to: — use a solid platform to lift the ball; anticipate the landing point; get there early and be on balance.

Fig. 250

Practices to Improve Passing (12-14 years)

Once players have mastered the simpler aspects of passing:
a) accuracy;
b) speed or weight of pass; and
c) disguise,

they should now concentrate on the **timing** of delivery.

The timing is largely determined by the receiving players who move into position just as the ball player is controlling the ball and gets his head up. Any runs made before the ball-player has the ball under control are wasted; similarly, runs made too late after the ball-player is ready to pass are largely wasted. The runs made by the receiving players should dictate the exact spot where they wish to receive the pass. They should aim at 'catching the ball-player's eye' an instant after he has controlled the ball and is in a position to pass it.

The timing of the run and the use of body language should be a major part of coaching with this age group.

1. 4 Vs 4 in an area four squares long, "Sentry Soccer". One sentry from each team patrols one of the end lines. The other three players in his team try to pass the ball to him. Award a goal for every successful pass. (Fig. 251)

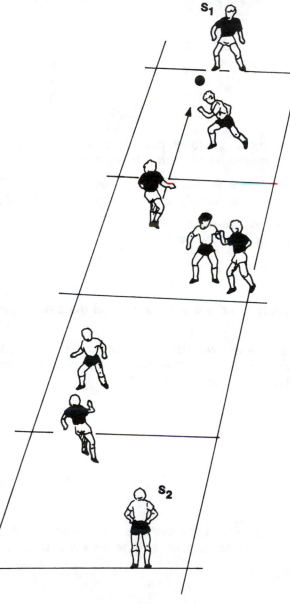

Fig. 251

Encourage the players to: — take up wide positions in order to make spaces through which the ball can be passed; take up a position that will allow them to make a good first time pass (if they need to); mark closely.

2. In two grid squares, 4 (2 plus 2) Vs 2 play "Keep Ball". Award a point for every 10 consecutive passes made by the 4 players. Whenever the 2 defenders touch the ball or force it out of the area, they change positions with the two attacking players responsible for losing the ball. (Fig. 252)

Fig. 252

Encourage the receiving player to: — **use all the space** available to give himself time to give and receive a pass; **position himself** so that there is always a clear 'line of sight' from him to the ball; move to a receiving position just before the passer is ready to release the ball.

3. 6 Vs 6, with four goals. Each team defends two goals and attacks at two. Use small, 3 yard goals, with no player allowed within three yards of any goal. (Fig. 253)

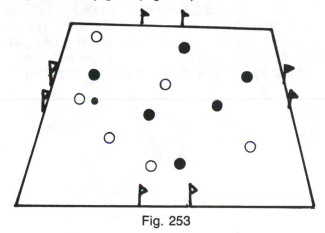

Fig. 253

Variations:
    a) Three consecutive passes must be made before a shot.
    b) Score either by scoring a goal or by six consecutive passes.

The ball is never out of play, but scoring is only possible from in front of goal.

Encourage the players to: — create good passing angles by getting a clear line between themselves and the ball; change the direction of attack; pressurize the player on the ball.

4. 4 Vs 4 in four grid squares (20 yards X 20 yards). One player from each team may position himself in each square. They play "Keep Ball" — how many consecutive passes can each team achieve? The team with the longest sequence wins the game. (Fig. 254)

Fig. 254

Encourage each player to: — draw his opponent away from the space into which the ball can be passed; try to imagine where and when his team mate intends to pass the ball, then dodge away from the line of the pass before returning to it quickly.

5. 4 Vs 4 in six grid squares (30 yards X 20 yards). One player from each team should position himself in each end square. C and D dribble or interpass so that they can pass over the vacant squares to G and H who try to do the same. Each time the ball crosses the vacant squares, from one pair in a team to the other pair, the team scores 1 point. If the other team gains possession of the ball, they try to achieve the same kind of sequence. The ball can be played in the air or on the ground. (Fig. 255)

Fig. 255

Encourage the players with the ball to: — position themselves to kick the ball first time over the vacant squares; pass the ball accurately with the right amount of pace on the ball for easy control; time their runs into receiving positions for when the passer is ready to kick the ball.

Encourage the players without the ball to: — position themselves to cut down passing angles; mark closely so they can intercept passes.

6. 4 Vs 1, guarding a cone. (Fig. 256)

Variation: 3 Vs 1.

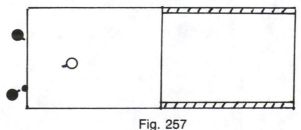

Encourage passers to: — create good support angles; judge how close they can get to the defender without risk; look for one touch passing.

Fig. 256

Encourage the defender to: — decide when to stay close to the cone or come out to challenge.

7. 2 Vs 1 in 2 grid squares 20 yards x 10 yards. The attackers aim to place a foot on the ball on either of the far side-lines. (Fig. 257)

Fig. 257

132

8.

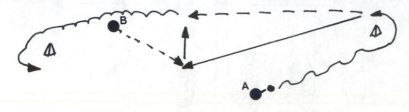

Fig. 258

Two players with one ball, 2 cones 20 yards apart. A dribbles round one of the cones and, as he turns, B moves to receive a pass. A plays it to B and immediately runs to receive a return pass and continues to dribble round the other cone. Repeat. (Fig. 258)

Encourage player A to: — look up as he turns round the cone; play the ball firmly and accurately into player B; accelerate into position to receive the return pass.

Encourage player B to: — time his run to receive player A's pass as player A's head comes up; be on balance in the receiving position; play the ball into player A's stride path.

9.

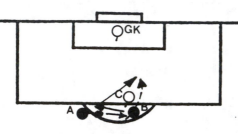

Fig. 259

Player A starts with the ball and passes to player B, who is marked by player C. Player B can either dribble, shoot, or play a 1-2 with player A. Player A is restricted to passing to player B only. (Fig. 259)

Coaching emphasis in this practice will focus on player B's play, dependent upon the actions of player C.

1. He must receive the ball under severe pressure.

2. He must use this pressure either to 'spin' on player C or play a quick 1-2 with player A and run into the space behind player C.

3. If player C's pressure is less than intense, he should turn to face the goal and try to create enough space to get a shot at goal.

It should be noted that 1-2's played near goal require a much greater degree of risk than those played in mid-field. Player B might have to consider turning to face player A (sideways-on to player C) and playing the ball with the foot nearest to player C; this might make player C lunge for the ball, at which point player B flicks it to player A and immediately gets into the space behind player C for the return pass. It is highly unlikely that player B will succeed with a 1-2 if he plays the ball to player A with the foot furthest from player C.

10. Four defenders Vs 2 attackers in each half of the field. The goalkeeper serves the ball to one of his defenders. The defense, opposed by the two forwards, interpass or run with the ball in order for one of them to take it across the half line to make a 3 Vs 4 situation. A point is scored each time a defender successfully crosses the half line in possession. The game continues in the other half of the field until the defense wins possession, at which point the additional player must return to his own half. Score 5 points each time a goal is scored. (Fig. 260)

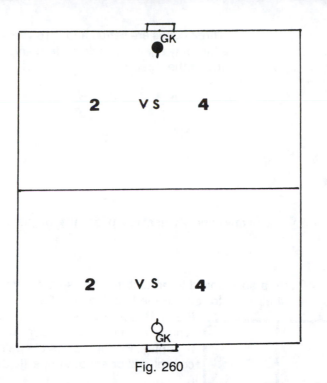

Fig. 260

Encourage the defensive players in possession to: — 'spread' out; offer receiving positions that provide a wide angle of awareness; calculate on the side of safety when in possession in their own half.

It should be pointed out that emphasis in the above practice could be focused on:

Marking, or
Covering, or
Goalkeeper distribution, or
Passing, or
Dribbling, or
Shooting, or
Shielding, etc.

The coach should concentrate his attention on one of these aspects during a practice.

It is also very simple to vary the practice e.g. by starting with 4 Vs 3 in each half or allowing any defensive player with or without the ball to move up in support of his forwards.

11.

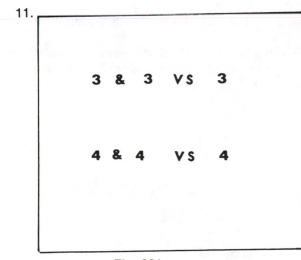

A group of players are divided into three teams, and two teams play "Keep Ball" against the third team. If one of the two teams in possession loses the ball, then it becomes the defensive team. (Fig. 261)
Score 1 point for 10 consecutive passes.

Fig. 261

Variations: Keep ball — two touch; or, no return passes to the same player.

Encourage the players in possession to: — create good support positions; time their runs; change the point of attack; 'spread' out; get the ball immediately under control; use body language.

12.

Three cones are set-up about 15 yards apart. Three players with a ball play against two defenders and try to kick it to knock down any of the three cones.

Fig. 262

Shots can only be taken within 2 yards of any cone. At least one pass must be played in every attacking move. (Fig. 262)

Variation: 4 cones, 4 Vs 3.

Encourage the attackers to: — form a solid shield to protect the ball; spin away from any challenge; create good passing opportunities; time their runs to receive the ball; look for 1-2 possibilities.

13.

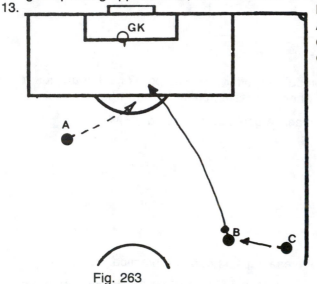

Player B receives the ball from player C in mid-field. Player A times his run to catch player B's eye just after the moment of control. Player B plays the ball to player A so that he can control and/or shoot in one fluid movement. (Fig. 263)

Fig. 263

Encourage player A to: — time his run when player B is ready to play the ball; run diagonally into the danger area; never lose sight of player B's intentions.

Encourage player B to: — set the ball up on his first touch; bend the ball into player A's stride path.

14.

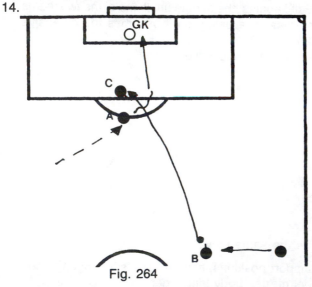

Player B receives the ball in mid-field and plays it to player C. Player C receives and either controls and/or shoots or lays the ball off for player A. (fig. 264)

Fig. 264

Encourage Player C to: — adopt one of the runs indicated in Fig. 222; time his runs for when B is ready to play the ball.

Encourage Player A to: — read player C's intentions; move into a support position dependent on player C's receiving position.

15. Five players with one ball play in an area 20 yards X 20 yards, bounded by six cones. The ball is interpassed first time and after a pass, the man who has played the ball sprints to the spare cone. (Fig. 265)

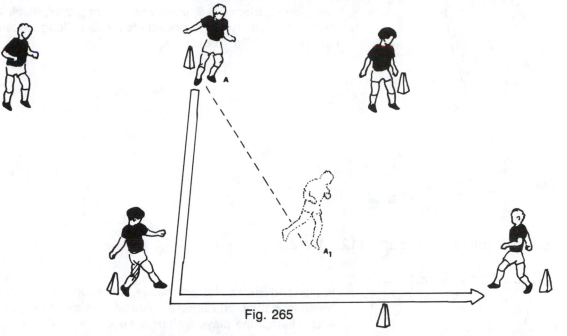

Fig. 265

16.

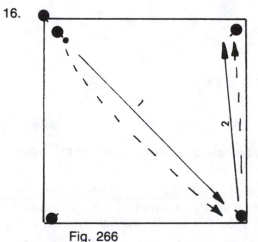

Fig. 266

Five players with one ball play in a 10 yard square. The player with the ball passes it to any of the other three players in the other corners and sprints to follow his pass. Count the number of consecutive first time passes. (Fig. 266)

17. Black 7 chips a ball from the goal line to a team mate, Black 8, downfield. He controls it, plays a 1-2 with a target man, Black 9, and shoots. He now plays a chip to the Black 7 who has run downfield, and the practice continues. (Fig. 267)

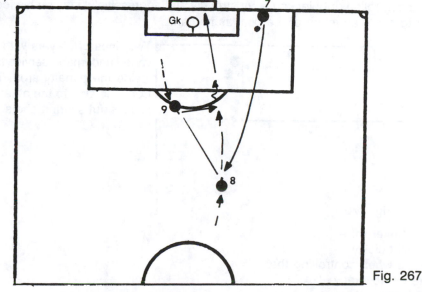

Fig. 267

18. Switching the point of the attack.

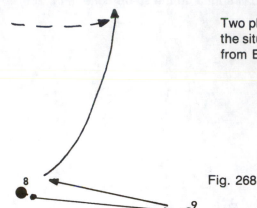

Two players, Black 8 & 9, interpass. A third player, Black 11, reads the situation and runs into position to receive a long crossfield pass from Black 8. (Fig. 268)

Fig. 268

Practices to Improve Shooting (12-14 yrs.)

1.
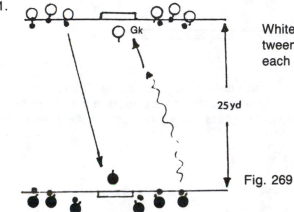

25 yd

Fig. 269

Whites and Blacks play alternately, with each player alternating between long shot, and dribble followed by a close range shot. After each attempt the players change ends. (Fig. 269)

Encourage the long-range shooters to: — concentrate on accuracy before power; hit the ball with the instep or outside of the foot; impart spin and swerve on the ball.

Encourage the close range shooters to: — dribble at controlled speed with minimum of touches; calculate how far ahead they can knock the ball without interception by the goalkeeper; be aware of the goalkeeper's movement so that they can choose whether to dribble round him, shoot low or chip the ball over him.

Encourage the goalkeeper facing long shots to: — anticipate early the line of flight of long shots; get into the intended flight path; decide whether to catch or tip the ball over the cross bar; let the wide or high shots pass by.

Encourage the goalkeeper facing close range shots to: — hold his position so that he cannot be chipped; swoop on any uncontrolled dribble; come out strongly and aggressively; stay on his feet as long as possible; spread himself to cover as much of the goal as he can.

2.
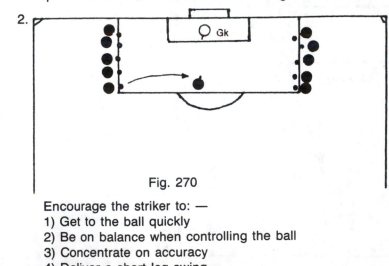

Two lines of players with a ball each provide a varied underhand service to a striker standing just inside the penalty area. The service alternates from one side to the other. Count the number of successful scoring shots. (Fig. 270)

Fig. 270

Encourage the striker to: —
1) Get to the ball quickly
2) Be on balance when controlling the ball
3) Concentrate on accuracy
4) Deliver a short leg swing
5) Keep his toe down.

3.

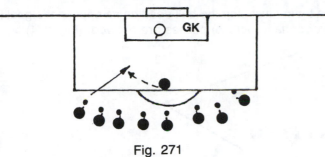

Fig. 271

A group of players with a ball each at their feet pass the ball to a striker in the penalty area, who must shoot for goal as quickly as possible with the minimum number of touches. (Fig. 271)

Encourage the striker to: —
1) Move onto the pass quickly
2) Hit first time shots whenever possible with either foot.
3) Control and turn in one action when the ball comes directly at him.
4) Concentrate on the accuracy of the shot.
5) Be aware of the goalkeeper's position.

4.

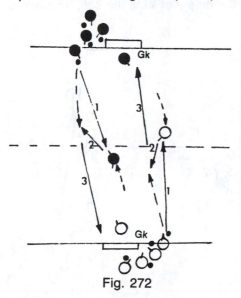

Fig. 272

Two groups of players with a ball each line up on either side of a goal 30-40 yds. apart. Two additional players take up a position about mid-distance between the goals.

The first player in a line passes the ball to one of the middle players and follows up for a return pass from which he must attempt a first-time shot at goal. (Fig. 272)

Encourage the middle player to: —
1) Move to the ball
2) Know what is behind him
3) Lay the ball off gently into the stride path of the shooter.

Encourage the shooter to: —
1) Pass accurately at speed
2) Delay his run until the ball nearly arrives at the middle player's foot
3) Adjust his strides so that he can shoot with power
4) Concentrate on accuracy

Practices to Improve Dribbling (12-14 years)

1. Player B passes the ball to player C who tries to dribble to reach the end line behind player A. Both player A and player B are restricted to their grid squares. On player C's second touch, player D may come into the game and defend along with players A and B; he may go as far as the middle grid only. (Fig. 273)

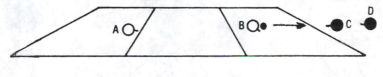

Fig. 273

Encourage the dribbler to: — attack at speed by using acceleration to go past player B; use changes of speed and direction.

2. Two teams each defending a goal-line. To score a team must stop the ball dead on its opponent's goal-line. No player may pass the ball forward. Only back or square (across) passes are allowed. (Fig. 274)

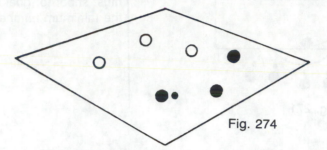

Fig. 274

Encourage the players to: — attack the defender with the least cover; develop fakes and deceptions; spin away from any challenge if double teamed and pass to an unmarked team mate.

3. In 6 grid squares, 30 yards X 20 yards, play 1 Vs 1 at each end with a goalkeeper. A defender at one end starts off with a pass to his attacker at the other end, who has to turn with the ball, beat the opposing defender and score past the opposing goalkeeper. After a goal, a miss or if the defender wins the ball, he starts off a move by passing to his attacker at the other end. (Fig. 275)

Fig. 275

Encourage the receiver to: — take up good receiving positions; roll-round on his defender; develop good close control, fakes and change of direction.

Encourage the passer to: — play the ball in accurately, with the correct speed and timed so that the dribbler receives it when he is ready.

4. Two cones are placed 20 yards apart on a line. One player with the ball at his feet attempts to knock over either cone with the ball. The defender, who must stay on his side of the line, shadows the dribbler and may only cross the line within one yard of each cone. (Fig. 276)

Fig. 276

Encourage the dribbler to: — run parallel with the line with the ball on the foot furthest from the defender; develop spin turns with acceleration.

To effect a spin turn, the dribbler must get over the ball. In the illustration, (Fig. 276) he places his left foot alongside the ball, then sweeps the ball back with the outside of the right foot almost falling back in the reverse direction. Immediately, he transfers the ball onto his left foot and runs for the other cone.

This movement can be reversed, whereby the dribbler steps up to or past the ball with his right foot, then pivots away from the defender and plays it with the inside of the left foot.

In executing the fake, the dribbler must get over the ball. He takes his foot outside the ball, across the front and back inside to play the ball with the inside of the foot and immediately gets into stride for the quick acceleration. (Fig. 277)

If he reverses the foot movement over the ball, his leg will arrive at the contact point with the knee pointing outwards and the hip joint in an open position, making acceleration difficult.

Fig. 277

An important consideration for players of this age is to know when and where to dribble — and when and where not to dribble. As a general yardstick, the guidelines set in Fig. 278 should apply for **where** to dribble.

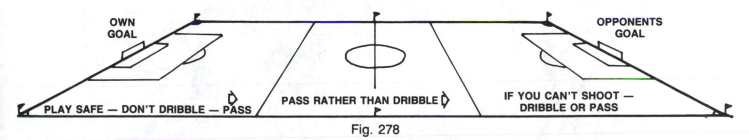

Fig. 278

It is also important that the coach uses small-sided games to help the players understand **when** to dribble. An example would be:

Here, White 1 can attack the defender, as the supporting defender is in a bad position. White 1 should attack Black 1 with the ball and seek the shaded space behind him. Players can be shown, and can understand, this type of situation that occurs many times in all areas of the field.

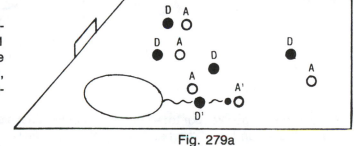

Fig. 279a

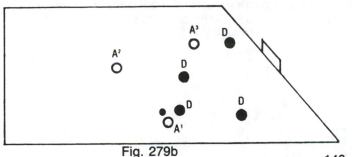

Fig. 279b

White 1 has the ball, but the defense is covering well, with pressure on the ball and with the supporting defender correctly positoned. White 1's best move would be to play the ball back to White 2, who can pass to White 3, leaving two defenders protecting the sideline.

140

5. Three cones are placed in a triangle 15 yards apart. 2 Vs 2, the pair in possession trying to knock over any of the three cones with the ball. There are no side-lines and the play is continuous. (Fig. 280)

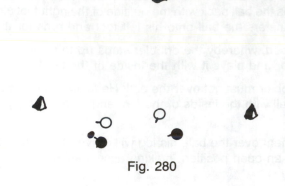

Fig. 280

Variations: Each time a player wins the ball, he must — try to outrun his immediate opponent; or play the ball with the foot furthest away from the defender; or include a spin or a fake; or include at least one pass; or include a 1-2; or must shield the ball.

6. 3 Vs 3, with 4 cones set up in a square.

Encourage the attacking players to: — work hard to retain possession by turning away from defenders; offer good receiving positions; look for 1-2's and take-overs.

Encourage the defenders to: — force the play towards the furthest cone; cover and communicate.

Practices to Improve Goalkeeping (12-14 years)

1. In pairs, 5 yards apart. One player gently kicks the ball along the ground to the side of his partner (the goalkeeper) and follows up. The goalkeeper dives to make a save at the feet of his partner.

Fig. 281

Encourage the goalkeeper to: — get down quickly on his side; get his chest behind the ball; pull the ball into him; roll over on top of the ball to protect it. (Fig. 281)

2. Several players with one ball form a circle about 20 - 25 yards in diameter around a goalkeeper. The outside players cross the ball over the goalkeeper to a player on the other side of the circle to meet it first time and 'score' past the goalkeeper. (Fig. 282)

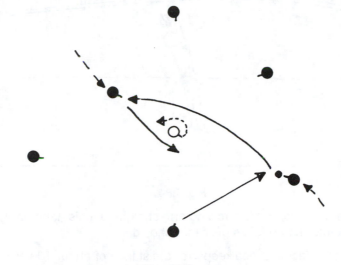

Fig. 282

Encourage the outside players to: — pass accurately with the right speed on the ball for their colleagues to hit it over the goalkeeper; read the movements of the player about to kick the ball and anticipate the height and direction of his kick; attack the ball and knock it down with head or feet past the goalkeeper.

Encourage the goalkeeper to: — pivot and instantly make a good 'ready' position; get balanced so that he can react quickly to the first-time shot.

3.   Three goalkeepers with one ball face a wall on which a target is marked. The goalkeeper with the ball throws the ball from as far away as possible to hit the target and the next goalkeeper tries to catch the rebound. (Fig. 283)

If a wall is not available, the goalkeeper should play 'piggy in the middle'. If any thrower fails to deliver an accurate throw, he goes into the middle. (Fig. 284)

Fig. 283

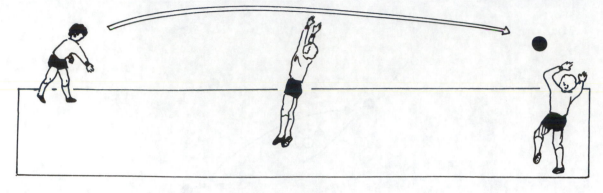

Fig. 284

Encourage the goalkeeper to: — keep his throwing arm straight; get his hand firmly behind the ball; use the non-throwing arm as a pointer as he looks over that shoulder.

4. A player with one ball stands facing a goalkeeper at a distance of about 10 yards. A third player stands a yard or so in front of the goalkeeper. The first player throws head and shoulder-high balls at the third player, who ducks out of the way at the last possible moment. (Fig. 285)

Fig. 285

Encourage the goalkeeper to: — get his hands behind the ball; hold, rather than parry, the ball.

Shots close to the body can often cause bigger problems for a goalkeeper than those requiring more difficult acrobatic saves. With the hard low shot between the hips and the ground, the technique is to 'collapse' on the ball, rather than dive for it, getting the legs out of the way quickly so that the hands and body can be behind the ball. (Fig. 286)

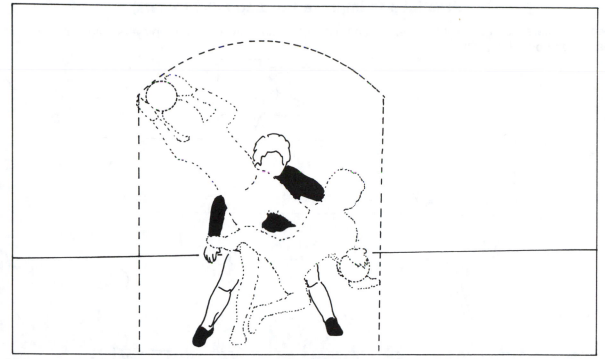

Fig. 286

5. A goalkeeper stands on a stretch of grass (or sandy or earthy ground) facing a wall. He should wear appropriate protection-thick warm-up pants, thigh and knee pads, etc. Two players with one ball stand about 10 — 15 yards behind him and, at an angle, throw or kick ball at the wall so they rebound within handling distance of the goalkeeper. (Fig. 287)

Fig. 287

Encourage the goalkeeper to: — fall on his side; get his hands behind the ball.

Practices to Improve Heading (12-14 years)

1. Two defenders stand under the crossbar and head chip shots away. Several players chip balls from outside the penalty box. (Fig. 288)

Fig. 288

Encourage the players to: — attack the ball; power their headers high and away from goal or over the bar or round the post.

2. 6 Vs 6 including goalkeepers in an area 60 yards x 40 yards with two goals. Attack by alternate heading and catching and throwing (a side may make two consecutive headers, but not catches). A team may only score with headers. Defenders may only intercept with their heads, and then the first to grab the ball wins possession for his side. (Fig. 289)

Fig. 289

3. One player with a ball faces a wall. He throws it in the air and heads it towards the wall. (Fig. 290)

    Variation: Throw the ball against the wall and head the rebound.

Fig. 290

Encourage the player to: — keep one foot in front of the other, lean back, tense the neck muscles and hit the ball with the forehead.

4. Two players with one ball face each other with a space marked by two lines 5 yards apart between them. They head the ball back and fore until eventually one fails to return it or it drops inside the 5 yard space. (Fig. 291)

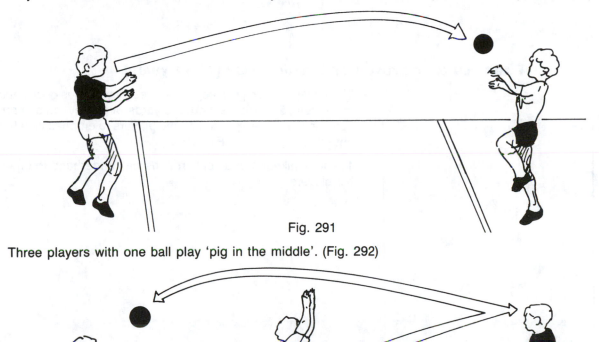

Fig. 291

5. Three players with one ball play 'pig in the middle'. (Fig. 292)

Fig. 292

Encourage the players to: — build-up power by use of legs, trunk and neck.

6. A ring of players round a 'target man' with one ball. The ball is played in the air to the target man who executes a variety of headed passes, including the angled flick-on (A), the back header (B) and the basic knock-down (C). (Fig. 293)

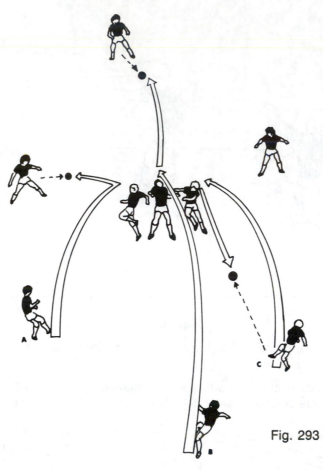

Fig. 293

Practices to Improve Combination Play (12-14 years)

1.

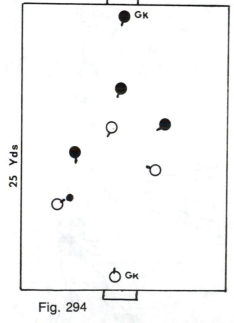

Fig. 294

Three players plus goalkeeper Vs three players plus goalkeeper in an area 25 - 30 yards long x 20 yards wide. Several different conditions can be imposed on the players to emphasize different coaching points. (Fig. 294)

1. The goalkeeper may only roll the ball underhand to one of his players.

2. The goalkeeper may only lob the ball in the air to one of his players.

3. Players receiving the ball can only dribble or shoot; no passing. Defenders should be encouraged to double-up on the attacker with the ball.

4. No offside law.

147

5. The player receiving the ball must make at least one pass before shooting.

6. A take-over, 1-2, spin turn or fake turn must be played before a shot is taken.

7. Shoot with the left foot only, etc.

    Variation: 2 Vs 3, 4 Vs 3, 4 Vs 4, etc.

    The players should be encouraged to: — shoot whenever an opportunity arises; concentrate on accuracy before power.

2.

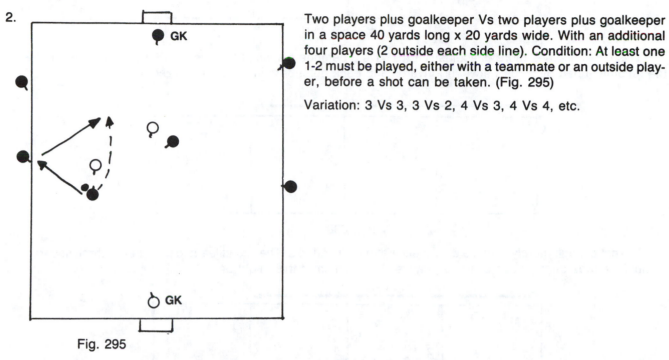

Two players plus goalkeeper Vs two players plus goalkeeper in a space 40 yards long x 20 yards wide. With an additional four players (2 outside each side line). Condition: At least one 1-2 must be played, either with a teammate or an outside player, before a shot can be taken. (Fig. 295)

Variation: 3 Vs 3, 3 Vs 2, 4 Vs 3, 4 Vs 4, etc.

Fig. 295

Encourage the attackers to: — play the ball accurately off the front foot; commit the nearest defender; accelerate into the space behind the defender by running on his blind side.

Encourage the outside players to: — take up a good receiving position to play a 1-2; decide whether to make a return pass or hold the ball.

Encourage the defenders to: — track down any runs made by the attackers into the space behind them; resist following the ball.

The Consolidation of Team Play (12-14 yrs)

The remaining 6 principles of play —

Compactness in Defense, Width in Attack, Balance in Defense, Mobility in Attack, Patience in Defense, Creativity in Attack — must now be introduced, again through small-sided games to the 12-14 year olds.

Compactness in Defense

A well-organized defensive team will only allow limited space to develop between and behind players. The player challenging for the ball must be closely supported by covering players.

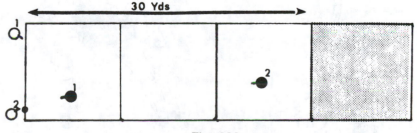

Fig. 296

This coaching point is easily demonstrated (Fig. 296) where, while White 1 and White 2 are asked to get past Black 1 and to get into the shaded area, Black 1 and Black 2 are restricted to playing in their own squares.

148

If we change this practice and allow Black 2 to move forward to cover Black 1, then White 1 and White 2's task becomes much more difficult (Fig. 297).

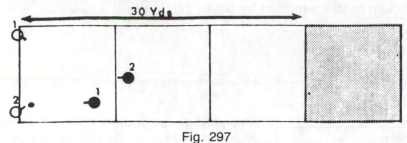

Fig. 297

This task becomes more difficult still if we have 3 defenders spaced out over 30-35 yards. (Fig. 298) This is the recommended distance between forwards and back defenders in a well-organized team.

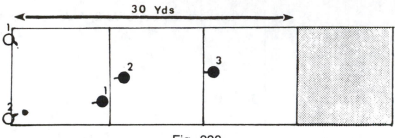

Fig. 298

It is not enough merely to place defenders within their squares. They must learn to play, not as three separate individuals, but as units of two or three players. An example of this might be:

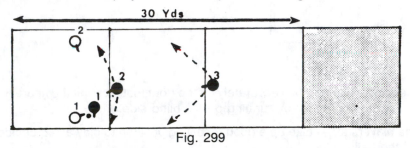

Fig. 299

Fig. 299, where Black 1 and Black 2 are playing as a pair. Black 1 has engaged White 1 and has shepherded him into a tight position near the side line; Black 2 covers Black 1 in such a way that he can tackle White 1 if he beats Black 1, or engage White 2 if White 1 decides to pass to White 2. Notice that Black 1 has closed down on White 1 and is facing him in the boxer's stance, sideways on (Fig. 300). Once he has engaged White 1 in this way, Black 1 must become relentless and he must continue to apply this pressure on White 1.

Fig. 300

Teams must attempt to achieve the same cover and compactness in defense as soon as they have drawn up their lines of confrontation.

In Fig. 301, White 2 is pressurized by Black 10. Players behind Black 10 are tightly marked, while Black 6 covers the space behind.

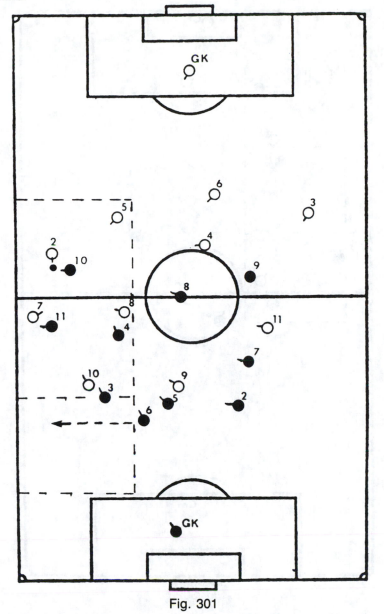

Fig. 301

If the defensive organization requires the team to defend in the opponents' half of the field, we may well see a situation as in Fig. 302.

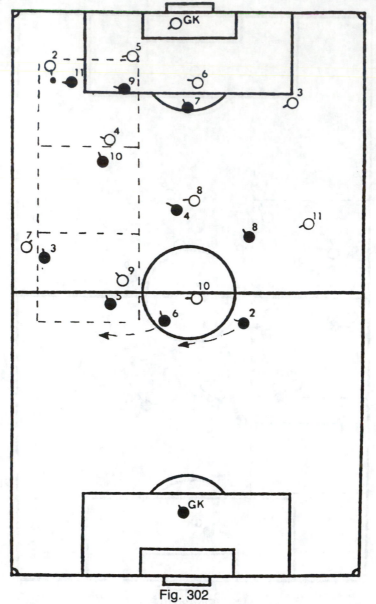

Fig. 302

The defensive team is involved in restricting space through which and into which attacking players can move with safety. Defenders aim to restrict the spaces through which passes can be made. Defenders cover, not only each other, but also the spaces for which the whole defense is responsible.

Players should be made aware of the difficulties of beating a concentrated defense in a confined space and defenders should be encouraged, especially when they are in any doubt, to retreat centrally, and as a result, concentrate in front of their own penalty area. In this way, if a full back is beaten in mid-field close to the touch-line, he should not get up and try to catch his opponent; rather he should retreat to a central defensive position. In Fig. 303, the White 2 has been beaten by the Black 11. As soon as this happens, the White 2 should get up and retreat on a line to his own goal so that he can take up a defensive position on the edge of the shooting area. At the same time, the White 4 who has been covering the White 2 should try to force the Black 11 toward the touch line, i.e. away from the danger area.

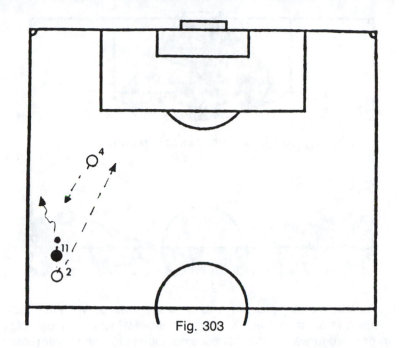

Fig. 303

Width in Attack

It will be remembered that the principles of play are based upon the considerations of defensive players guarding the spaces behind and in front of the defense to a position in which an attacking player may shoot at goal. If an attacking player collects the ball unchallenged in the space in front of the defense, his chances of making a good pass into the shooting area are increased enormously. In the same way, it should be realized that the space on the flanks of a centrally concentrated defense can be utilized by attacking players.

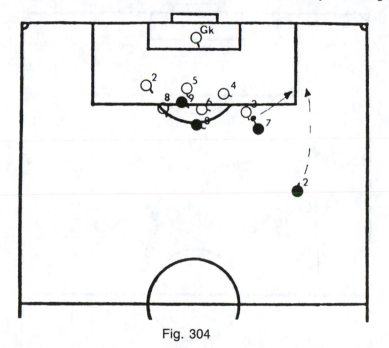

Fig. 304

In Fig. 304, the Black 7 has the ball and is confronted by a centrally concentrated defense. The Black 2, realizing that there is space outside the Black 7, moves down the wing to take a pass from the Black 7. Immediately this happens, either one of the defenders must move out to tackle the Black 2, or otherwise, the Black 2 can steady himself to make a good pass into the area in front of goal. From this, we can deduce that the attacking area in front of the defense can now be enlarged to include the spaces down the flanks and we arrive at a danger area similar to the build-up or preparation area in fig. 305, in which it would cause the defense great anxiety if an opposing player collected the ball unchallenged.

152

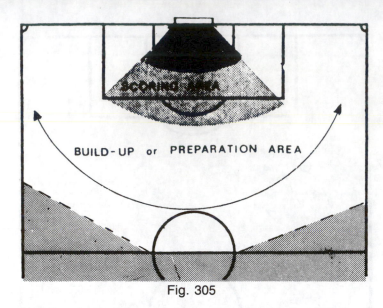

Fig. 305

In modern soccer, where teams may play only two or three forwards, width in attack may not seem necessary. There is little point in having two players wide on the touch lines when a team only plays two forwards. When a team is only playing two or three forwards, the first consideration is for the player receiving the ball to receive immediate support. In this way, if the center-forward receives the ball, his fellow strikers should move quickly toward him to give support, or if a winger receives the ball, the center-forward and the other winger should move across the field to support him, as in Fig. 306. By moving across to help the Black 7, the Black 9 and the Black 11 may cause the opposing defense to move over, thus making it possible for the Black 6 or Black 3 to break out quickly from defense and utilize the space on the left flank.

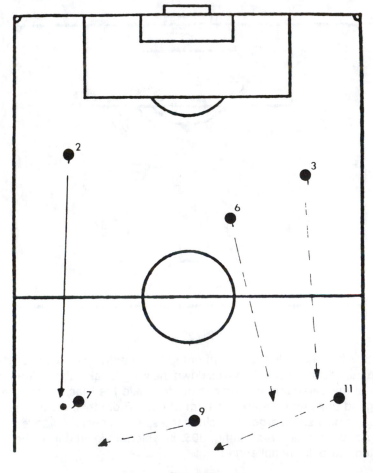

Fig. 306

Mobility in Attack

Most soccer coaches have found that it is extremely difficult to operate "set" attacking plays in the match situation. It is impossible to predict the movement of opposing players and even the simplest and best rehearsed of moves falls down because of the problems created by the opposing defense. It is much better, therefore, to allow attacking players opportunities of solving these problems, and they should be encouraged to react naturally and intelligently to out-wit the defense.

In attacking play, too much regimentation kills imagination; too much organization can be restrictive. When players are faced with the problems created by a defense, they must be allowed to experiment with solutions.

One of the simplest way of upsetting a defense is for the forwards to switch positions. A full back who is marking a winger on the same side of the field all the time has a comparatively easy task, especially if he has made a sound tackle early on in the game. One or two heavy tackles might very well put the winger out of game. If, however, the winger is continually switching positions with his other forwards, the full-back's problems will be increased, for he may have to contend with four or five different players during the game.

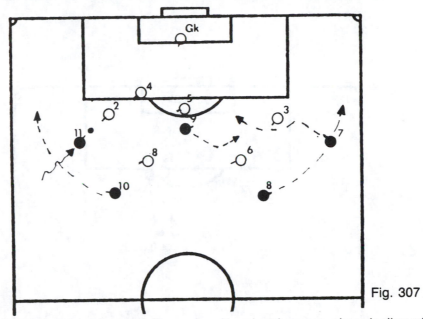

Fig. 307

An attacking team should make full use of diagonal and overlapping runs when dealing with an organized and compact defense on the edge of that defense's penalty area (Fig. 307). Here Black 11 has the ball and is challenged by White 2 who is covered by White 4. The Black 10 who is marked by White 8 makes a wide overlapping run outside of Black 11. At the same time, Black 7 makes a diagonal run to threaten the space just behind White 5 who might have been moved out of position by Black 9's run out of the central position. Black 8 will make an overlapping run into the space vacated by Black 7 and is likely to get free into this area as his marker, White 6, will, in all probability, be watching the ball.

We might, therefore, have our players in the following positions (Fig. 308).

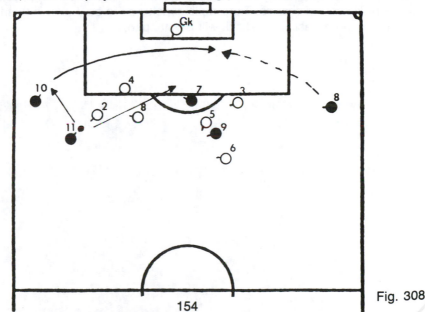

Fig. 308

The Black team has effectively destroyed the White defense's balance and cover by the use of diagonal and overlapping runs. Black 11 has now two good opportunities to create a scoring opportunity. He can either play the ball to Black 7, or he can play it to Black 10, who in turn, can cross into the danger area for either Black 8 or Black 7 to have a strike at goal.

All movements of attacking players near the danger area have to be watched closely and judged quickly by defenders. Defenders are never quite certain whether an attacking player is moving to receive a pass, or to tempt a defender away from a position in which some other attacker may receive the ball i.e. creating space.

Diagonal runs should be made precisely for this purpose, and an attacking player should run into positions in which he is an immediate danger himself, should he receive the ball, and in which, at the same time, he has opened up the possibility of a pass to a team-mate who is just as dangerously placed.

The more direct the attacker makes his run toward the opponents' goal, the more positive must be the reaction of the defender. A direct run towards goal by an attacker must be covered by a defender. But this type of run has two major drawbacks. First, it is often difficult to pass the ball to a player running directly towards the goal (Fig. 309);

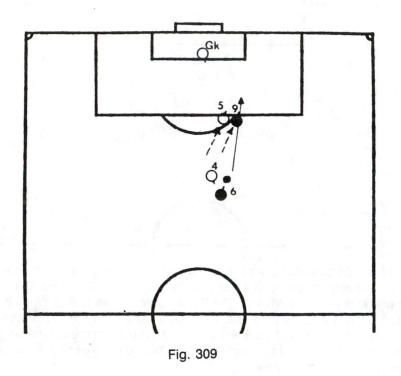

Fig. 309

and secondly, the problem of, or choice of, action is solved for the defender. But such a run, if it is successful, usually results in a goal scoring chance. The simple conclusion to be drawn is that the more often attackers adopt this kind of run, the more easily the attack will be stopped.

Much greater success can be expected if attackers make diagonal runs to threaten the space behind the defense (Fig. 310). Here the Black 9 runs diagonally forward into the space behind White 5. In this type of run, he should maintain eye-contact with Black 8. On no account should he turn his back on the ball. Black 8's task will now be to bend the ball round into the path of his run by using the inside of the right foot, or the outside of the left foot.

Black 9 could also threaten the space to the right of White 5 in which case Black 8 would have the responsibility of bending the ball with the inside of the left foot or outside of the right foot into Black 9's path (Fig. 311).

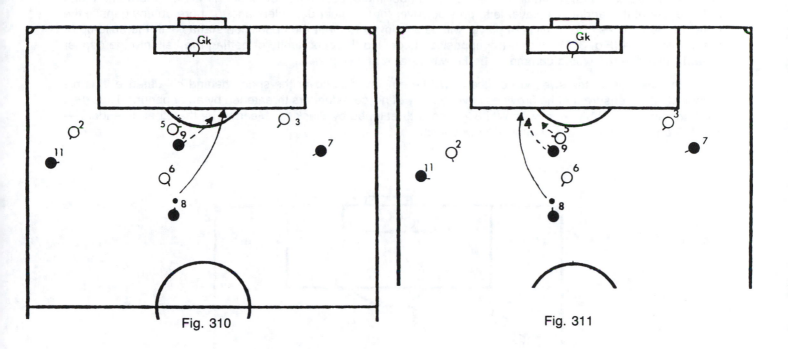

Fig. 310   Fig. 311

Not all diagonal runs should be made away from the ball-player. A great deal will be added to the attacking possibilities of a team if players in advanced positions near their opponents' goal make diagonal runs away from goal.

In Fig. 312, Black 9 has made a short diagonal run toward Black 8. In this way, he has drawn White 5 away from the area of greatest danger and enables Black 8 to play a short pass into him so that he can immediately feed Black 11, who is running into the space behind the defense. Note that Black 9 is half-turned toward White 5 so that not only does he see the movement of the defender, but he can also receive the ball with the foot furthest away from the defender, and at the same time, observe Black 11's run. It is much more difficult for Black 9 if he cannot see White 5 by having his back toward him.

BALANCE IN DEFENSE

It is apparent from our discussion of mobility in attack that defensive play must be concerned with the maintenance of cover at all times. Attacking players will make runs to draw defenders out of position in order to create space for themselves and other attackers, and it is imperative that the defense is balanced against these threats.

Probably the two most important factors in the maintenance of balance in defense are:
...the role of a free defender; and,
...tracking down players.

Most teams, when defending, hope to outnumber the opposition by at least one player. More often than not, the role of this additional player is to provide cover for the other defenders and to shore up any gaps in the defense. Sometimes, this additional player will be employed to meet the opposition's attacks in the build-up or preparation area (Fig. 305), so that the opposition is denied the opportunity of getting the ball into the danger area. In this role, he would commonly be known as a front sweeper.

In most cases, the sweeper, or libero, will be employed to cover the space behind his defense. It is his responsibility to ensure that he provides cover for any of his co-defenders threatened by an opponent. Thus (Fig. 313), the sweeper, White 4, covers White 2, who is threatened by Black 11. Meanwhile, the other defenders — Black 5 and 3 — mark their immediate opponents.

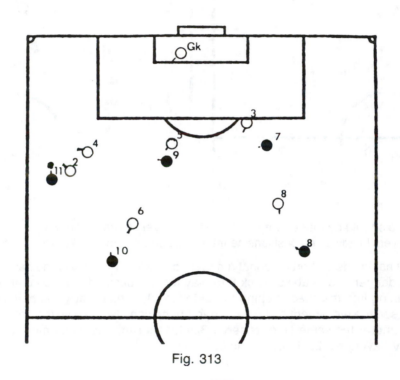

Fig. 313

The mid-field defenders — White 6 and 8 — have the responsibility to close down their immediate opponents if the ball is played to them by Black 11. They also have the responsibility to TRACK DOWN their immediate opponent should he threaten to run into spaces between and behind the defense. In Fig. 313, White 8 is particularly vulnerable if the ball is played back to Black 10, as White 8 might be caught ball-watching and allow Black 8 to run into the space behind him. In such circumstances, we might expect the sweeper to 'pick-up' any mid-field opponent who has not been tracked down (Fig. 314). An experienced sweeper in this situation might demand White 3 to cover the space threatened by Black 8 while he 'picked-up' Black 7, White 3's immediate opponent. Once the danger had passed, White 4 would ask White 3 to 'pick-up' Black 7 again so that White 4 could revert to his role as sweeper.

If an opposing player receives the ball unchallenged in the build-up or preparation area and 'attacks' the defense, it is the responsibility of the sweeper to come out to challenge him. In this way, the marking players can concentrate on marking their immediate opponents (Fig. 315).

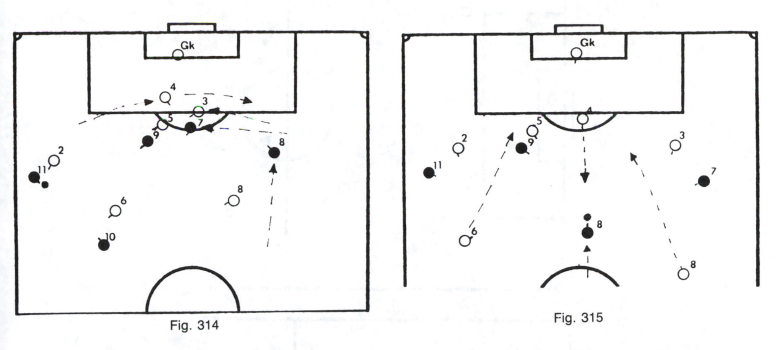

Fig. 314

Fig. 315

Here we find Black 8 in clear possession and the sweeper, White 4, comes out to challenge him. On no account should White 4 allow himself to be beaten by lunging into the tackle. Rather, he should concentrate on delaying the attack until White 6 and 8 have recovered into defensive positions, goal-side of the ball, so that the defense can re-establish its balance.

Creativity in Attack

To unlock modern defenses, we need players with skill, flair and imagination. The player who is prepared to do the unexpected, the unorthodox, is much more likely to succeed against well-organized defenses than the player(s) who is drilled and predictable.

All players should be encouraged to develop awareness and imagination during their soccer-formative years. Each player, particularly those in forward positions who are likely to be tightly marked, should develop a range of 'tricks' with the ball that are likely to deceive their immediate opponents.

Without doubt, the key to the development of creativity is **the total awareness of immediate opponents.** Players should make full use of their visual, audio and tactile senses to determine the exact position and intention of every immediate opponent. If they know where their immediate opponent(s) is positioned and what his likely intention will be, then they can call on their repertoire of 'tricks' or skills to deceive this opponent.

For most forward players, it is good planning to allow themselves to be tightly marked just before the ball is ready to be played forward. In this way, they will establish the starting position of the defender through using their eyes (they will need to be slightly sideways-on to their opponent) and through touch (by leaning against him).

In Fig. 316, Black 2 has received the ball off Black 6, but is not yet ready to play it forward. Black 9 advances as far as possible towards the White goal, making White 5 mark him closely, and, at the same time, forcing White 6 (the sweeper) to play square. In this position, Black 9 can dictate the line of the White defense, and, at the same time, create a space (bounded by White 4, 5, 6 and 10) in which he will eventually receive the ball from Black 2.

When Black 2 has the ball under control and is ready to play it forward, Black 9 makes his move to receive the ball. As he 'comes off' White 5, the pressure on his arms and side will indicate to him how closely White 5 will follow. At the same time, he should face the side-line so that he can receive the ball with White 5 in view out of the corner of his left eye. Some players will also pick up cues (or information) of White 5's movements by listening to the sounds of his foot beats.

We might now expect a situation such as illustrated in Fig. 317 to have developed.

158

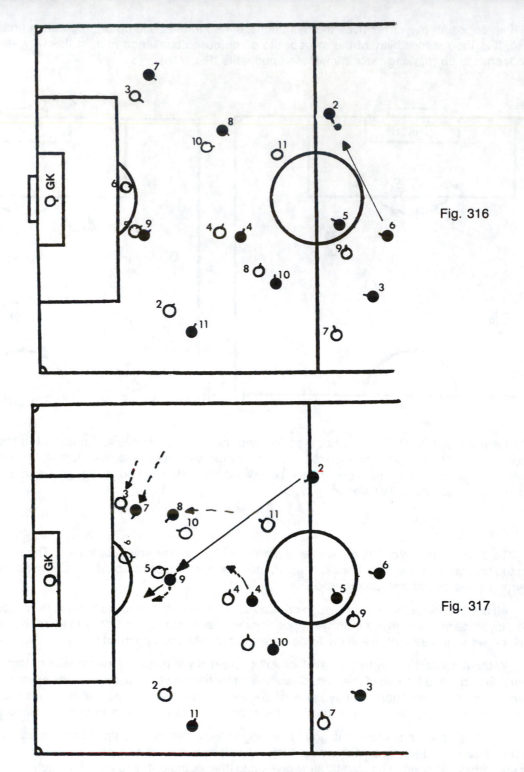

Fig. 316

Fig. 317

Black 9 comes off White 5 and receives the ball from Black 2 facing the side-line. From visual and tactile cues, he knows that White 5 has tracked down his run and is marking him very tightly. He also sees that Black 7 and 8 have initiated penetrative runs to get into the space between White 3 and 6. Black 9 is, therefore, faced with 3 major options:

1. He can flick a pass onto Black 7 or Black 8;

2. He can hold the ball and lay it off to Black 4; or

3. He can step over the ball and pivot to beat White 5.

The inventive, creative player will recognize all three options and will not only have the technique to carry each option out, but also the skill to recognize which will be most effective.

Players should frequently be challenged and encouraged to do the unorthodox, particularly when they are outnumbered by defenders.

159

Patience in Defense

Too often, defenders give up sound defensive positions because they become impatient and go for balls which cannot be won. It should be recognized that a defender's three priorities are:

1. Interception;

2. Challenge and tackle;

3. Delay and contain.

In Fig. 318, the ball has been played forward to Black 9 to a position where it is difficult for White 5 to attempt an interception.

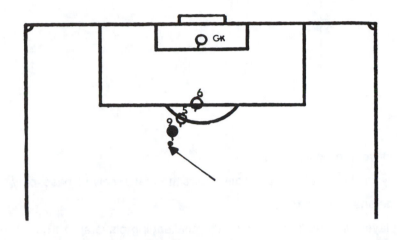

Fig. 318

In this situation, it would be foolish for White 5 to commit himself to a challenge, as this might give the Black 9 the opportunity of pivoting and beating him. Rather, he should restrain his actions and be content to maintain the numbers-up situation which he and White 6 enjoy.

Again, in Fig. 319, White 2 should be content to keep Black 11 facing the side-line and prevent him turning to face the danger area. This will allow White 4 time to recover into a covering position, and only when commanded to do so by White 4 should White 2 attempt to challenge and win the ball.

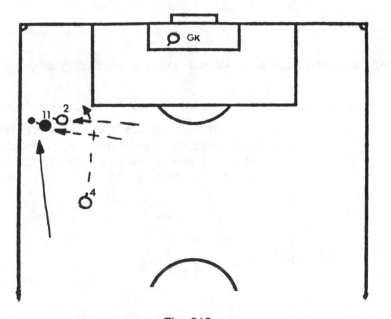

Fig. 319

Too often in this situation, defensive players allow the attacking player to collect the ball and turn to face the danger area. No attacking player should be given the freedom to turn if it is at all possible to keep him facing away from the danger area.

160

Practices to Consolidate Team Play (12-14 years)

1.

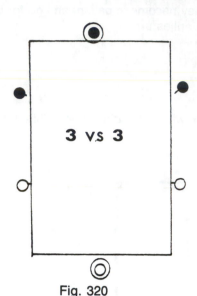

Fig. 320

Twelve players in and around an area 30 yds x 20 yds. Six players play 3 Vs 3 inside the area with the object of trying to get the ball to either end players. They may use the outside players for support in order to play 1-2's or 1-3's. (Fig. 320)

Encourage the players in possession to: —

Protect the ball by shielding; take up positions where they can receive a pass; play the ball off the front foot.

Encourage the defensive players to: —

pressurize the player with the ball; to cover the challenging players; to track down any forward runs.

2.

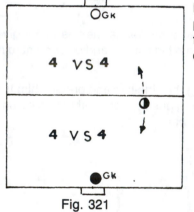

Fig. 321

Four attackers versus four defenders plus goalkeeper in each half. All these players are restricted to playing within their space. One free player joins forces with the four attacking players in possession thus creating rapidly changing 5 Vs 4 attacking situations. (Fig. 321)

Encourage the four attacking players to: — create space for the additional player to make penetrative forward runs.

Encourage the free player to: — seek penetrative forward positions to get himself into scoring areas.

3.

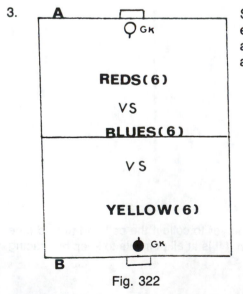

Fig. 322

Six players (Blue) in an area 50 yds x 40 yds attack a goal on line A defended by six Reds and a goalkeeper. If the attack fails Reds take the ball and attack the goal on line B defended by six Yellows and a goalkeeper, and so on. (Fig. 322)

161

Encourage the attacking players to: — make a quick transition from defense to attack; take up good support positions; make forward runs into the danger area; shoot, whenever possible.

Encourage the defensive players to: — make a quick transition from attack to defense; pressurize the opponent with the ball; to cover and support the pressurizing player; to communicate and play as an unit; track down any opponent making forward runs.

4.

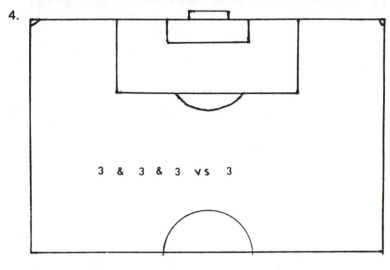

Twelve players in four groups of three in a half field. Each group wears a different colored training apron. Nine players combine to play 'Keep Ball' against the fourth group, which tries to win the ball or kick it out of the area.

Fig. 323

The player responsible for losing the ball, and his two colleagues, become the defending group. (Fig. 323)

Variations:

1) The receiving players may not give a return pass to the same player.

2) Play two-touch.

3) Ten consecutive passes mean that the defending group has to win the ball twice.

4) As above, but the ball has to be played through the middle at least once and not continually around the sides.

Encourage the defending players to: — work hard to pressurize the player with the ball; support each other and work as a defensive unit of three.

Encourage the attacking players to: — control the ball quickly by setting it up on the first touch; support the player with the ball by moving to a position with a clear line between themselves and the ball; develop an awareness of what is behind them; play simple, quick passes.

5.

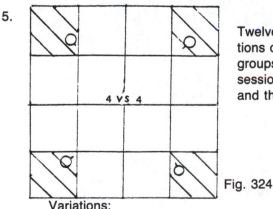

Twelve players in three groups in an area 40 yd x 40 yd. One group positions one of its players in each of the four corners, while the other two groups play 4 Vs 4 in the unshaded grid squares. The four players in possession play 'Possession Soccer' or "Keep Ball" using their colleagues and the four corner players. (Fig. 324)

Fig. 324

Variations:

1) Ten consecutive passes equals one goal

2) Three-touch soccer

3) Each passing movement must include at least a 1-2 or wall-pass within the attacking groups of four.

Encourage the attackers to: — continuously seek to get into good receiving positions; change the point of the attack; control the ball quickly; disguise their passes; run past their immediate opponent.

Encourage the defenders to: — pressurize the man on the ball; support the pressurizing player; track down any player who runs into the space behind them. 162

6.

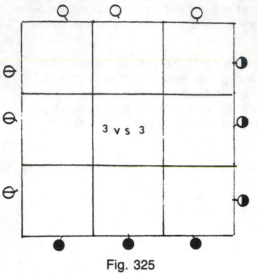

Fig. 325

Eighteen players in six groups of three in an area 30 yd x 30 yd. One group positions itself outside each of the four sides while the remaining two groups play 3 Vs 3 inside the area. One player from each of the four outside groups supports the group in possession in playing 'Keep Ball'. The first group to accumulate seven consecutive passes wins the game and the losing group is replaced by one of the outside groups. (Fig. 325)

Encourage the defending players to: — work together as a close-knit unit; force play into one of the four corners; mark on a man-to-man basis.

Encourage the attacking players to: — protect the ball when in possession; look for simple, quick passes; take up good receiving positions; spread-out by using the full width of the area.

7.

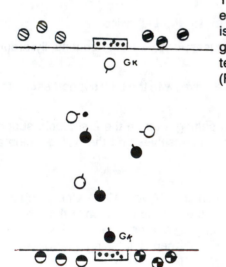

Fig. 326

Twenty players divided into six teams of three players and two goalkeepers in an area between two goals 20 yards apart. A supply of soccer balls is placed in each goal. Two teams play 3 Vs 3 while the remaining four groups are deployed along the goal lines and behind the goals. The first team to score two goals wins the game and the losing team is replaced. (Fig. 326)

Variation:

1) A team must accumulate three consecutive passes before taking a shot.

2) A 1-2 or wall pass must be included in each attacking move.

3) No passing so the ball player is faced with a 1 Vs 3 situation.

Encourage the attacking players to: — shoot at the earliest opportunity; concentrate on accuracy before power.

Encourage the defensive players to: — close down the player with the ball; exercise patience and not 'dive-into' tackles.

8.

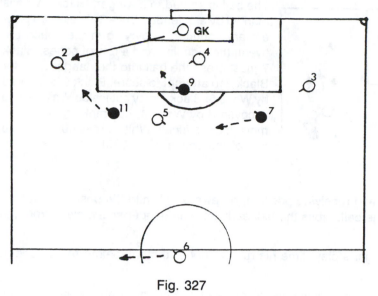

Fig. 327

A goalkeeper and four defenders against three attacking players in a half-field. A fifth defender is deployed just beyond the half way line. The goalkeeper serves the ball to any of the four defenders who must try to get the ball to the fifth player. (Fig. 327)

Encourage the defenders to: — receive and turn quickly to face most of the play; play long, accurate passes whenever possible; exercise care that they are not caught in possession.

Encourage challenging forwards to: — immediately pressurize the player with the ball; support each other; prevent forward passes.

9.

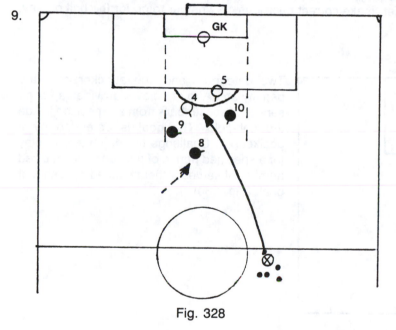

Fig. 328

Seven players in a half field. One attacking player merely provides a varied service of a supply of soccer balls from near the half-line. Two attacking players, Black 9 and 10 attempt to gain possession while two defensive players White 4 and 5 attempt to clear the ball. A third attacking player, Black 8 comes into action once the ball has entered the penalty arc but he is restricted to first time shots only. Play is confined to the area inside the dotted line. (Fig. 328)

Encourage the twin strikers to: — be first to the ball; get their bodies between opponent and ball; be aware of positions and runs of colleagues; be aware of positions of defenders; develop a gentle touch; try the unexpected — flick ons, fakes, take-overs, spin turns, 1-2's etc.

Encourage the support attacker to: — anticipate the actions of the twin strikers and defenders; position himself for any possible first-time shot; run behind the defense for possible through passes.

Encourage the defensive pair to: — be first to the ball; make their clearances high, wide and far; close down the attacker with the ball.

Encourage the goalkeeper to: — communicate with his defense; read the play in front of him and anticipate long shots or through passes.

10.

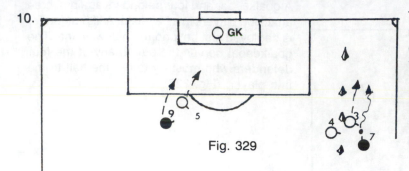

Fig. 329

The ball is served to a winger, Black 7 who is marked by a defender White 3. These two players are confined to playing in the space between the side line and a row of cones. Black 7 must cross the ball into the danger area for Black 9 to attempt to score. Black 9 is marked by White 5. Black 7 may cut inside White 3 who is covered by White 4 thus making the inside move more difficult. White 4 may not cross the line of the cones. (Fig. 329)

Encourage the winger to: — take up a good receiving position; be aware of White 3's position when he receives the ball; develop fakes and feints on the ball; cross the ball early into the danger space away from the goalkeeper.

Encourage the striker to: — read the winger's play; time his runs to get to the ball before the defender; attack the ball; hit first time shots.

Encourage the challenging full back to: — close down the winger early; force the winger away from the danger area; exercise patience and not fall for fakes and feints.

Encourage the covering full back to: — communicate with the challenging full back; read the play and take-up a good inside covering position.

Encourage the central defender to: — read the winger's play; be aware of the movements of the striker; get to the ball first; make his clearances high, wide and far; listen and obey the instructions of the goalkeeper.

Encourage the goalkeeper to: — read the play; take up a position where it is difficult to beat him at the near post; communicate with his central defender; make correct decisions on whether to go for the ball or stay, whether to catch or punch.

11.

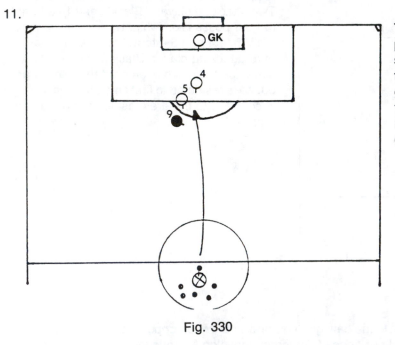

Fig. 330

Two defenders and one attacker near the penalty arc. A fourth player provides a varied service of soccer balls from any position inside the half-field. The goal is defended by a goalkeeper. Challenge the defenders to play for a specified period of time or for a specified number of serves without conceding a shot at goal. (Fig. 330)

Encourage the defensive players to: — play as a pair — one to challenge, the other to cover; get to the ball first; clear it high, wide and far; communicate with each other; exercise patience if the attacker gets the ball.

Encourage the attacker to: — fight for every ball; get his body between opponent and ball; develop fakes, feints and dummies.

Encourage the goalkeeper to: — read the play in front of him; position himself against possible long shots or service over the top of his defenders.

12.

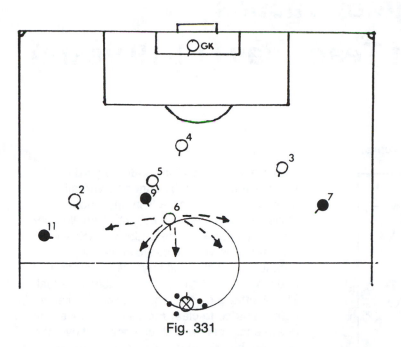

Fig. 331

Five defenders and a goalkeeper against three attackers. An additional player (or the coach) provides a varied service of soccer balls. Three defenders — White 2, 5 and 3 mark on a man-to-man basis while White 4 plays as a covering player. Meanwhile White 6 plays the role of front sweeper whose main responsibilities are:

1. to intercept the service to the attacking forwards

2. to sandwich any forward with the ball between himself and the marker. (Fig. 331)

Encourage the front sweeper to: — anticipate the service; get into the line of flight early; move quickly to challenge any receiving player; obey the instructions of the defenders.

Encourage the marking players to: — mark closely on the inside line between the ball and the goal; prevent attackers turning with the ball; challenge aggressively whenever possible.

Encourage the covering player (back sweeper) to: — cut off all through passes; give early cover to the challenging player; obey his goalkeeper; communicate with his fellow defenders.

Encourage the attacking players to: — interchange positions; make runs towards and away from the ball; look for penetrative flick-ons; support each other.

Encourage the goalkeeper to: — commmunicate with his defense; be alert for through passes behind the defense.

CHAPTER FOUR

The Age of Tactics
The Development of Team Play (14-19 years)

Practices to Develop Team Play (14-16 years)

1.

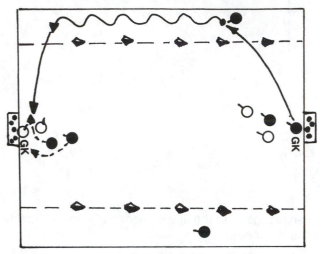

Fig. 332

On a field 70 yards long x 60-70 yards wide, a grid is marked out by cones 10 yards infield from each side-line. A winger, unopposed, plays inside each grid area, with a goalkeeper and 2 attackers vs 1 defender at each end. A goalkeeper serves the ball to either winger who dribbles within the grid towards the other goal and crosses the ball across the face of the foal. The 2 attackers attempt to score while the defender tries to clear the ball. Whenever the goalkeeper gets the ball, or it goes out over the end line, he serves it to one of the wingers. A supply of soccer balls should be placed in each goal. (Fig. 332)

Variation: 2 Vs 2, 2 Vs 3, 3 Vs 3, etc. in front of goal.

The above practices can be used to emphasize a number of important coaching points. For example, they can be used to:

I) Develop the goalkeeper's distribution. He should be encouraged to:

   a) throw the ball so that the winger can receive it on the fly i.e. it should not bounce just in front of the winger.

   b) throw the ball so that the winger can immediately control it and take it forward at speed.

II) Develop the winger's receiving position. He should be encouraged to:

   a) have his back to the side-line in such a way that he can see the opposing goal.

   b) control the ball immediately with his first touch so that he can immediately accelerate towards the opposing goal.

III) Develop the goalkeeper's communication. He should be encouraged to:

   a) make an early decision of whether to come for the ball or not and let his defender know by shouting either 'Keeper' (if he is coming for it) or 'Away' (if he wants the defender to go for it).

IV) Develop the goalkeeper's ability to deal with crosses. He should be encouraged to:

   a) adopt a starting position about mid-way between each goal post, close to the goal line, facing the line of the cross.

   b) attack the ball at its highest point.

   c) get his hands in a 'W' formation behind the ball.

   d) take off one foot to achieve height in his jump.

   e) punch the ball if he cannot catch it because other players are in the way.

   f) punch the ball with both fists to send the ball high, wide and far. (Fig. 333)

Fig. 333

V) Develop the attackers' ability to meet crosses. They should be encouraged to:

  a) read the winger's movement just prior to the cross so that they can predict the angle and flight of the ball.

  b) co-ordinate their runs so that they don't take each other's space.

  c) time their runs so that they meet the ball while on the move.

  d) make near post runs to get ahead of the defender as the ball passes through the near post area. Bent runs, finally moving towards the ball, are usually more successful. (Fig. 334)

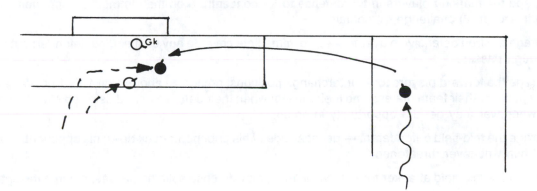

Fig. 334

  e) concentrate on accuracy rather than power in re-directing the ball towards goal with their head, foot or body.

  f) get above the ball and head it downwards towards the goal line.

VI) Develop the winger's ability to cross the ball. He should be encouraged to:

  a) hit the space between the retreating defender and the goalkeeper.

  b) where possible, drive the ball just above head height across the face of the goal.

  c) if he has more time and gets up over the ball to clip it to the near post area or send it all the way across to the far post area. Where possible, he should miss out the middle goal area. Neither should he try to place the cross on a forward's head; rather he should hit the space for the attacker to run onto the cross.

VII) Develop defensive play. The defender should be encouraged to:

    a) read the winger's movement prior to the cross and try to predict the angle and flight of the ball.

    b) get to the ball before a forward and attack it to send it high, wide and far from his goal.

    c) Listen to instruction from his goalkeeper — 'Keeper'' or ''Away'' — and respond accordingly.

2. Three forwards and four defenders restricted to half a field. Goalkeeper at each end with two players (1 Vs 1) allowed to play the full length of the field. (Fig. 335)

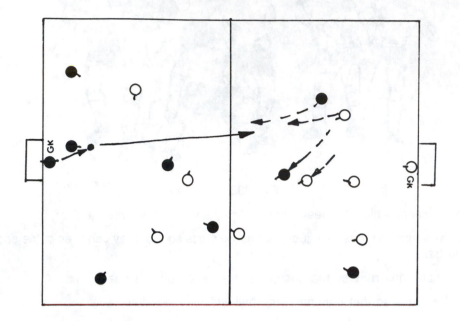

Fig. 335

Encourage the marking players in the defense to: — concentrate on their immediate opponent so that they can 1) intercept, 2) challenge, 3) contain.

Encourage the free defensive player to: — give immediate cover to any challenging defender; cut off avenues for through passes.

Encourage the forward players to: — interchange positions; recognize and exploit 1 Vs 1 or 2 Vs 2 situations; create space for their team mates; time their runs for when their defense or mid-field can play the ball forward; shoot whenever they get the opportunity to do so.

Encourage the mid-field defender to: — get goal-side of his opponent; track down his opponent into the space behind him whenever threatened.

Encourage the mid-field attacker to: — look for 1-2's; play defense splitting passes; run into the space behind his opponent.

Variations: There are literally hundreds of variations of the above practice which can all be weighted to produce different coaching points. e.g.

1) Allow the defender who plays the ball forward to join the attack.

2) Allow any defender to join the attack.

3) Limit the defense to two touches.

4) Restrict the forwards to a maximum of two passes.

5) No offside, etc. etc.

3. A server, Black 6, plays the ball into the space between the defender, White 5, and the goalkeeper. Black 9 gives chase and tries to harass White 5 and the goalkeeper into making mistakes. (Fig. 336)

Variation: 2 vs 2 in front of goal.

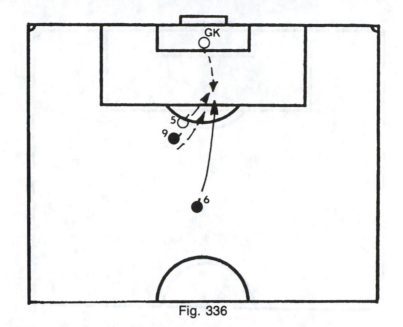

Fig. 336

Encourage the goalkeeper to: — make an early decision of whether he can get to the ball first or the defender will get it; communicate his decision to the defender; if he decides to go for the ball, he must get it and hold-on to it; if he decides that the defender can get it and play it back to him, then he must 'set' himself ready for the back pass; if he decides that he cannot get it and the defender is under severe pressure, then he should instruct the defender to clear the ball — 'Away'.

Encourage the defender, White 5, to: — position himself so that he can recover quickly into the space behind him; try to observe both the ball and the goalkeeper as he runs towards his goal; be aware of the proximity of the Black 9's challenge; if he has time, he should play the ball back accurately to his goalkeeper; if he is severely pressurized, he should clear the ball away over the side-lines.

4. A winger has a supply of balls and dribbles at speed along a corridor marked between cones and the side-line. As soon as he passes the end cone, he crosses the ball across the face of the goal for two Black attackers to try to score goals. The goal is defended by one White defender and a goalkeeper. (Fig. 337)

Variations: Add more defenders.

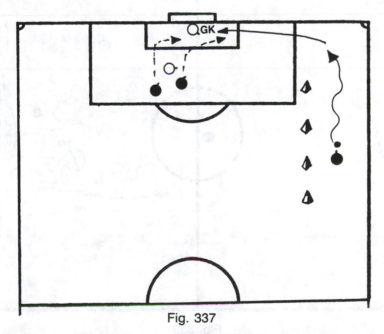

Fig. 337

Encourage the goalkeeper to: — make an early decision of whether to go for the ball or not; communicate this decision to his defender — 'Keeper' or "Away''; if he decides to go for the ball, whether to catch or punch; attack the ball and take it as early as possible.

Encourage the winger to: — hit his crosses across the face of the goal to threaten the near and far post areas; (Fig. 338), avoid hitting crosses at catchable height in the middle goal area.

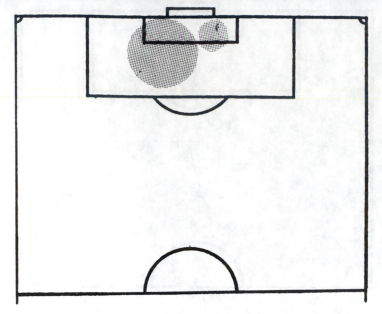

Fig. 338

Encourage the forwards to: — read the winger's movements and predict the angle and height of the cross; make curved runs to meet the ball, particularly at the near post; redirect the ball accurately towards the goal with the head or foot.

Encourage the defender to: — adjust his position dependent upon information received from the goalkeeper; read the winger's movements and predict the angle and height of the cross; prevent blind-side runs by the forwards; avoid being beaten by the near post run.

5. Two teams of eleven players on a full field. The White goalkeeper is served the ball and the Black defense has to reorganize. The game continues until the Black team wins possession. (Fig. 339)

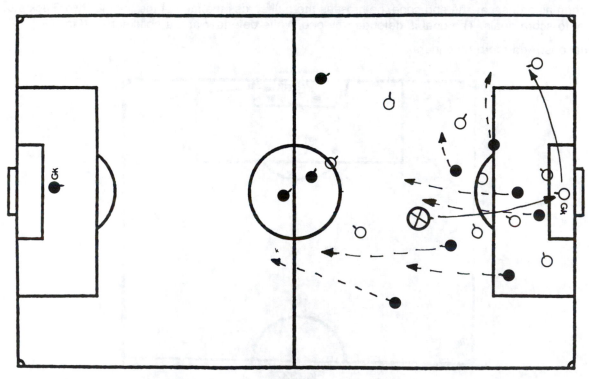

Fig. 339

Encourage the Black team to: — make a challenge on the ball by the nearest player; if the ball can be won, to support the challenging player; if not, then recovery runs to predetermined lines of confrontation. (Fig. 340)

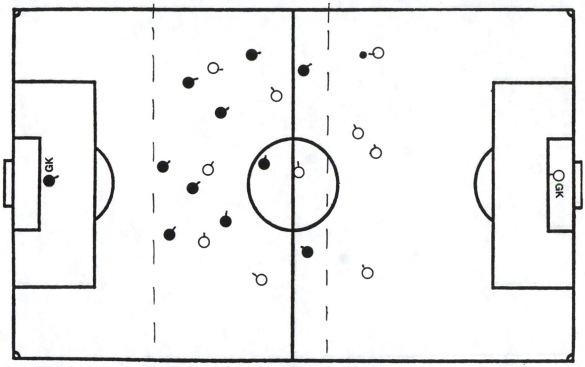

Fig. 340

6. The Black team should be organized to play against a team playing a 4-4-2 system. This organization should be designed to dominate three vital areas. (Fig. 341)

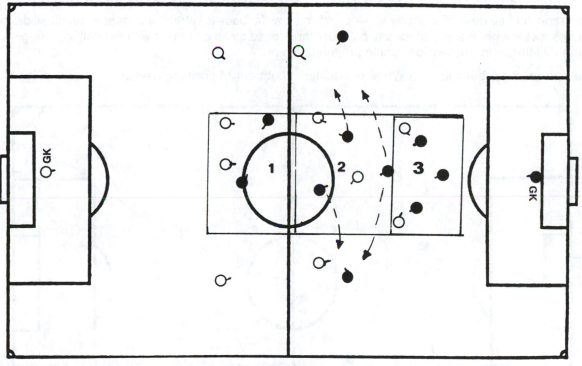

Fig. 341

1) 2 Vs 2 in Build-up area immediately in front of opponent's goal.

2) 3 Vs 2 in mid-field Build-up area.

3) 3 Vs 2 in defensive area.

4) It will leave the Black team with 2 Vs 1 situation on each wing but this can always be countered by the third mid-fielder moving across the cover.

7. Six Black attackers play against seven White defenders and a goalkeeper. The White mid-field unit tries to prevent the opposition from playing the ball forward. (Fig. 342)

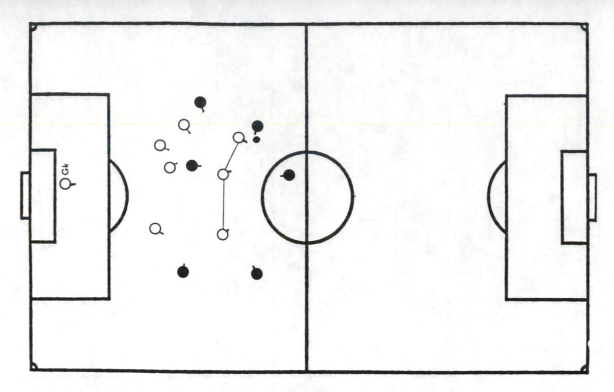

Fig. 342

Encourage the White mid-fielders to: — close down their immediate opponent so that whenever he gets the ball, they can pressurize him; force any opponent in possession to go away from goal or across the field.

Encourage the free defensive player to: — decide on how far back to retreat or advance; cut off all dangerous avenues for through-passes; cover any defender threatened by an opponent with the ball; challenge any opposing mid-fielder in possession running at the defense.

8. As above practice, but with one White mid-fielder caught out of position, having to recover. (Fig. 343)

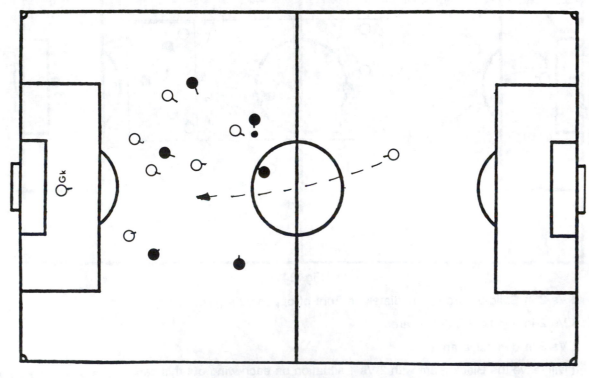

Fig. 343

Encourage the White mid-field to: — regain 'balance'. This is usually achieved by the nearest player challenging and the other two, covering. We can detect two distinct shapes in this balanced mid-field defense. Firstly, a triangle, whereby the challenging player is covered by his two colleagues, (Fig. 344)

Fig. 344

and secondly, a dog-leg where one of the wide mid-field defenders is covered by the other two. (Fig. 345)

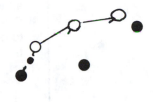

Fig. 345

9. Three forwards Vs four defenders in each half of the field, plus 3 Vs 3 covering the whole field. (Fig. 346)

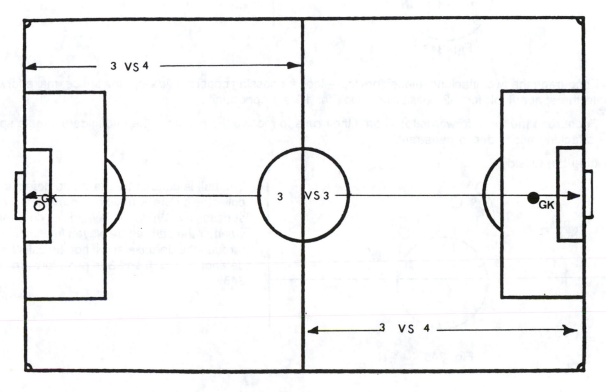

Fig. 346

Coaching emphasis should be placed on one of:

a) Defensive marking and covering.

b) Communication of defenders — passing-on and tracking down.

c) Distribution of defense.

d) Responsibilities of free defenders.

e) Runs and receiving positions of forwards.

f) Mid-field play.

174

The Development of Team Play (16-19 yrs.)

1. Exploiting the mid-field space:

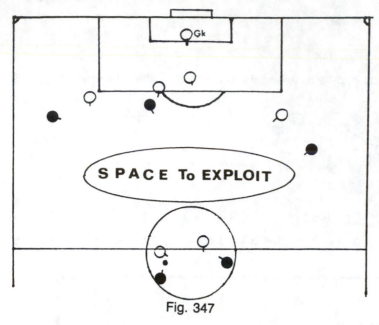

2 Vs 2 in the center circle, with four White defenders plus goalkeeper versus three Black attackers just outside penalty area. The two Black attacking players in the center circle try to get clear possession in the space between the two lines of White defenders. (Fig. 347)

Fig. 347

Encourage the two attacking midfielders to: — look for passing opportunities into the space; make forward runs into the space; look for 1-2 possibilities; look for 1 Vs 1 opportunities.

Encourage the three forwards to: — time their runs to receive the ball from the midfielders; create space for the attacking midfielder to penetrate.

2. Setting the Offside Trap:

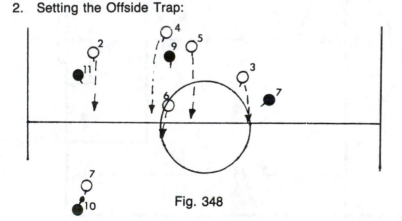

The ball is cleared by the White defense and collected by Black 10 who is immediately pressurized by White 7. White 4 determines whether the ball can be played forward over or through the defense and if not, he calls his co-defenders 2, 5, 6 and 3 to push forward. (Fig. 348)

Fig. 348

Encourage the pressurizing player to: — close down and refuse to be beaten by a fake or dribble; force any passes to go backwards or square.

Encourage the covering player to: — read the actions of the pressurizing player; make an early decision on whether to hold or push forward; give his decision in a clear and positive manner.

Encourage the other White defenders to: — obey the instructions of the covering player; push forward at speed.

3. Beating the Offside Trap:

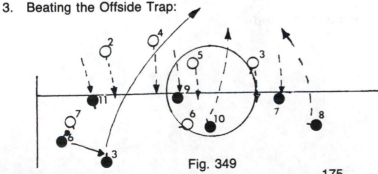

The White defense having cleared the ball up-field immediately push forward to play the Offside Trap. Black 6 is immediately pressurized by White 7, but lays the ball off to Black 3 who hits it over the top of the advancing White defense. The Black midfield players recognize the opportunity of beating the offside trap and make positive forward runs from their own half of the field. It is essential that **all** Black forwards retreat in front of the White defense. (Fig. 349)

Fig. 349

175

Another method of beating the Offside Trap is for one player to dribble through the line of advancing defenders. More often than not he will only have to beat one or two players to beat the whole defense as it will probably be caught very square across the field. Again it is imperative that **all** forward players remain Onside by retreating in front of the advancing defense.

4. Switching Play:

Two attacking players against three defenders in an area about 15 yd x 10 yd. near the half-way and side lines. If the two attackers fail to get through the area with the ball then they have the option of playing it back to a support player who must immediately transfer a long crossfield pass to a fourth attacker. (Fig. 350)

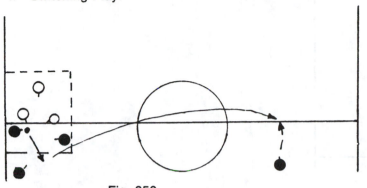

Fig. 350

Encourage the two attacking players to: — look for and exploit 1-2's or 1 Vs 1 situations; lay the ball back to the support player so that it can be kicked first-time.

Encourage the support player to: — read the play in front of him and adjust his position accordingly.

Encourage the fourth player to: — read the play and time his run forward dependent upon the activity; control the ball immediately.

5. Establishing Midfield Defensive Balance (3 players):

Normally, a midfield defensive unit of three players will adopt a triangular formation with one player, sometimes referred to as the anchor man, in a more withdrawn position at the apex of the triangle. (Fig. 351a)

If the opposition attacks down its right flank then we could expect the triangle to readjust to a situation similar to that in Fig. 351b.

Similarly if the attack occurs on the opposite flank then we would expect the players to reform (Fig. 351c)

If the opposition attacks through the middle we might expect the anchor man to move forward while covered by his two colleagues (Fig. 351d).

If however, the opposition changes its point of attack from the flank across-field to the center we might see an inter-change of position between the anchor man and one of his colleagues. (Fig. 351e)

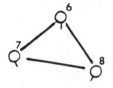

Fig. 351a

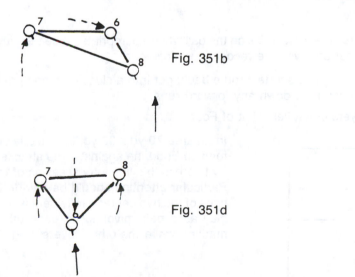

Fig. 351b

Fig. 351d

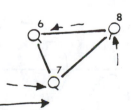

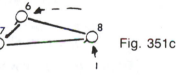

Fig. 351c

Fig. 351e

Teams should practice the redeployment of their mid-field defense by playing six forwards Vs seven defenders and a goalkeeper.

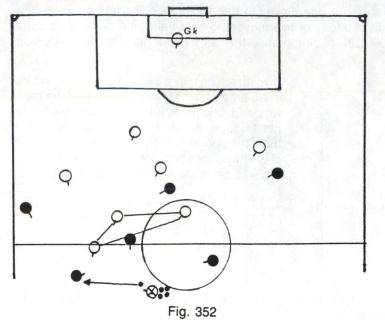

The coach serves the ball to any of the Black midfielders and the game continues. The White midfield defenders should constantly be encouraged to readjust their positions and communicate with each other. (Fig. 352)

Fig. 352

6. Re-establishing Mid-field Balance (3 players):

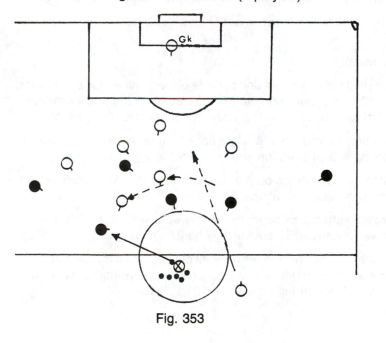

The coach plays the ball to one of the three Black mid-fielders. Two White defensive midfielders close down the play and try to delay until the third White midfielder has recovered into position. (Fig. 353)

Fig. 353

Encourage the two defensive midfielders to: — pressurize on the ball when appropriate; force the play backwards or square; communicate with each other and with the recovering midfielder.

Encourage the recovering midfielder to: — take shortest route back; get into a close covering position to form a triangular shape with his two colleagues; track down any forward runs.

7. Defensive responsibilities of Center Players in Midfield Unit of Four:

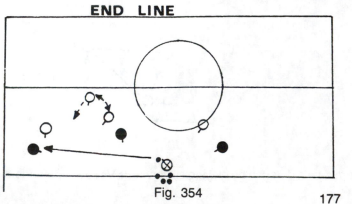

END LINE

In an area 70 yd x 30 yd, four midfielders defend an End Line against three attackers who try to cross this line in possession of the ball. Particular attention should be paid to the actions of the two center midfielders who should play as a pair, pivoting on each other, one marking while the other covers. (Fig. 354)

Fig. 354

177

8. Re-establishing Midfield Balance (four players)

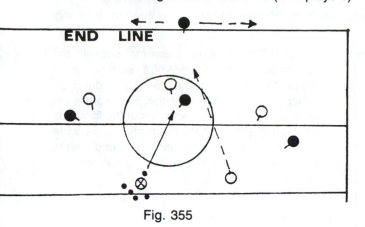

In an area 70 yd X 30 yds. four midfielders defend an End Line, outside of which a fourth attacker plays. The three attacking players attempt to get the ball to the fourth attacker. One of the center midfield defenders has been caught on the wrong side of the ball and has to get back to join his colleagues. (Fig. 355)

Fig. 355

Particular attention should be paid to the actions of the three defensive midfielders and the recovery run of the fourth midfielder.

9. The Role of the Sweeper:

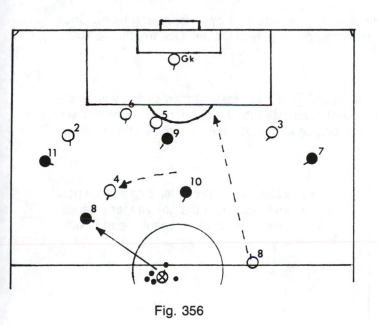

The coach with a supply of soccer balls plays the ball to one of five Black attackers who are marked by five White defenders and a goalkeeper. A sixth defender has been caught out of position but he can make a recovery run as soon as the ball has been played forward. (Fig. 356) Particular attention should be paid to the action of the back sweeper or libero (White 6).

Fig. 356

He must control his defense by:

1) Deciding whether to hold the line, push everyone forward or withdraw.

2) Dictating to other defenders how tightly to mark, which angle to take, and to track down any forward runs.

3) Offering cover to any challenging player.

4) Challenging any attacker who breaks through.

5) Communicating with his co-defenders, particularly White 4 and White 8 (Fig. 356).

Lines of Confrontation:

10. All good teams should know where to draw up their lines of confrontation once the ball has been irretrievably lost.

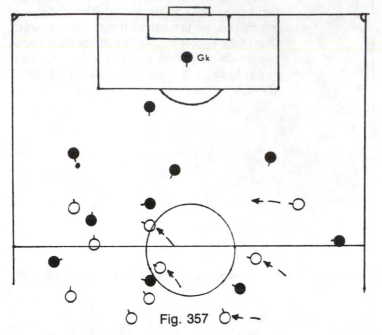

In fig. 357 the ball has been lost deep in the opponents' half and the White team has withdrawn to an area about 15-20 yds deep on either side of the half-way line. The team is set up in a 4-4-2 formation with one of the forwards defending either flank, supported by a wide midfield player and a full back. Two midfielders guard the middle, supported by two central defenders.

Fig. 357

Teams should practice falling back into these positions and being attacked by an opposing team. Once the opposing team has brought the ball within 5-10 yds. of the front line, or played the ball forward, then a 100% effort should be made to regain possession.

11. Defending at Goalkicks:

To often, teams push too far forward when facing opponents' goalkicks, making themselves vulnerable to back players being beaten in the air or the ball traveling over the defense into the danger area behind them. Good teams will usually place a midfield player in the expected landing area of the ball so that he can challenge for it while covered by a triangle of defenders. (Fig. 358)

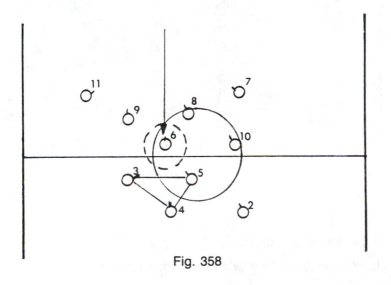

Teams should practice defending against goal kicks and kicks from the goalkeeper's hands, in which case they will probably need to withdraw a further 10-15 yds.

Fig. 358

Particular attention should be paid to the positional play of White 6 and the cover he is given by White 3, 4 and 5. Attention should also be focused on White 6's heading ability who could easily convert a defensive situation into an attacking opportunity with well-placed headers to White 11, 9 or 8.

12. Central Defenders:

Two defenders and a goalkeeper guard the channel immediately in front of the goal. A group of attacking players take it in turn to send waves of attack using either one, two or three players. Particular attention should be paid to the actions of the two central defenders and how the goalkeeper links up with them. They must be able to adjust quickly to whichever situation confronts them:

1) Challenging aggressively for the ball.

2) Communicating and encouraging each other.

3) Covering. (Fig. 359)

Fig. 359

The goalkeeper's positional play is of vital importance. He must not be beaten by any long shots that sail over his head and yet he must be alert to any through passes played into the space behind the two defenders.

13. Creating Space for Others:

Players should recognize that, playing against teams who employ tight-marking tactics, they can dictate to their immediate opponent where they will defend. Attackers should seek opportunities of taking their immediate opponents out of good defensive positions thus creating space for team mates to exploit. A typical example might be Fig. 360 where the White team is playing the ball out of defense.

White 2 has the ball but his passage forward is blocked by Black 11 and 3. The White players (7 and 8) however, recognize that if they make diagonal runs forward then they are likely to be tracked down by Black 11 and 3, thus creating space for White 2 to go forward.

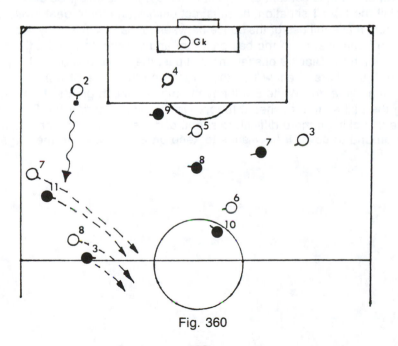

Fig. 360

CHAPTER FIVE

Phases of Play

It is always a dangerous practice to breakdown a game into parts, but from experience it is found that similar situations occur in soccer over and over again. These situations, or phases of play should be practiced regularly so that all the players understand the possibilities that exist in them for both attacking and defending players.

One Against One

Players should receive plenty of opportunities of practicing 1 vs 1 situations near a goal. Thus, in Fig. 361, the Black 9 has received the ball with only the White 5 between him and the goal. If he can beat White 5, he will create an excellent scoring chance.

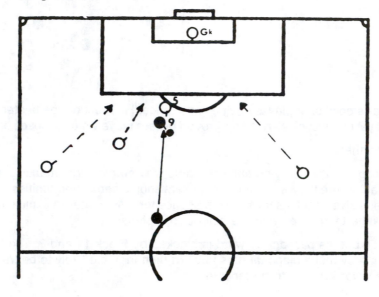

Fig. 361

White 5, on the other hand, is content to contain Black 9 until his fellow defenders get back to cover him. If the Black 9 is to exploit the 1 Vs 1 situation, he must act quickly and try to beat White 5 as soon as possible. In order to do this, he must make full use of the space between him and White 5 by taking the ball at speed and then, if he can get him off balance, push the ball past him and accelerate to take the ball on toward the goal for a shot. The angle at which the Black 9 pushes the ball past the White 5 is of vital importance; the closer the ball brushes past White 5, the more direct will be the threat, and the easier it will be for the Black 9 to make a shot (Fig. 362). At the same time, the White 5 will have to make a much greater turn, but he will have a better chance of intercepting the ball as it is pushed through. On the other hand, if the Black 9 pushes the ball well wide of the White 5, he is making it more difficult to shoot, and the White 5 has only to make a small turn. The White 5 also has less ground to cover if he wishes to keep on a line between the Black 9 and the goal.

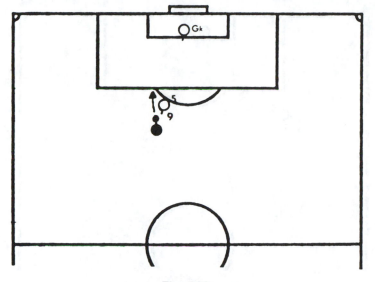

Fig. 362

If a forward has only one defender between him and the goal, he should, therefore, be encouraged to try to beat the defender. He should make full use of the space between himself and the defender so that he can go past the defender "on the burst". Once he has managed to get the ball past the defender, his impetus should mean that he gets to the ball before the defender.

Defenders should ensure that, if they are stranded in a 1 Vs 1 situation, they position themselves so that (1) they can intercept, (2) challenge and tackle, (3) contain and delay. This does not mean that they rush at a forward whenever he gets the ball. There is no easier defender to beat than the one who comes charging in. The good defender will ensure that he has closed the gap between himself and the forward as the ball is being played to the forward. He will also prevent the forward who has his back to the goal from turning to face him. Thus, in Fig. 363, if the ball has been played to Black 9, who has his back to the White 5, the White 5 will ensure that the Black 9 is kept facing his own goal. On many occasions, however, a forward will have made room for himself to turn and "attack" the defender. The defender's first thought should now be to take the ball off the forward, but he should not attempt to tackle until he is absolutely certain of winning the ball. If he is outside the shooting area, a defender can fall back in front of the forward, and this inevitably results in the forward slowing down, which makes the defender's task of winning the ball much easier. Again, an intelligent defender will "invite" a forward to go past him on one side; if the forward is essentially a right-footed player, the defender could encourage him to go past him with the ball on his left foot. Thus, in Fig. 364, the Black 9 is essentially a right footed player and the White 5 is encouraging him to go past him on his left foot.

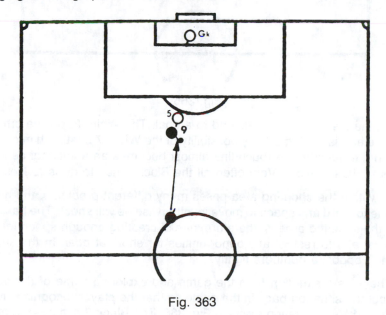

Fig. 363

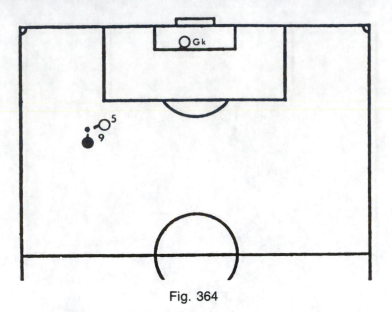

Fig. 364

The fact that the White 5 is nearly standing sideways also means that he can make a quicker turn for any ball pushed past him.

The position adopted by the defender is often of vital importance especially if he is near the goal line or one of the touch lines. For example, in Fig. 365, the White 2 is facing the Black 11 square-on, which give the winger the option of beating him on either side.

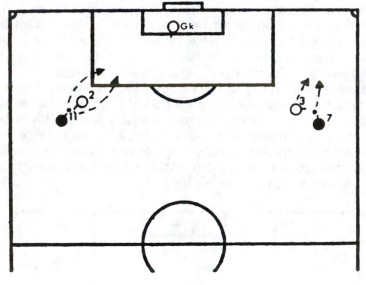

Fig. 365

If he beats him on the inside, it may well lead to a goal. The White 3, on the other hand, is inviting the Black 7 to go down the line and is cutting off any possibility of the White 7 beating him on the inside. If the White 7 does try to beat him on the outside, the touch line almost becomes an additional defender by restricting the space in which the White 7 has to work. Very often all the Black 3 has to do is to kick the ball out of play.

A 1 Vs 1 situation within the shooting area poses many different problems, the most obvious being that a defender cannot give the forward any space to move in; otherwise he will shoot. The basic problem for a forward who receives the ball in the shooting area is, therefore, one of creating enough space for himself to shoot. Conversely, the defender must aim to restrict any opportunities for shots at goal. In the shooting area, therefore, defenders must mark their opposite numbers tightly.

Having isolated the 1 Vs 1 situation from the game and exploring some of the possibilities that exist in it, the coach must now put the situation back in the game so that the player recognizes it when it occurs during match play. For example, a 1 Vs 1 situation exists in Fig. 366. The Black 2 has passed to Black 7 who has only the White 3 between him and the goal. Here the Black 7 should be encouraged to take on the White 3, unless another forward is in a position to receive a pass for a shot at goal. Very often, forwards refuse to accept the responsibility of taking on a man and pass to other players who are in a less advantageous position. Too frequently, we find a player receiving the ball in a position similar to that taken by the Black 7 who passes the ball back to Black 8.

183

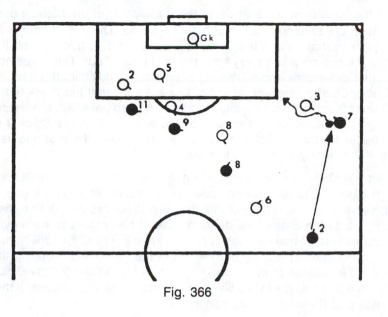

Fig. 366

2 Vs 1

A situation which occurs frequently in a game of soccer is that of 2 Vs 1, and young players should often be exposed to this situation so that they can understand and appreciate the possibilities that exist in it. In Fig. 367, the Black 9 and Black 10 are opposed by White 5. The Black 9, who has the ball, has two alternatives; he can either pass to Black 10, or he can attempt to beat White 5. This is an extremely favorable position for the forwards to find themselves in, and they must learn how to make full use of the situation before the other defenders can get back to help White 5.

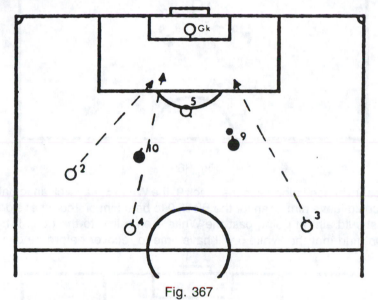

Fig. 367

The fact that the other defenders are going to race back to help White 5 implies that Black 9 and Black 10 must beat the White 5 quickly if they are going to take full advantage of the 2 Vs 1 situation. The Black 9 cannot dally with the ball and should "attack" the White 5, who must not be allowed to slow down the attackers. If the Black 9 passes the ball early to the Black 10, it means that the White 5 will have time to move to his right to cut off the Black 10's path to goal (Fig. 368(a)). Again, if the Black 9 takes the ball too close to the White 5, the intended pass to the Black 10 might be intercepted (Fig. 368b). The Black 9 should, therefore, release his pass just before the White 5 can tackle him or possibly intercept a pass to the Black 10 (Fig. 368c).

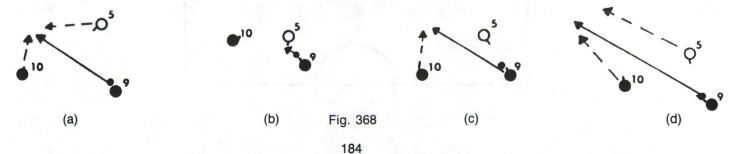

(a)   (b)   Fig. 368   (c)   (d)

It is essential that the pass from the Black 9 to the Black 10 is of the highest quality. Too often scoring chances in a 2 Vs 1 situation are squandered through poor passing. The pass from the Black 9 to the Black 10 should be in the latter's path so that he can take it in his stride toward goal for a shot. If the pass is too strong, the Black 10 has to chase the ball on a line away from the goal (Fig. 368d). This gives not only the White 5 time to recover, but also the other defenders who have been caught out of position. If the pass is too weak, the White 5 may well tackle the Black 10 as he receives it. Again, it is essential that the Black 9 disguises his intention of passing the ball to the Black 10 until the last possible moment. A push pass with the inside of the foot often gives the White 5 early warning of the direction of the pass by the way in which the Black 9 sets himself up, and in this situation, it is often better for him to flick a pass with the outside of the foot nearest to his partner, as this gives the defender very little warning of where the pass will go.

Whenever a situation such as that presented in Fig. 367 is experienced, the Black 10 should always offer himself as an option for the Black 9 to pass to. He should present himself in such a way, without getting offside, so that the White 5 can see him all the time and thus use him if necessary. All that the Black 10 needs to do in Fig. 368 is to keep along side the Black 9 ready for a pass. If he decides to run anywhere else, he reduces the Black 9's passing possibilities and makes it easier for the White 5. Thus, (Fig. 369) if he runs on a line between the Black 9 and White 5, he is virtually putting himself out of the game and reducing the 2 Vs 1 situation to a 1 Vs 1 situation. If the Black 9 decides to pass, it will be extremely difficult for the Black 10 to control the ball as he is moving away from the ball and the White 5 will be in a good position to tackle. If the Black 10 runs forward too soon, he will be offside and the whole move spoiled.

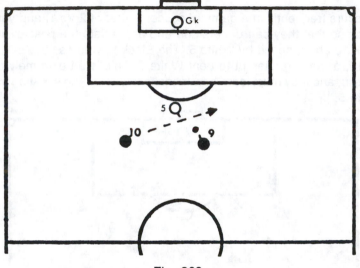

Fig. 369

If the Black 10 presents himself alongside the Black 9, the White 5 may well anticipate the pass being made to the Black 10, and this could leave him open for the Black 9 to beat him on the other side (Fig. 370). If the Black 9 decides to do this, he should aim at going past the White 5 on a line to the goal. If he pushes the ball wide past the White 5, he might find that the White 5 will have time to recover before he can take a shot (Fig. 371).

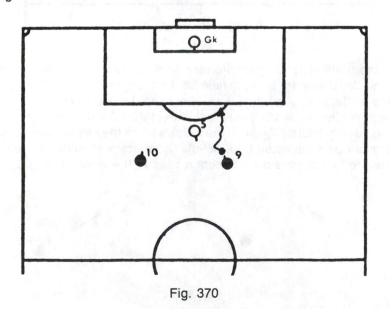

Fig. 370

185

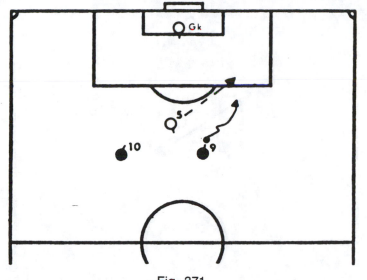

Fig. 371

The coach should also suggest ways in which the defender can cope with 2 Vs 1 situation. The defender should know that there are only two courses of action open to the players in possession that will cause him any real concern; firstly, if the forward dribbles past him, or secondly, if the ball is passed to the 2nd forward to take on and shoot. If either of these movements are performed quickly, then there is a good chance that the forwards will score. The defender's first concern, therefore, is to slow down the attackers so that his other team mates may have time to get back to cover him. It may prove that merely retreating toward his own goal will be sufficient to slow down the attackers. Again, the defenders can slow down the attackers by encouraging them to pass early so that two or more passes might be made before the defender has to commit himself to tackle.

The more passes the forwards make, the greater will be the chance of them losing control, and more important still, the more time will they take in getting past the defender.

It might prove sound advice for a defender, especially if he is quick on the turn, to position himself in such a way that there is only one course of action left open to the ball player. Thus, in Fig. 372, the White 5 has positioned himself in such a way that it is difficult for the Black 9 to make a good pass to Black 10. The White 5 is inviting the Black 9 to attempt to beat him knowing that he will have a good chance of tackling the Black 9 if the attempt is made. The White 5 is already half-turned to make a quick start for the ball that is pushed through, and he has the added advantage of knowing that the Black 9 has further to run than he does, and all he has to do is to kick the ball clear.

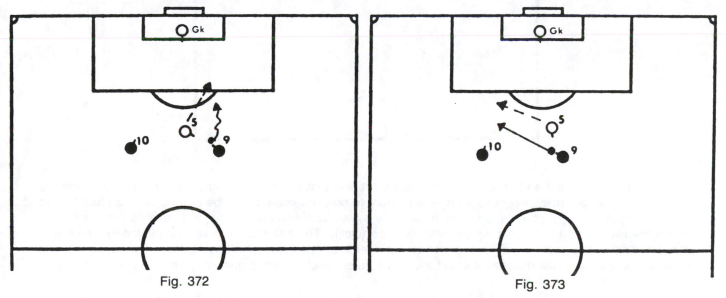

Fig. 372   Fig. 373

Again, the defender might decide to position himself in such a way that would make it difficult for the Black 9 to beat him. He would invite the Black 9 to pass to the Black 10 and then move across quickly to force the Black 10 away from the goal (Fig. 373). He might very well get away with this, especially if the Black 9's pass is too strong for the Black 10 to take in his stride and the ball is played out toward the edge of the penalty area. Here the White 5 could very well cut off one forward from the other (Fig. 374).

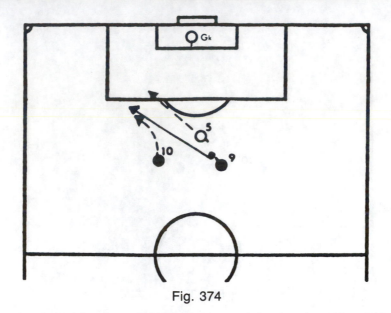

Fig. 374

Possibly the best piece of advice that could be given to a defender placed in a 2 Vs 1 situation just outside the shooting area is not to sell himself with a desperate, lunging tackle. If he is beaten, a goal will inevitably follow. On the other hand, if he can "jockey" the forwards, encouraging them to pass or invite them to attempt to beat him by dribbling, he might well force them into errors and redeem a hopeless situation.

Short Corners

Soccer statisticians have found that, proportionately speaking, far more goals are scored from short corners than from long corners. The reason for this is simple; if an attacking team can get a player with the ball close to, or even into, the shooting area, then it is comparatively easy for him to make a good pass for another forward to shoot at goal (Fig. 375). The Black 11 can guarantee to make an accurate pass into the shooting area far more often than if he centered the ball from the corner.

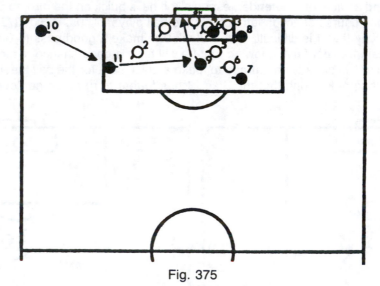

Fig. 375

If a team is to use a short corner, the first essential is that two players should go to the corner with the ball as quickly as possible. Very often they will be able to play the short corner before the defense has time to get itself organized or send defenders out to stop the move. Well organized sides will have its players briefed so that the two nearest to the corner can take the kick quickly. The ball should always be played to the second man standing on the goal line, as this immediately places the rest of the team onside. If no defender has come out to challenge the forwards, then the ball should be taken quickly toward goal, and either a shot at goal or a pass to another forward to shoot should follow.

More often than not, defending sides will send out one defender when the opposing side threatens to take a short corner. This immediately becomes a 2 Vs 1 situation, and all the possibilities of this situation are apparent except that the forwards have the added difficulty of working in a confined space. As soon as the Black 11 pushes the ball to the Black 10 (Fig. 376), he should move into position for a return pass from the Black 10. At the same time, the Black 10 should turn and take the ball at the defender. The Black 10 then has the option of either trying to beat the defender or passing to the Black 11 who can then move into the shooting area.

187

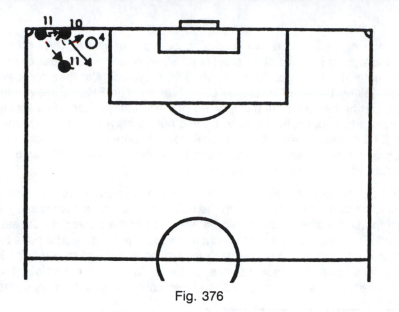

Fig. 376

It is often a good plan to have a left wing corner taken by a right footed player and vice versa. This often means that if the winger receives a return pass from the second player, he is in a position to make a shot at goal. For example, if the Black 11 (Fig. 376) possessed a good right footed shot, he would be able to take a shot at goal after he had beaten the White 4.

Teams should also think positively of the outcome of having a 2 Vs 1 situation in the corner. There is a very good chance that a goal will be scored if the remaining players can position themselves intelligently. At most corners, defenses expect a high center to be made and often they can be caught unaware if a low pass is made into the shooting area. The remaining players should position themselves for this low pass, especially the one made into the 6 yard box. At least two players should, therefore, position themselves in the six yard box, for not only could they 'unsight' the goalkeeper, but also they will be in a position to shoot home any blocked shots or rebounds. The remaining attacking players should position themselves on the 18 yard line in front of goal, ready to move into any space left vacant by a defender who goes out to challenge the winger. We might then expect to find the attacking players taking up positions something similar to those illustrated in Fig. 377. Very often in this situation, the ball can be played straight-away to the Black 3, who can move for a shot at goal. If this happens, however, the forwards will have to take care in case they are caught offside.

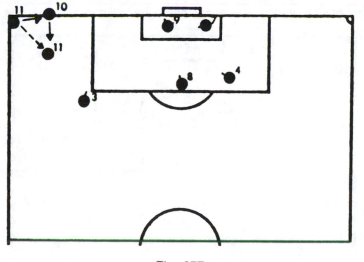

Fig. 377

A side should always have its defense organized to meet a short corner. At least two defending players should meet this threat and one of these should be the defending winger on the side where the corner is taken. This means that only one defender has to come out of the space in front of goal.

188

Overlapping

This is a term recently introduced into soccer to describe a player coming through from behind to give support to another player. This type of move is often seen in mid-field where a defender or mid-field player uses the space alongside a team mate to move into. Thus, in Fig. 378, the Black 4's passing possibilities are restricted, and he is prevented from taking the ball forward by the White 10. The Black 2 moves forward into this space alongside the Black 4 so that he can take the ball forward or pass unchallenged to a forward player. It is a good plan to encourage defenders to support in this way, as this puts a player in clear possession of the ball in the build-up area. Admittedly, he is a long way out, but he has plenty of time to pick his spot for a pass into the shooting area. Again, having players supporting from behind in this way makes it much easier for the defense to play the ball out safely and cuts down the risk of losing possession in mid-field.

It is essential that both the player with the ball and the one supporting from behind know what to do. The player running from behind should let the player with the ball know that he is overlapping as soon as he decides to move forward. The supporting player's run should be well wide of the player in possession so that the risk of the pass being intercepted is eliminated. In order to reduce this risk even further, the pass to the supporting player should be made early, before the opposing player can move close enough to tackle (Fig. 379). It is vital that this pass is of the highest quality so that the Black 2 can take the ball forward in his stride. If it is too strong, it could well go out of play, or if it is too weak, the supporting player could be caught in possession.

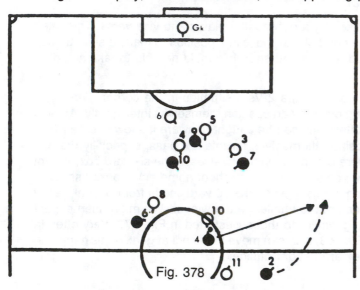

Fig. 378

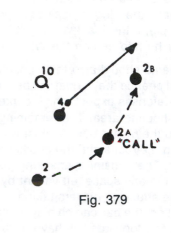

Fig. 379

As soon as the supporting player has made the overlap and moves forward with the ball, it is important that he displays the same level of skill as a player normally found in that position. Thus, in Fig. 380, if the Black 2 moves forward with the ball, it is essential that he is competent at crossing the ball accurately from the right. Too often we find defenders having made the overlaps cross the ball over the goal line or straight to a defender.

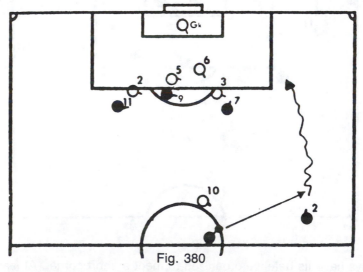

Fig. 380

Black 2 overlaps on the outside of Black 7 (Fig. 381). The timing of Black 2's run is very important. If he goes too soon, he may get caught offside. Again, if he goes too late, he may find that White 3 has already closed in to tackle Black 7. Black 3 should, therefore, tell Black 7 to release the ball as he runs into the shaded area, and here the call is of vital importance as Black 7 is often unaware that Black 2 is going to overlap.

189

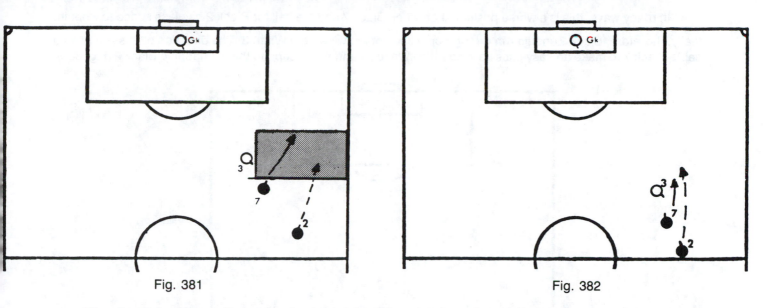

Fig. 381   Fig. 382

The direction of Black 2's run is also important. If he runs through on a line that passes close to White 3, then Black 7's pass will have to pass close to White 3. This makes White 3's task of interception considerably easier (Fig. 382). It is unlikely that Black 7 would attempt to make such a pass, however, the likelihood being that he would push the ball through wide of White 3. But this makes Black 2's task more difficult as he will now take the ball on his outside (Fig. 383).

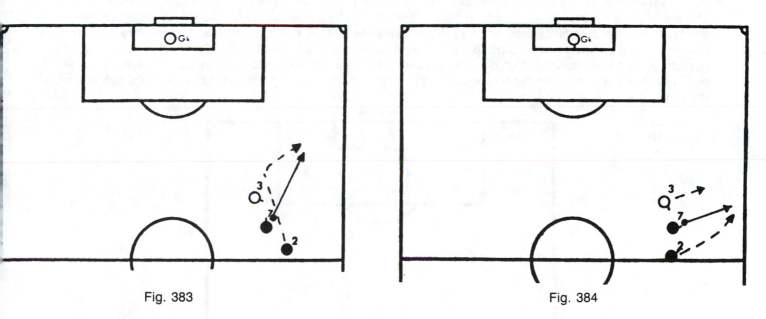

Fig. 383   Fig. 384

This gives White 3 the opportunity to fall back and keep Black 2 close to the touchline. Again, if the line of Black 2's run is well wide of White 3, it will enable White 3 to fall back to a position between Black 2 and the goal (Fig. 384).

In many ways, this is a worse position than when Black 7 had the ball for Black 2 has less space to work in.

Ideally, therefore, Black 2 should run through on a line not too wide from White 3. The direction of this run should enable Black 7 to make an easy pass i.e. one which White 3 cannot intercept, to the overlapping Black 2 (Fig. 385).

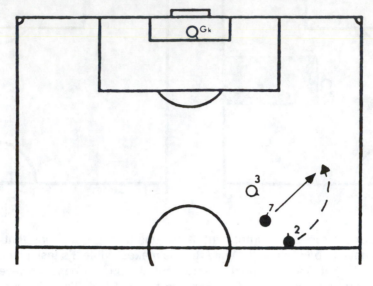

Fig. 385

Wall Passes

Wall passes, sometimes known as 1 - 2's or give-and-goes, can be played in various parts of the field. However, there are profound differences between a wall pass played in mid-field and a wall pass played in and around the danger area near goal.

A wall pass in mid-field is essentially used in a 2 Vs 2 situation. The two attacking players try to get one of them in clear possession in the space behind the two mid-field defenders. In Fig. 386, Black 6 has the ball and takes it under control towards White 10. Black 8 realizes that the wall pass is on and moves into a receiving position, timing his run to catch Black 6's attention. Black 8's run might well draw White 4 into a tight marking position and so it is important that Black 8 takes up a final stance side-ways on to White 4 where he can see him. If White 4 does not come into a tight marking position, then Black 8 might decide to turn with the ball towards the White goal.

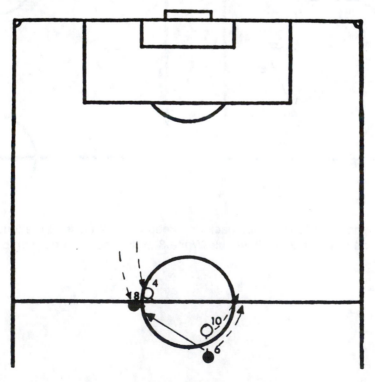

Fig. 386

Notice that in Fig. 386 Black 8's final position allows him to receive the ball on the foot furthest from White

4. This means that, even with poor control, he might retain possession of the ball by forming a wide screen between White 4 and the ball.

Black 8 can, therefore, decide on one of several options if he receives the ball sideways-on to a tight marking White 4, and where he can see him. Firstly, he can play the ball first-time into the space behind White 10 and into Black 6's stride-path; secondly, he can hold the ball, wait for Black 6 to get behind White 10 and then play the ball into his stride-path; thirdly, he can take the pass and spin on White 4 to take the ball into the space behind the mid-field defense.

Black 6's role in playing the wall pass is very important. He must approach White 10 at controlled speed in order to commit him. Then, disguising his intentions, he should play the ball just before White 10 can make a challenge. (Fig. 387)

Fig. 387   Fig. 388

The easiest way to achieve this disguise is to play the ball off the front foot. The disguise will be even greater if the ball is flicked-off the outside of the front foot, allowing Black 6 to continue running without breaking stride. White 10 will receive advance warning of Black 6's intentions if he tries to play it off his back foot. (Fig. 388).

Black 10 should concentrate on delivering a firm accurate pass into Black 8's right foot. As soon as this accurate pass is delivered, Black 6 should accelerate into the space behind White 10. Almost without exception, the direction of this run should be on the blind-side of White 10. It is remarkable how often poor mid-field defenders will respond to Black 6's pass by following the ball. Even turning their heads should give Black 6 enough time to get into the space behind White 10.

Good defenders combat the wall pass in mid-field by adjusting their play. In Fig. 389 White 4 has taken up a defensive position that allows him:
1. To intercept any bad pass from Black 6, and
2. Prevent a return pass from Black 8 to Black 6.

At the same time, White 10 resists the temptation to follow Black 6's pass and concentrates on tracking down Black 6 as he runs forward. If need be, White 10 should turn to face Black 6 and run with him, even at the expense of losing sight of the ball. This tracking down action by White 10 forces Black 6 to run wider (and further) in order to get into the space behind the mid-field defense.

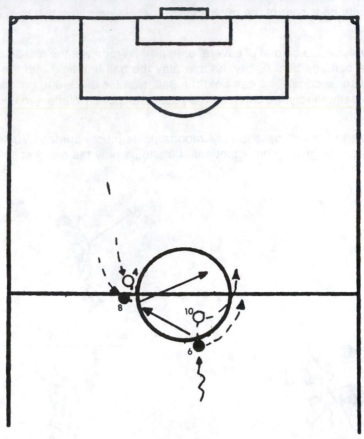

Fig. 389

The closer the wall pass is attempted to the opponents' goal, the flatter (or squarer) the ball will travel. A wall pass in and around goal is essentially used by two attackers to get behind two or more defenders.

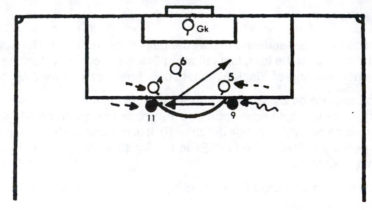

Fig. 390

In Fig. 390 Black 9 has the ball and Black 11, realizing that a wall pass is on, moves towards him. As Black 11 gets across the line of White 4, he sets himself up to receive a pass with the foot furthest away from White 4. His movement, therefore, must be sideways-on to White 4 so that he can recognize many of the options available to him. Some of these are a first-time pass into the space between White 5 and 6; hold the ball and look to play the ball, after a delayed run by Black 9, into the space between White 5 and 6; shoot at goal; fake a pass, and spin or step over the ball to attack the space outside White 4.

Although Black 9 might initially receive the ball with the foot furthest away from White 5, he is unlikely to be able to play the ball off to Black 11 and get into the space behind White 5. The latter will be very concerned about the space behind him and will have adequate warning of Black 9's intentions to counter the run. On the other hand, Black 9 might well get into the space behind White 5, if he is prepared to risk playing the ball with the foot nearest to the defender. This move might lure White 5 forward to make a challenge for the ball and immediately Black 9 flicks off the ball accurately to Black 11 and 'falls', in stride, into the space behind White 5, Fig. 390 to receive a return pass.

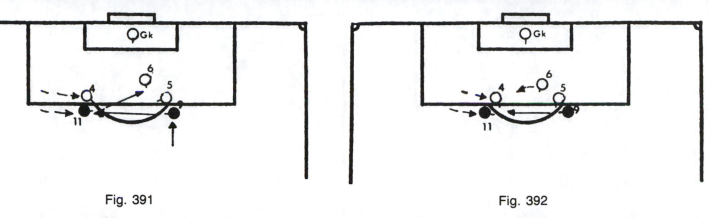

Fig. 391   Fig. 392

The timing of Black 11's run to set up the wall pass is of critical importance. If it is made too early (Fig. 391), then it will give White 6 time to adjust his covering position, and White 4 to adjust his marking position; if it is made too late (Fig. 392), he will probably be off balance as he receives the ball and his passing angles will be cut off.

Take Overs

Take-overs can be played in various parts of the field, but as defenders are likely to mark more tightly the closer they get to their own goal, there are differences between take-overs played in mid-field and those in and around the opponents' goal.

Before any take-over can be played, the ball-carrier must attempt to **out-run** his immediate opponent with the ball and threaten the space diagonally behind him. The first priority for the ball carrier is to be able to run with the ball at speed outside the line of his body on the side furthest away from the defender. (Fig. 393) As soon as the second player recognizes that a take-over is on, he attempts to move towards the ball player along the line of the latter's run. (Fig. 394)

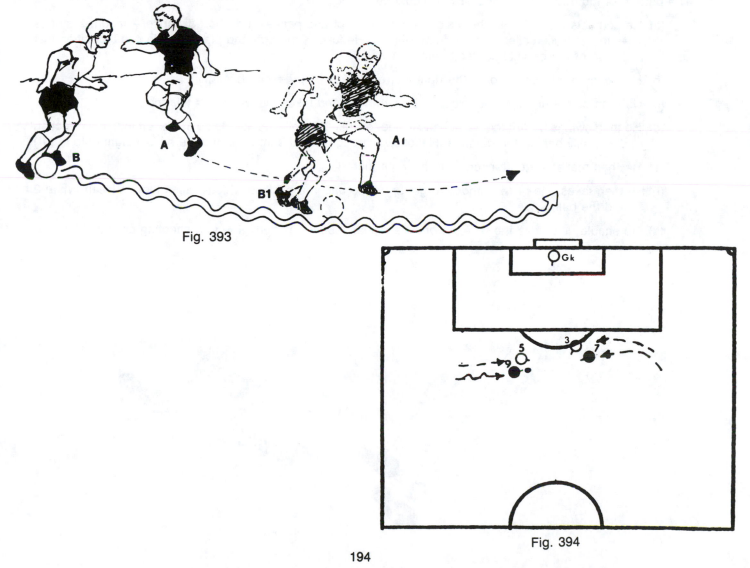

Fig. 393

Fig. 394

194

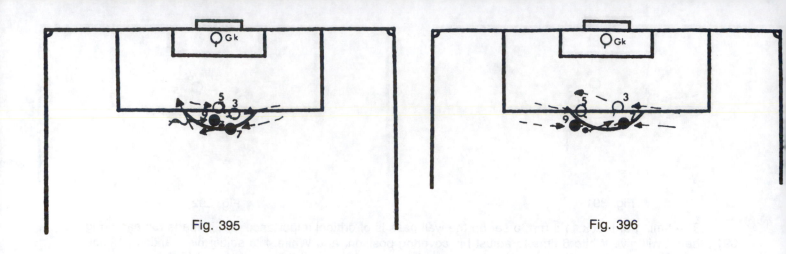

Fig. 395   Fig. 396

At the point of take-over Black 9 leaves the ball for Black 7 to take it with his right foot and then immediately transfers it to his left foot. If the take-over is well executed, then Black 7 will be able to take the ball into the danger zone with his second touch. (Fig. 395) Very often, the take-over is unsuccessful as Black 9 tries to pass the ball to Black 7. This leaves too much space between the two defenders for the take-over to be executed and for Black 7 to get into the space behind the two defenders (Fig. 396). This will result in the receiver, Black 7, taking the ball further away from the danger area.

When properly executed, the ball should be left by the ball-carrier for the receiver to take-over. No verbal communication should be required. Rather, through frequent practice and from a knowledge of each other's movements, both players should develop an understanding.

The pattern of foot movements of Black 7 should be as Fig. 397:

   (a) He contacts the ball with the inside of the right foot and pushes it a short distance — about 2 strides — in a direction slightly away from White 3. He follows through and places his foot in a position just ahead of the original contact point. (a¹)

   (b) He transfers his weight onto the right foot and takes a stride with his left.

   (c) He then plants his right foot close behind the ball and takes his weight on this foot.

   (d) He then swings his left foot round and inside to strike the ball with the inside of the left foot in a direction diagonally behind the defense. He follows through with the left foot, transfers his weight onto it. (d¹)

   (e) He then makes a quarter turn with his right foot.

   (f) He then takes one or two strides to get up to the ball in a position which places him between White 3 and the ball.

   (g) He should now have the ball just outside the left side of his body line in a shooting position.

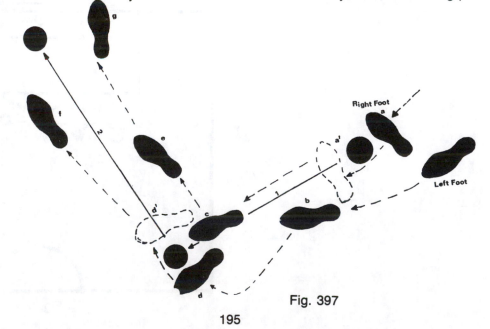

Fig. 397

CHAPTER SIX

Functional Practices

When a player has become proficient in the basic techniques of the game, it is sensible to let him practice these techniques in typical situations relating to his position on the field. There are phases of play and certain uses of technique and skill which are particular to each team position. This is called functional training.

Goalkeeper

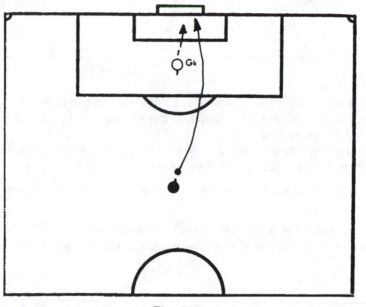

Fig. 398

The goalkeeper stands on the penalty spot and a player with a ball tries to chip it over his head from 25 yards. (Fig. 398)

Fig. 399

Fig. 400

The goalkeeper has to decide if he can catch the ball or, while going backwards, help the ball on over the crossbar. (Fig. 399)

Fig. 401

Fig. 402

A goalkeeper has to deal with an onrushing player who has the ball at his feet. (Fig. 400) The goalkeeper should be encouraged to: a) Decide how far to come off his line so that he cannot be 'chipped' (Fig. 401), but at the same time, narrow the angle. (Fig. 402)

b) Anticipate the attacker's movements and stay in the 'ready' position for as long as possible. Far too often, goalkeepers go down at the attacker's feet too soon.

c) To spread himself as wide as possible when he goes down at the attacker's feet.

Full Back

The goalkeeper serves the ball to his full back who quickly takes it forward to about the half-way line. He looks for the opposite winger to break into the middle and plays a long pass to him so that he can shoot or control/shoot in an instant. (Fig. 403)

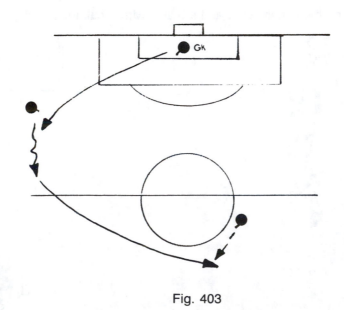

Fig. 403

Encourage the full-back to: — receive the ball facing infield; run with it with his head up; set the ball up for a long pass; hit a long, accurate cross-field pass with back spin to meet the winger's run.

Center Back

A player with a ball serves a variety of high balls towards two opposing players some 25 yards from goal. (Fig. 404)

Encourage the defender to:
a) Mark so that he can:
1) Intercept,
2) Challenge, and win the ball,
3) Contain.
b) When heading the ball to aim for:
1) Height,
2) Width,
3) Distance.

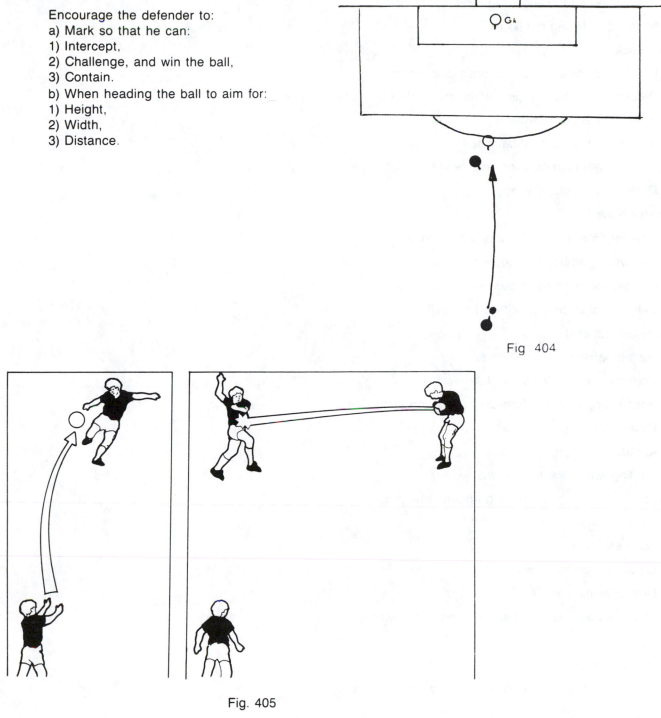

Fig 404

Fig. 405

Center Forward

A player with a ball throws a two handed under-arm lob to a second player standing 10 yards away. The second player allows the ball to bounce once, then volleys it towards goal guarded by a goalkeeper. (Fig. 405)

Encourage the kicking player to: — place his supporting foot as far from the ball as possible to allow the full extention of the kicking leg; develop a swivelling movement of the body, a sort of cork-screw motion, which takes him through 90⁰ or more to make contact; get his head as near to the ball as possible; get the knee of the kicking leg above the ball.

Here is a selection of further functional practices.

Goalkeeper

1. Assessing when to catch or punch a high cross.
2. Distribution by throwing and kicking.
3. Methods of faking goalkicks.

Full Back

1. Interception of a cross-field pass to a wingman.
2. Defending on the goal line when the goalkeeper is out of goal.
3. Defending against throw-ins.
4. Dealing with 2 Vs 1 situations.
5. Dealing with high crosses near goal.
6. Defending against a winger.

Center Back

1. Heading from the goalkeeper's clearances.
2. Recovering after being beaten by a forward.
3. Interception of through passes.
4. Ball control in dealing with a high ball.

Sweeper (Libero)

1. Judging offside.
2. Communication with other defenders.
3. Responding to a numbers-down situation in mid-field.
4. Passing-on players.

Mid-field

1. Dealing with 2 Vs 1 situations.
2. Tracking down and covering against wall passes.
3. Support play.
4. Long shooting.
5. Quick service for forwards.
6. Defensive heading.
7. Throw-ins and corner kicks — attack and defense.

Winger

1. Dribbling to beat an opposing full-back.
2. Interpassing with mid-field player and center forward.
3. Ball control from a variety of services.
4. Running in to goal to shoot past a goalkeeper.
5. Heading and shooting from crosses from the other wing.
6. Throw-ins and corner-kicks — attack and defense.

Center Forward

1. Shooting opportunities when tightly marked.
2. Ball control from a variety of services.
3. Countering the offside trap.
4. Laying-off balls to support players.
5. Meeting crosses.

CHAPTER SEVEN

SET PLAYS

Free Kicks

A direct or indirect free kick within 20 - 25 yards of the goal represents a real goal scoring chance. Attacking teams should be organized to take the free kick quickly, if allowed to do so by the referee, or if not, to have a rehearsed and practiced move in which all players know their role.

The first decision to be made is which player takes the shot at goal. He should be chosen for his consistent accuracy in bending balls round 'walls'. He should spend time in practicing these shots from a variety of angles and distances within 20-25 yards from goal. A typical practice would be (Fig. 406)

Fig. 406

A barrier, such as a vaulting box, is lined up in front of goal to resemble a wall. The player with a supply of balls swerves shots around and over the box.

Variation: Have a second player push a short pass to the kicker.

Encourage the player to: — strike the ball off-center to impart spin; emphasize accuracy before power.

A typical planned free kick might be (Fig. 407)

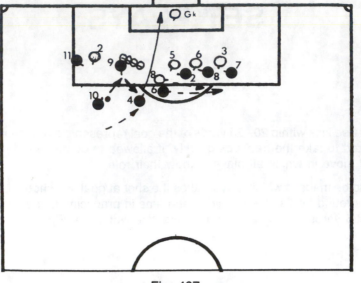

Fig. 407

A Free Kick is awarded just outside the Penalty Area slightly wide of the goal. The defense sets up a wall of 4 players, with one defender, White 2, guarding the near side and three defenders, White 5, 6 and 3, guarding the open side of the goal. Another defender, White 8, guards the area near the ball.

Attacking players are given the following responsibilities:

a) One player, Black 11, is given the task of occupying the near side of the wall so that he commits White 2.

b) Three players, Black 7, 8 and 2, are given the task of occupying the open side of the wall so that they commit White 3, 6 and 5. They also follow-up any shots at goal seeking any rebound possibility.

c) Black 6 is required to run into a dangerous position at the last moment so that White 8 has to go with him.

d) Black 10 plays the ball accurately to Black 9 who lays-it off diagonally for Black 4 to shoot at goal. Remember that Black 4 should strive to approach the ball at an angle so that he can strike it with power and accuracy.

Another play might be: (Fig. 408)

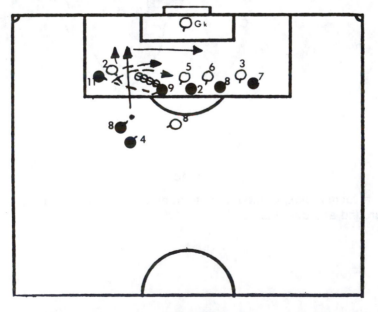

Fig. 408

Black 11 takes White 2 out of the near post area by moving into the dangerous space on the open side of the wall. Immediately, Black 9 'rolls' around the wall and the ball is played to him by Black 8. Black 9 crosses the ball across the face of the goal for the on-rushing Black attackers to shoot into goal.

201

Teams should also be organized to defend against free kicks given against them within 20 - 25 yards from their goal. They should establish:

a) How many, and which, players go into the wall (during practice).

b) The goalkeeper should indicate if he wants a 2, 3 or 4 - man wall.

c) One player should be designated to line-up the wall. He should know which player to line-up in the wall in relation to the ball and the near post.

d) Once he has lined up the wall, this player should seek to get into a position where he can threaten the short or quickly taken free kick.

e) All remaining players should mark opponents on both the near and open side of the wall.

f) They should take up a position on a line with the wall and refrain from getting behind the wall.

g) The goalkeeper should keep his concentration on the ball and not be deceived by quickly taken free kicks.

h) Neither should he allow any defenders to drop back into the space between him and the wall.

Corner Kicks (For)

It is essential that each team has a player who can take accurate corner kicks from either wing. Generally speaking, opposing goalkeepers and defenses have far more difficulty in coping with inswinging corners — a left-footed corner from the right wing or a right-footed corner from the left wing. The inswinging corner is usually much more dangerous if it is played into the near post area.

Although short corners run the risk that the ball may be lost before it is crossed, they have the added advantage of enticing defenders out of the danger area and, if successful, playing the ball into the goal area from a better angle.

Two attackers can easily beat one defender as follows:

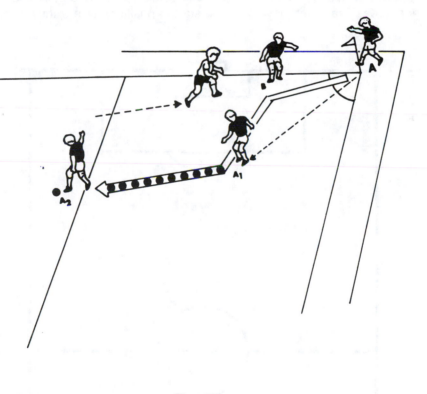

Fig. 409

while three attackers can beat two defenders by: (Fig. 410)

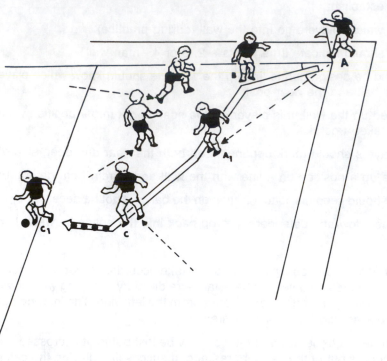

Fig. 410

Once a team has established that it has a consistently accurate corner-kick taker and/or a successful short corner play, it should establish the positions that the other attacking players adopt. One of these should almost certainly be directly in front of goal so that he unsights the goalkeeper and is in position for deflections, flicks or rebounds in the goal area. The other players should start in positions where they threaten the near and far post areas. (Fig. 411)

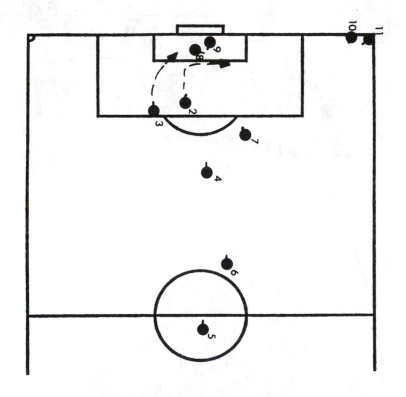

Fig. 411

The remaining players of the attacking team also have a responsibility that they do not leave themselves open to a quick counter-attack and they should deploy at least two players, Black 4 and 7, to stop the fast break.

203

Corner Kicks (Against)

Once a corner kick has been given against a team, there is very little that it can do to prevent the ball being crossed into the danger area. It can, however, reduce the threat by stopping the opposition playing a short corner and guarding the vulnerable near and far post areas.

The defense can be organized in many ways. Certain players can be detailed to mark dangerous opponents while the remaining defenders mark dangerous spaces; or a team might use all its players to mark dangerous spaces (Fig. 412).

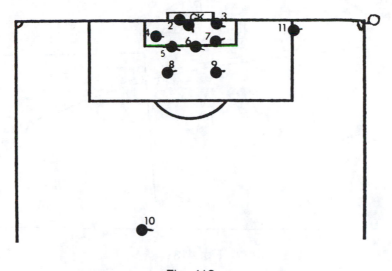

Fig. 412

Here all the team have been deployed in certain positions. Black 11 is stationed 10 yards from the ball on the probable line of the cross. Black 3 guards the near post, while Black 2 guards the far post. Four players, Black 4, 5, 6 and 7 form a curved line about 6 yards from goal with the responsibility of attacking any cross in the area immediately in front of them. Black 8 and 9 guard the area outside the goal area with the responsibility of tracking down any opponent running into the goal area. Black 9 should also be responsible for supporting Black 11 should a short corner be played. Black 10 should stay upfield and commit as many defenders as possible.

The Throw-In

Every team can expect to take anywhere between 20 - 60 throw-ins during a game. Yet the throw-in remains a largely neglected aspect of tactical play. Most players and many coaches regard the throw-in as merely a mechanism for getting the ball back into play, rather than as a springboard for positive action. This is particularly so in the middle third of the field where both attacking potentail and danger seem distant.

This casual approach is caused by a combination of several factors. The throw-in is a comparatively common restart and familiarity breeds contempt; it lacks the immediate drama of a free-kick near goal or a corner-kick, when players, aware of the pressure, are 'psyched-up'; there are a multitude of options available to the thrower encouraging players to feel that someone else will make themselves available, to convince themselves that they are too closely marked.

In theory, each throw-in presents the chance to start an attacking move. The basic concern at throws-in should be to retain possession, although there are obviously occasions in the attacking third of the field when possession has to be risked for the potential reward of achieving penetration and a chance at goal.

In the defensive third, safety should be the priority at the throw-in. One of the safest throws is to the goalkeeper, provided other defensive players have cleared the space for him to receive the ball. (Fig. 413)

Fig. 413

An alternative would be for the thrower to throw the ball to the defender standing deep near the corner flag.

In the middle third of the field, keeping possession still remains the priority, but risks may be taken in trying to get one of the receiving players going goalwards with the ball and into more penetrative positions. This can often be achieved through the simple ploy of two players interchanging positions. (Fig. 414)

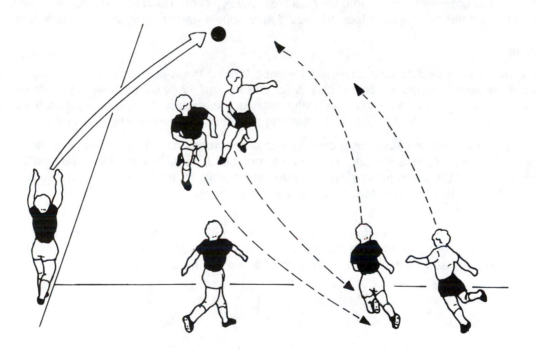

Fig. 414

A variation of the above interchange would be for the winger to move towards the thrower, drawing his marker in tight, then check infield to receive the ball in space. (Fig. 415)

Fig. 415

In the attacking third, the basic aim should be to get the ball into the danger area as quickly and positively as possible. Defenders are likely to lose concentration when the ball goes out of play and are vulnerable to the quick throw. It is often a good plan to have the nearest man to the ball take the throw-in and for the other players in the vicinity to look for good positions that will achieve penetration.

A fairly simple movement can create enough space necessary to get the cross in to the danger area with a first or second touch from the receiver.

If the receiving player does not get away from his marker because the latter is concerned about the space behind him, then a simple alternative is for the thrower to throw the ball directly at the receiver. The ball should be aimed at the receiver's feet (or head) so that the ball can be played back first time to the thrower. On no account should the throw bounce just in front of the receiver. It should be the responsibility of other attacking players to clear the space so that this simple return pass can be played. (Fig. 416)

Fig 416

Fig. 417

Attacking principles at throw-ins are:

   a) The nearest player should quickly throw the ball in.

   b) The other players should immediately offer good receiving positions.

   c) In the defensive and middle thirds, calculate on the side of safety; aim to retain possession.

   d) In the attacking third, calculate on the side of risk; aim for penetration.

   e) Remember that players cannot be offside when they receive the ball directly from a throw-in; they should seek to exploit the spaces behind defenders.

   f) Clear the space close to the thrower. Too often, players stand within 5 yards of the thrower, which makes it almost impossible to make a legal throw. (Fig. 417)

   g) Move into the receiving position when the thrower is ready to throw the ball.

   h) The throw-in should be viewed as a simple pass. The thrower should strive for: accuracy, speed of pass, timing and disguise.

Defensive principles at throw-ins are:

   a) Do not lose concentration when the ball goes out of play. Mark-up quickly.

   b) Judge the length of the throw and do not let the ball be thrown into the space behind you.

   c) Mark your immediate opponent on the inside line between him and your goal. Your position should follow the classic marking principles so that you can:

   1) Intercept

   2) Challenge

   3) Contain

   d) Free players should be concerned with not only the space behind, but also the space in front of receiving players.

   e) Track down players moving into dangerous positions.

207

Fig. 418

Black 8 moves to receive a throw-in from Black 6. Black 8 has two main options if he is to be successful

1. He moves away from Black 6 then cuts back sharply, or

2. He moves towards Black 6 then he cuts diagonally away. (Fig. 418)

Black 8 is likely to be much more successful if from the beginning he learns to position himself so that by vision (and touch) he knows what is behind him. There is a much greater chance of him being unsuccessful if he runs square across the line of the throw or if he does not know what is behind him.

Encourage Black 8 to: —

1. Make his move when Black 6 is ready

2. Cut sharply either towards or diagonally away from Black 6

3. Coast to a halt when receiving the ball after cutting towards the thrower.

4. Develop good first touch control

5. Adjust his stride pattern and immediately move onto the ball when cutting away from the thrower.

Encourage the thrower to: —

1. Throw the ball accurately and at the right time to the exact place dictated by the receiver's body language.

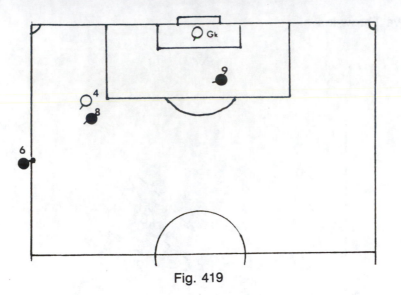

Fig. 419

2. As above, but now Black 8 is marked by White 4. Black 8 has three main options:

   1. He plays a return pass to Black 6.

   2. He comes off White 4, receives the ball and turns to attempt to beat White 4.

   3. He cuts diagonally away to receive the ball in the space behind White 4.

   In each option the object should be to get the ball as quickly as possible to Black 9 to shoot at goal. (Fig. 419)

Encourage the thrower to: —

1. Throw the ball accurately to the precise spot indicated by the receiver's body language

2. Disguise his throw

3. Time his throw to give the ball to the receiver exactly when he wants it

Encourage the receiver to: —

1. Delay his run until the thrower is ready

2. Move one way then cut sharply in the opposite direction keeping his central focus on the ball and his peripheral vision on the opponent

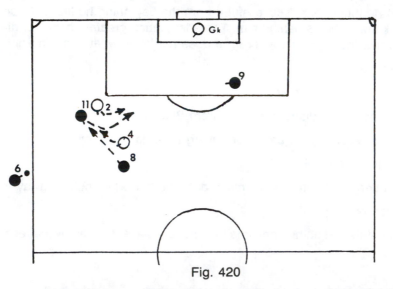

Fig. 420

  3.   As above but with two attackers and two defenders. As well as moves to receive the ball by cutting towards or diagonally away from the thrower, the receiver may now look for opportunities to interchange positions. It is remarkable how often such a simple ploy is effective particularly when the two attackers run towards each other before breaking away.

     Again, the coaching points made in the earlier practices are most important if the attacking players are to succeed.

CHAPTER EIGHT
Defensive Systems

The majority of practices previously featured in this book have been in the main concerned with attacking play. This is rightly so as the creative qualities of the game should be encouraged by all coaches. Nevertheless, it should be recognized that the defensive skills of top-class defenders can also be admired. The player with the ability to mark, cover and dispossess opponents is a valuable member of any team.

It could even be argued that the better the skills of defenders then the more the attackers will have to strive to perfect their skills.

A noticeable trend in the modern game is the emergence of all-round players, capable of both attacking and defensive skills. It is important for today's coaches to give equal attention to both aspects of the game. Remember that BALL POSSESSION DETERMINES EVERYTHING, and a good team will include a number of ball-winning players.

Much of the re-thinking that has gone into modern soccer tactics has been based on the tactics of basketball. Indeed, there is much in common between the two games and many of the expressions used in basketball have lately crept into soccer. Man-to-man marking, zone defense, switching, sagging, fast breaks, etc. were all expressions once exclusively reserved for basketball, but now many of them are expressions found in soccer.

Perhaps there are two vitally important lessons that soccer coaches should take out of the basketball game. The first is that the space near the basket (or goal) is of vital importance and no forward should be allowed into this space unless he is tightly marked. In Fig. 421, Black 7 should not be allowed to move into the space behind the defenders; he should be tracked down by White 3, who should be in a position to intercept if Black 8 plays the ball through. In the same way, White 5 should "track down" Black 9 while White 4 moves across to cover. By far, the greatest number of goals are scored from inside this space, and it is imperative for any defense to prevent any forward from entering this space unmarked.

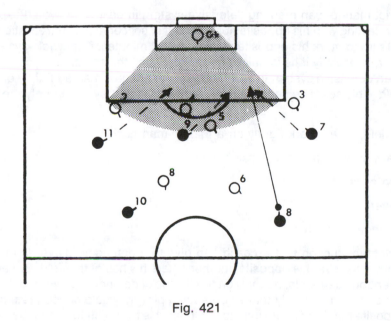

Fig. 421

Secondly, basketball coaches, having realized the importance of this space, evolved two methods of defense: the first, known as man-to-man marking, and the second, known as zone defense, in which players would retreat to defensive positions and concern themselves with filling spaces into which opposing players would eventually move. There are arguments for and against using both methods of defense in soccer.

Zone Defense

Exponents of the zone defense method would not be concerned with restraining individual opponents by marking them. They would be concerned with getting players to retreat into defensive positions as soon as their opponents gained possession of the ball. In this way, certain players would be responsible for defending areas when the opposing side gained possession. Each player's area would overlap (Fig. 422) so that at any time, two, three and sometimes four players would guard an approach to the goal.

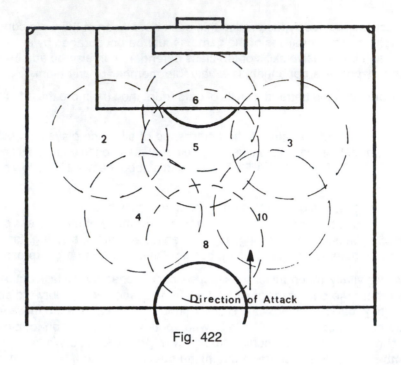

Fig. 422

Man-To-Man

Exponents of a strict man-to-man marking defensive system in basketball would expect each player in a team to be responsible for dealing with his opposite number. But in soccer, this is unrealistic and it is far too much to expect each man in a team to mark his opposite number for 90 minutes. The whole system is destroyed if an opponent beats a defender, especially if he is quick enough to exploit the situation. Soccer coaches have, therefore, evolved a man-to-man defensive system in which opponents are only marked tightly on a man-to-man basis in certain areas of the field. This seems a sensible approach, provided they can supply the answers to 5 simple problems.

1. In which areas of the field do we mark tightly on a man-to-man basis?

2. How many players mark on a man-to-man basis?

3. Which players mark on a man-to-man basis?

4. What do the other players do?

5. What happens if a defender is beaten?

Probably the simplest instruction that a coach can give to a defending player is to instruct him to mark his opposing number tightly whenever his opposite number enters his half of the field. But again, this is unrealistic, as it would make tremendous demands, not only on the fitness of defending players, but, perhaps more important still, on their concentration. It is unlikely that all defending players would concentrate sufficiently to be able to stick closely to their opposite numbers for 90 minutes. If, then, it is too much to expect defenders to mark strictly on a man-to-man basis over half a field, then the area in which they mark closely must be reduced. Some coaches would prefer their defenders merely to mark tightly whenever opponents get within shooting distance, but this can often lead to trouble, as the shot will have been made before the defender is in position to tackle. Obviously, some compromise is needed, and the method usually adopted by coaches is to ask defenders to mark tightly in the last 1/3 of the field. Thus, in Fig. 423, the side defending the White goal would mark tightly in the area marked 1, while in the area marked 2, they would mark their opposing number less tightly, but still be in position to close mark if the opponent entered the area marked 1.

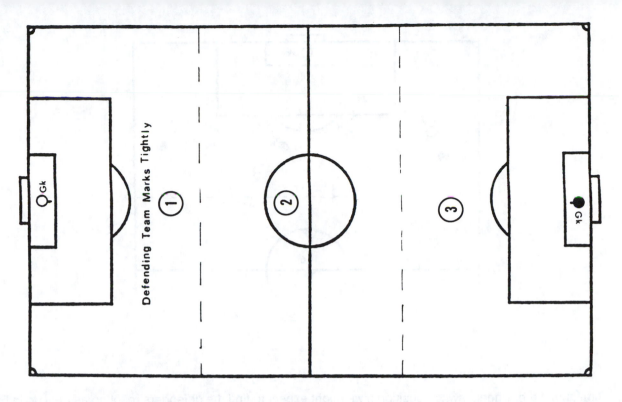

Fig. 423

Thus (Fig. 424), we might expect the White 2, 5, 4 and 3 to mark tightly, but the White 6 can afford not to close mark the Black 8 until he enters the last third of the field.

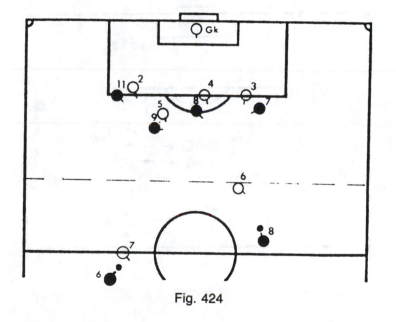

Fig. 424

The number of players who should mark on a man-to-man basis will depend largely on the number of players the opposition will throw into attack. If they play three players in their forward line, obviously at least three defenders must be detailed to mark them. Similarly, if the opposition play 4 or 5 players up front, 4 or 5 players must be detailed to mark them. Thus, we might expect to find (Fig. 425):

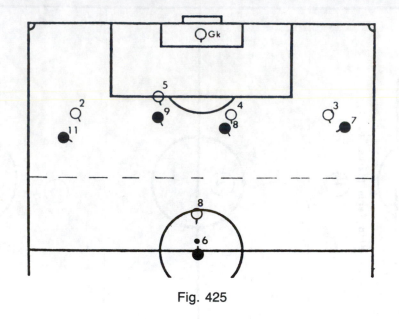

Fig. 425

Similarly, if the wingers switch positions, we might expect to find the defenders reacting as they do in Fig. 426. In other words, each defender takes up a position on a line between his immediate opponent and the goal so that whenever the opponent receives the ball, he must beat him to reach the goal. This type of defensive system demands considerable concentration from the defenders, and the exponents of the zone defense method reckon that it has grave disadvantages.

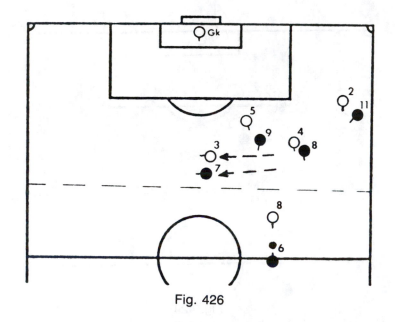

Fig. 426

Many players are born "ball-watchers" and are attracted to the ball like a pin to a magnet. As this happens, the man-to-man system breaks down as the clear forward will move on the blind side of the ball-watcher and take up a position near the goal. In Fig. 427, the White 6 is ball-watching and the Black 8 has moved on the blind side of him and taken up a dangerous position.

213

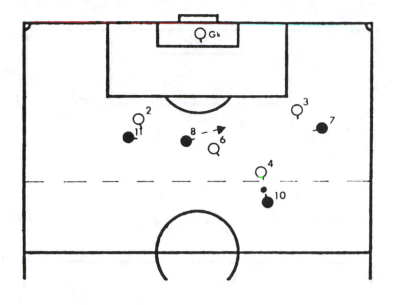

Fig. 427

A sensible approach to a man-to-man defensive system is to detail all defenders and mid-field players to mark certain opponents. Thus, with a side using a back four system with a mid-field unit of two, we might expect a picture similar to that presented in Fig. 428.

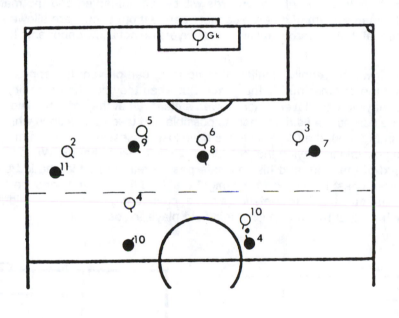

Fig. 428

The captain of the team can inform his defenders and mid-field players which opponents to mark as they line-up for the kick-off; or if the coach knows the strength and weaknesses of the opposing players before the game, he can arrange his defenders accordingly. For example, if the opposition has a very fast winger, he might choose a defender who is a very good close marker and a strong tackler to mark him. Again, if his opposition has a forward who is very good in the air, the strongest defender in the air can be detailed to mark him.

The remaining four players who have not been given specific men to mark have an important role to play in the defensive system of their team. The role is best described in the simple word — delay. It is the forwards' job to ensure that the opposing defenders take a long time in playing the ball forward. It is the forwards' task to slow down the opposition until their defenders have had time to recover and find the man they should be marking. The time of this delay may only take a few seconds, but that is sufficiently long for defenders to retreat to a position between their immediate opponent and the goal. If a coach can get his forwards to work in this way, it will make the task of his defenders considerably easier.

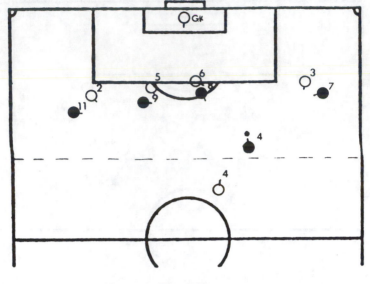

Fig. 429

The greatest problems that any defense, based on a man-to-man system, has to solve is when an opponent is allowed to "attack" them unchallenged. Thus, in Fig. 429, the Black 4 has broken clear and is bringing the ball at the White defense, who are all marking their opposite numbers tightly. The Black 4 has the choice of picking his spot and pushing a pass through for either his Black 7 or 8 to run onto, taking the ball forward and shooting, or go through himself. At some time or other, it will be necessary for one of the defenders to come and challenge him, but as soon as this happens, one of the forwards will be left unmarked and the man-to-man system destroyed. Clearly, a man-to- man system of defense cannot operate if opponents are allowed to attack them in this way. It is, therefore, essential that forwards and mid-field players do not allow opponents to go through and attack their defense.

At the same time, it will be readily admitted that no team can prevent the opposition from entering their half of the field at some time or other during the game. But when they do, the defending mid-field players and forwards should ensure that the ball player is not allowed a clear run at the defense. They should aim to get the opposition to pass square across the field as often as possible and take up positions which only allow a slow attacking build up. Thus, in Fig. 430, the Black forwards have lost possession and are aiming at making the White defense take as long as possible in playing that ball forward. It is unlikely that the White 2 will take any unnecessary risks in the last third of the field, and his only safe pass is either into the shaded area i.e. back to White 5 or GK. If he tries to dribble past the Black 11, he might well lose the ball and concede a goal. If he does pass back, this will take time and give the Black defenders a chance to re-organize. Again, mid-field players must prevent any direct approach at goal by an opposing mid-field player or defender.

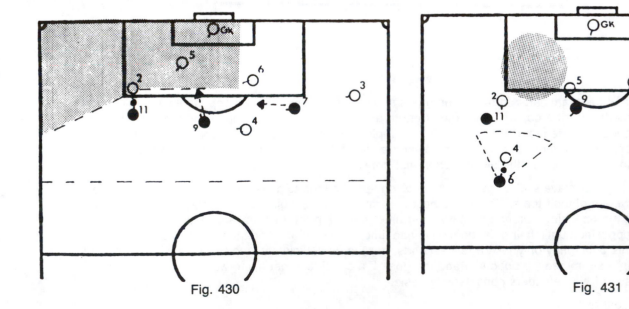

Fig. 430

Fig. 431

215

It would be a highly dangerous situation if the Black 6 was allowed to push the ball through into the shaded area for Black 11 and 9 to run onto (Fig. 431). The White 4 has made the task of the White 2 and 5 considerably easier by cutting out this possibility so that Black 6 now has to look for an alternative pass. This might mean that the Black 11 has to come back toward the Black 6 and go nearer the touch line to receive the ball from the Black 6. This obviously is far less dangerous a situation than if the Black 11 received the ball in the shaded area.

If any man is beaten in a man-to-man defense, his first task is to get back into a position between his opponent and the goal. It is essential that this recovery be made as quickly as possible, and it is well worth while spending some time in training players who have made unsuccessful tackles to get up and get back with speed. The remaining defenders are unlikely to allow the forwards free access to the goal and the nearest defender will be confronted by 2 forwards. His task should be to delay them sufficiently long for the beaten defender to recover. Thus, in Fig. 432, White 2 having been beaten, should recover as quickly as possible on a straight line back towards his own goal. The White 5 should move across to intercept the Black 11, but, at the same time, making sure that the Black 11 cannot get a pass to the Black 9. This might mean that he invites the Black 11 to go down the line rather than into the middle, and the further the Black 11 goes down the line, the more time it will give White 2 to recover. When the White 5 sees that the White 2 has recovered to mark the Black 9, he can then attempt to dispossess the Black 11.

It will be seen from the above example that unless the defenders are well-drilled, a man-to-man marking system can often be an unsafe, if not dangerous, method of defense. Many coaches are unwilling to accept the risks involved in playing a strict man-to-man defense and employ a SWEEPER to make the defenders' tasks easier.

In modern day soccer, there are two types of sweepers. The first known as the back sweeper, and the other known as the front sweeper. Most teams which use a man-to-man defense employ either a back sweeper or a front sweeper.

We have already seen that the main dangers for a defense using a man-to-man system arises out of a forward receiving the ball in the danger area; a player attacking the defenders; or simply one of the defenders being beaten. To overcome these disadvantages many teams employ a back sweeper so that we may expect the following formation (Fig. 433), with the White 4 acting as a sweeper and the other players marking on a man-to-man basis. Many pundits will argue that this system only leaves a team with three forwards, but it should be remembered that these three will be marked by four defenders only, and everything else being equal, the three playing against 4 should create more scoring opportunities than should six against seven, if only for the simple reason of having more space to work in.

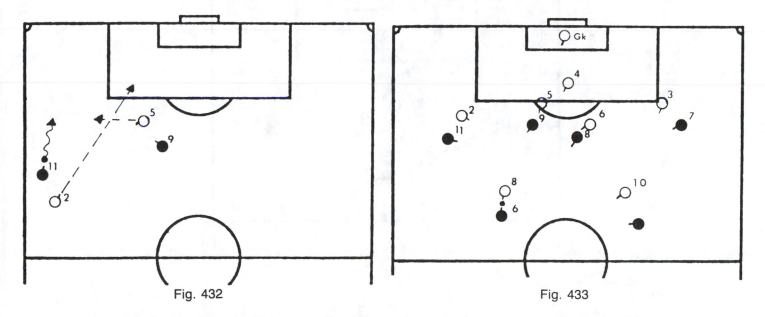

Fig. 432   Fig. 433

In choosing a back sweeper, the coach should look for a player who reads the game well. He should not be a ball watcher, but should be prepared to step into any gap left by his colleagues. Thus, in Fig. 434, the Black 4 has broken through and is attacking the White goal, so the back sweeper comes out to meet him. Alternatively, he should instruct either the White 5 or 6 to go and meet the Black 4, and he should then slot in to mark either the Black 9 or 8. Again, if any defender is beaten, then the back sweeper should be in position to mark that man so that the beaten defender can then recover and become the new back sweeper. For example, in Fig. 435, the Black 11 has beaten the White 2 so the back sweeper (4) steps in to challenge him while the White 2 recovers on a line to his own goal and becomes the new sweeper.

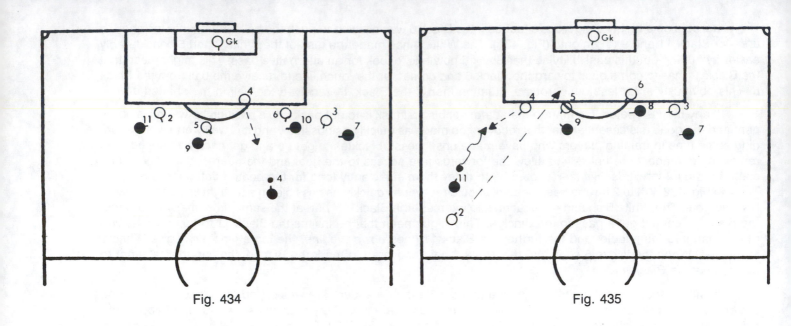

Fig. 434   Fig. 435

Teams which use a front sweeper work on the principle that, although most goals are scored in the area marked A (Fig. 436), they generally originate from passes made from the shaded area marked B. It is argued that any defense is in trouble if an opponent is allowed to collect the ball unmarked in area B and play it unhurriedly into area A. For this reason, a front sweeper, White 4, is used to make it as difficult as possible for an opponent to collect the ball unmarked in area B and play into area A.

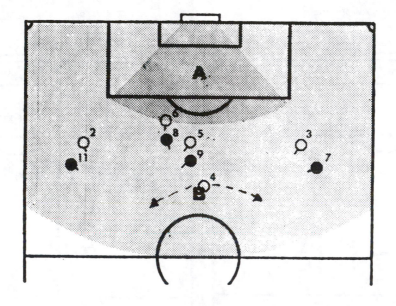

Fig. 436

Obviously, the use of either form of sweeper will make defenders' jobs considerably easier, especially if forwards and mid-field players contribute defensively by delaying and harassing. The problems for the coach seem to be to decide:

217

1. Do his players need the extra support of a sweeper?

2. Can his forwards afford to play a man short?

3. If a sweeper is to be used, which role should he fill, and,

4. Which player does he play as a sweeper?

The advantages of man-to-man marking can be summed up as:

     a) You can choose your defenders to match-up in order to nullify the opposition's strength.

     b) It is simple and requires less thinking and understanding. It could be argued that a good defender must be able to play man-to-man defense before he can play zone defense.

     c) It covers for lack of skill and understanding.

     d) It applies immediate pressure on an opponent.

The disadvantages of man-to-man defense can be summed up as:

     a) The defense can become unbalanced.

     b) It is sometimes difficult to spring counter-attacks.

     c) There can be unequal match-ups.

CHAPTER NINE

Coaching Defenders

If we are to base our defensive work on a man-to-man system of defense, our first task is to drill our defenders into concentrating on their immediate opponent rather than on the ball. This might seem a dangerous method of approach to many coaches, but really, the main problem for any coach introducing a man-to-man system of defense is to get the players to concentrate sufficiently to mark their opposite numbers.

Probably the simplest method of introduction is that illustrated in Fig. 437. The coach stands on the edge of the last 1/3 of the field with a supply of balls.

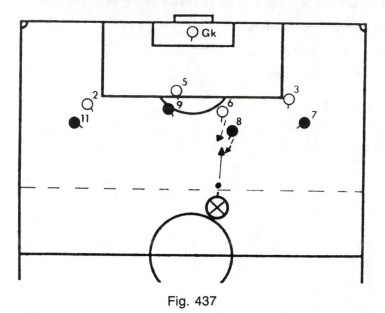

Fig. 437

He pushes a short pass to any of the four forwards who comes to collect it. Whichever forward comes for the ball, the opposing defender must come too. The defender prioritizes his position so that (1) he can intercept the pass; if not (2) to challenge and win the ball; if not (3) to mark tightly and contain his opponent.

The coach should insist here that, once a forward receives possession of the ball while facing away from goal, on no account should he be allowed to turn. The defender should stay close to the forward and, if the forward is foolish enough to turn, then the tackle should be made. Few forwards will attempt to turn with the ball when a defender is breathing down his neck, as this puts the forward at a great disadvantage — whenever he turns, he will have a less stable base than the defender, who will thus be in a position to make a strong tackle. Most forwards will, therefore, pass the ball back and this will buy time for the defenders so that they can get more men back in defense.

If the coach passes the ball to a forward near the touch line, the defender should maintain a position between that forward and his own goal (Fig. 438). In this way, even if the Black 11 or 7 receives the ball before the defender gets a chance to tackle, the avenue of approach to the goal and into the area of greatest danger will be blocked. Thus, if the ball is pushed to the Black 11, he will be unable to move the ball onto the Black 9 or turn in time to take on the White 2. The winger's safest approach will be back toward the coach or toward the touch line, both approaches which confront the defense with considerably fewer problems than if the Black 11 was allowed to turn with the ball or even flick it on to the Black 9.

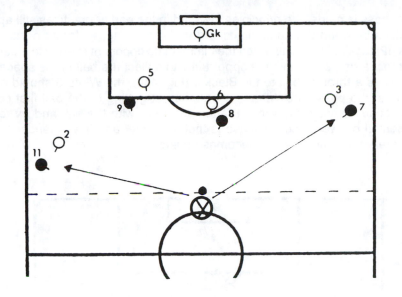

Fig. 438

The same principle applies to players in the central defensive areas (Fig. 439). At all times, they should take up a position between their own goal and their immediate opponent, and they should also position themselves so that, if the opponent goes deep to collect the ball, then that opponent should only be allowed to move with the ball away from the danger area. On no account should the Black 8 or 9 be allowed to turn to face the White goal; they should be kept moving toward the touch line or back into their own half of the field.

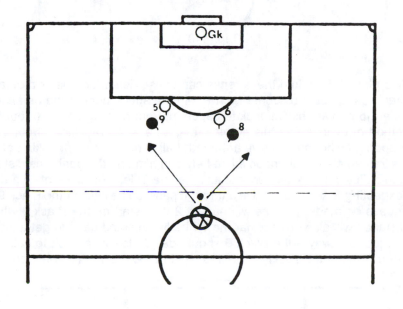

Fig. 439

A coach should spend a great deal of time with his defenders on this particular aspect of play and should insist that each of his defenders concentrates on marking his opposite number out of the game.

After defenders have had the opportunity of solving the problem involved in a forward going back to collect a pass, they should be exposed to the situation in which forwards receive a variety of passes from the coach (or server). Thus, the coach (or server) will serve long balls down the middle, through balls behind the full backs, short-balls, etc. and the defenders will be expected to react so that their goal is exposed to the least amount of danger.

Whichever type of pass is made, the principles involved in the earlier practices still apply. Defenders must always position themselves between their opponents and their goal, and, as far as possible, they should be in a position to (1) intercept, (2) tackle, (3) contain when their immediate opponent is likely to receive a pass. Defenders should also ensure that forwards never have the opportunity to collect the ball in the space behind them. Thus, if the coach (or server) plays a through ball to the Black 9 (Fig. 440), the White 5 should ensure that the Black 9 is not allowed to run onto the pass. The White 5 should aim at getting to the ball first so that he can push it back to his GK. On no account should the White 5 attempt to turn with the ball and try to dribble his way out of danger. The first essential of every good defense is that it is safe, and if a defender takes an unnecessary risk in his own penalty area, then the defense becomes unsafe.

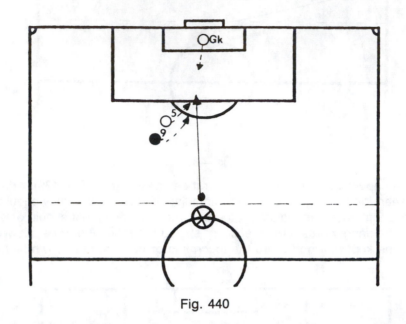

Fig. 440

The pass which is played deep into the defense can cause defenders major problems. It will be remembered from Fig. 436 that most goals are scored from within the space behind the defense and every defender must be continuously alert to prevent his immediate opponent from running onto a through ball pushed into the danger space. The method of overcoming this problem might be a contradiction of our earlier coaching, but a defender marking an opponent who may receive a through ball should not mark "skin tight". Rather, he should be in "contact" with his immediate opponent on a line between him and the goal. The distance of this "contact" will vary according to the ability of the defenders but as a general rule, a distance of 2 yards may be used. Thus, in Fig. 441, White 5 is expecting Black 9 to receive a through pass, so he lays off the Black 9 sufficiently to ensure that, should a through pass be made, then he will have a 2 yard start on the Black 9 when the ball is pushed through. This 2 yard distance will also ensure that the White 5 can stand back to get a clear view of the picture being built, and it is not too far away if the Black 9 should decide to move back to collect a short pass. If the White 5 is alert, he can still move up quickly enough to be in a position to (1) intercept, (2) tackle, (3) contain as the Black 9 receives the ball.

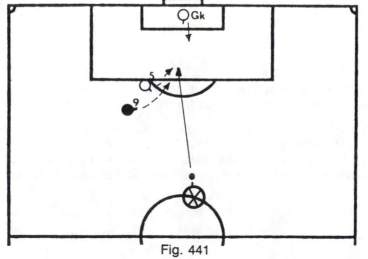

Fig. 441

The ability to mark a man close enough in order to be first to the through ball and still be in position to intercept or tackle when the short pass is made is of vital importance to any defense employing a man-to-man system. The time spent in showing players how closely to mark and where and in what circumstances to tackle is often of far greater importance to any defense than instruction in the techniques of tackling. Of course, it is still necessary for defenders to be able to tackle correctly when they decide to do so, but instruction in the techniques of tackling should only be given when weaknesses arise naturally out of the game situation.

Defenders should also learn to use the touch lines and goal-lines as additional "defenders". Thus, in Fig. 442, Black 11 has the ball near the touch line. The White 2 "invites" the Black 11 to take the ball down the line and positions himself so that it is difficult for the Black 11 to cut in toward goal. What is happening, of course, if that the Black 11 is moving further away from the danger area and the White 2 is cutting down the space in which the Black 11 can play in. When the Black 11 moves down the line, the White 2 can then make his tackle and, if necessary, push the ball out of play.

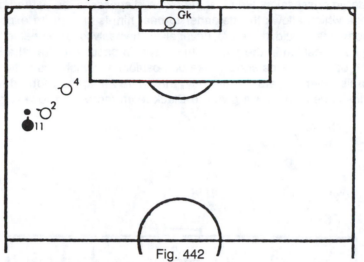

Fig. 442

We saw from the preceding chapter that one of the first principles of a good defense is DELAY! Once a side has lost possession, its first task is to get its defense organized so that it is not vulnerable to a quick counter attack by the opposition. The forwards and the mid-field players should ensure that the opposition takes a long time in building up its attack so that the defense can be quickly organized.

In Fig. 443, the White 8 and 11 have lost possession to Black 6 deep in the opponents half, and the ball is played quickly to the Black 10, who is confronted by White 4. The White defense is thus outnumbered 6-5 and it is the task of the White 4 to delay the Black attackers until the White 7 and 10 can recover into defensive positions.

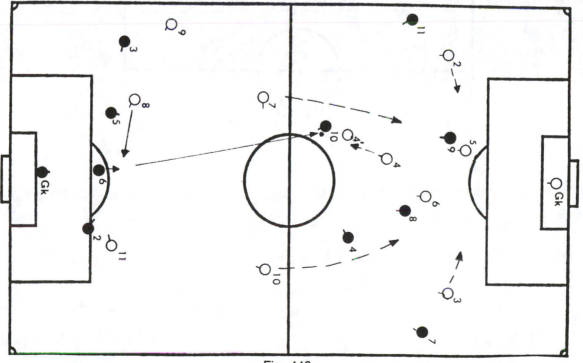

Fig. 443

There are a number of ways in which he can do this. In Fig. 443 he has taken up a position between the Black 10 and Black 4 so that the Black 10 can either move with the ball toward the Black 11, or make a square pass to the Black 4.

In either case, the White 4 will be achieving his aim of gaining time; as in the first case, a pass made to the Black 11 will be a pass made away from the danger area and a square pass to the Black 4 will achieve nothing in penetration. Clearly, the attackers will want to achieve penetration as quickly as possible while they still retain a numerical advantage, and the Black 10 must "attack" the White 4 so that he can then push the ball to the Black 4, who can, in turn, attack the defense (the problems involved — a 2 Vs 1 situation were discussed in Chapter 5).

It is obvious, the deeper inside the opponent's half that delaying tactics are used, the longer will be the time that the defense will have to get organized. It is, therefore, vital that all forwards realize the importance of tackling back. Whenever possession is lost, the forward nearest to the defender must become the "delay" man by confronting the defender in possession. He must, if he can, dispossess the defender, but it should be remembered that a wild challenge which allows the defender to beat him is enough to expose other members of the defending side. Delaying forwards should, therefore, never allow themselves to be beaten by making wild challenges. Rather, they should take up a position in the path of the player in possession, as the Black 11 has done in Fig. 444. At the same time, the other forwards should take up positions in which it is difficult for the White 2 to pass the ball forward safely to his other players. In this way, the White 2 might be forced to pass square to White 5 or back to his GK, both instances which will give the Black team more time to re-organize.

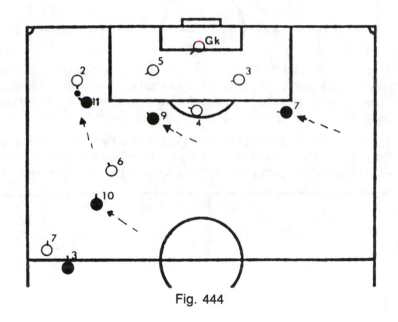

Fig. 444

CHAPTER TEN

Coaching the Game

Very often, soccer coaches discuss techniques, skills and tactics without any clear understanding of the definition of each term.

Technique - is **how** to perform an action,

Skill - is **where and when** to apply a particular technique, while

Tactics - is the means of using techniques and skills to a team's best advantage, while nullifying the opposition's strengths.

Techniques, skills and tactics follow a logical order. It is very difficult to have skills without good technique, and almost impossible to develop tactics without skills. A good coaching program should reflect a logical and progressive development plan.

From the preceding chapters, we have established: a) The demands made by the game, and b) what aspects of the game should be introduced at different age levels (or levels of maturation). We must also establish how to teach or convey our understanding of the game, at each age level, to our players. In particular, we must look at how people learn.

Much of the thinking in theories of learning originated from the work of Pavlov, a Russian physiologist. From experiments conducted with animals, Pavlov conceived the Stimulus-Response theory. He found, for example, that when a dog was fed and a bell was rung at the same time, then eventually, even when the food was withdrawn, the dog would salivate on hearing the bell. Pavlov deduced that all learning was developed in this way, i.e. repetition of stimuli would produce a conditioned response.

Indeed, much of Pavlov's theory is appropriate for learning such activities as putting the shot, or driving a golf ball. By and large, the environment and stimuli are consistent in both activities and the quest is to produce a perfect mechanical response.

What we failed to find out from Pavlov is that his experiments were unsuccessful when a whistle was blown or a different bell was rung. In other words, the stimuli had to be repeated exactly to produce the desired response.

In soccer, we can never exactly reproduce the same stimuli. The game is made up of a series of unpredictable situations in a constantly changing environment.

A survey of other researchers investigating theories of skill learning would suggest that Thorndike's Theory of Identical Elements is much more appropriate for soccer. Thorndike stated, "The amount of transfer between a practice situation and a match situation is dependent upon the degree of similarity between the practice and the match. The greater the degree of similarity, then the greater the degree of transfer."

Thorndike is simply making a commonsense statement. To learn to play soccer, we must play (or practice) soccer. As coaches, we must place our players during practice sessions in situations which resemble as closely as possible those situations in which they find themselves in during the game.

If exposed to such situations, a player will learn to focus his attention on relevant cues within the display that will lead him to take a successful course of action.

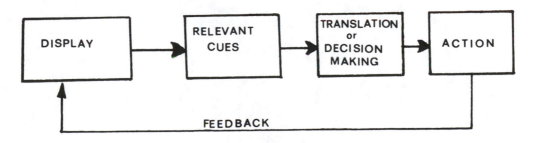

Fig. 445

These cues are translated within his mind and a decision is reached which leads to a certain action. Further cues then become available based on the success, or otherwise, of his course of action (feedback). (Fig. 445)

Our coaching must follow this model. The coach cannot make the decisions. He can help set up the display (create the practice); help the player to recognize, choose or ignore cues; give him options to use in solving problems; but at no time can the coach make the decisions or determine the course of action to be taken by a player. A program of drills in which the player is not allowed any freedom of decision is restrictive and harmful.

To achieve the optimal transfer of training from practice to match situations, we should have the following ingredients in each practice:

A ball

Decision making by the player

Rules of the game (or modified rules)

In addition, we should seek to include as many of the following ingredients as possible:

Opposition

Team mates

Area

Direction

Goal or target

The younger the player, then the fewer opponents and teammates should be included in the practices (and matches).

All practices in this book have included as many of the above ingredients as possible. Each practice has been accompanied by information on the encouragement the coach should give to the player(s) to improve his response to the problem presented. It should be stressed, yet again, that whenever possible each player should find his own successful solution to the problem inherent in the practice.

No player should be drilled in practice, or required to produce the coach's interpretation of the technique or skill demanded by the practice. Drills lead to unimaginative, regimented players and teams, and REGIMENTATION KILLS IMAGINATION.

Encourage your players to be **The Best They Can Be** through enjoyable, stimulating and challenging practices where the players themselves find solutions to the demands of the game.

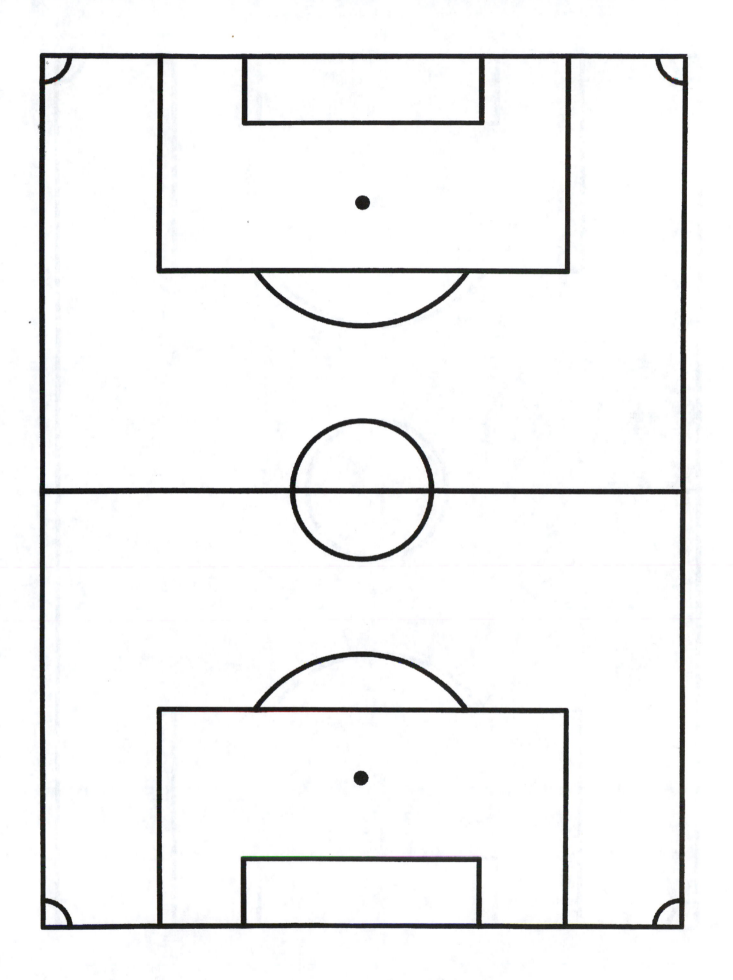

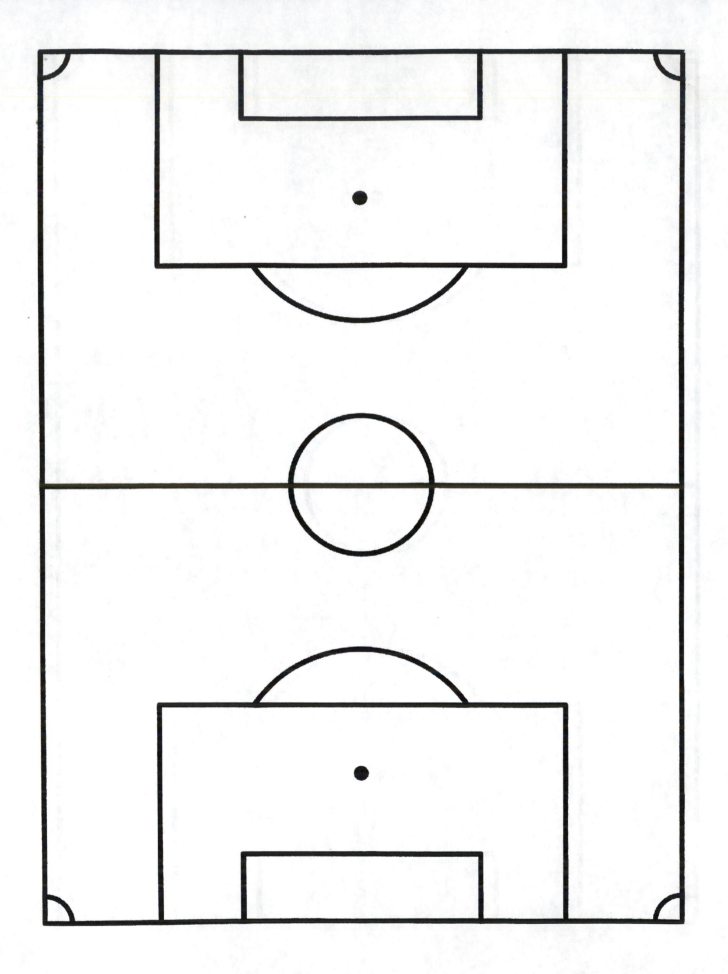

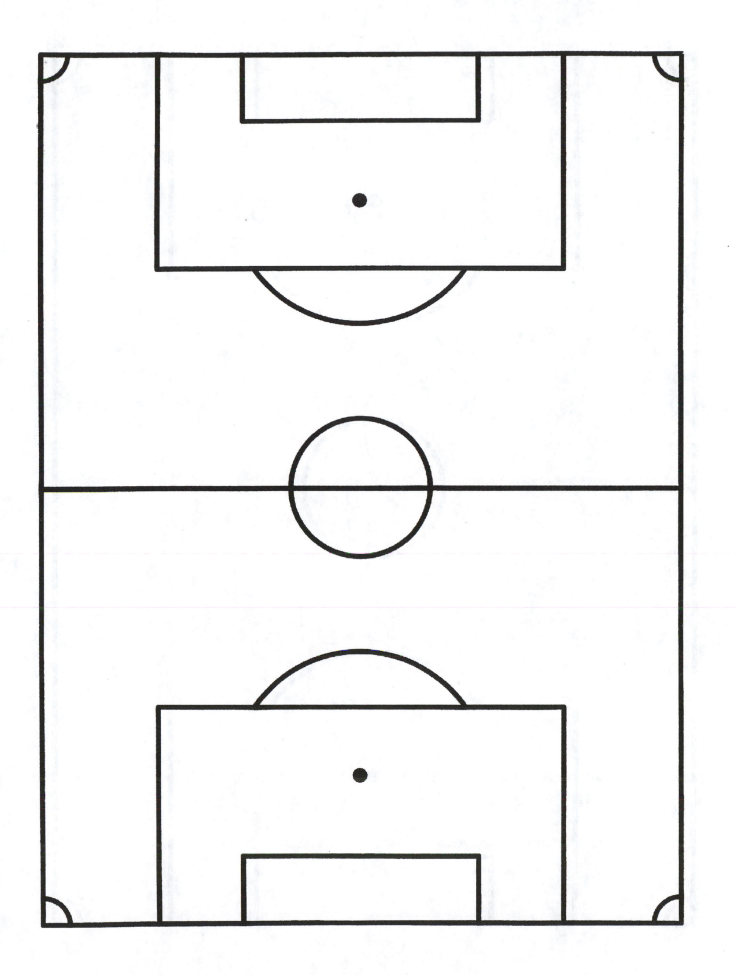

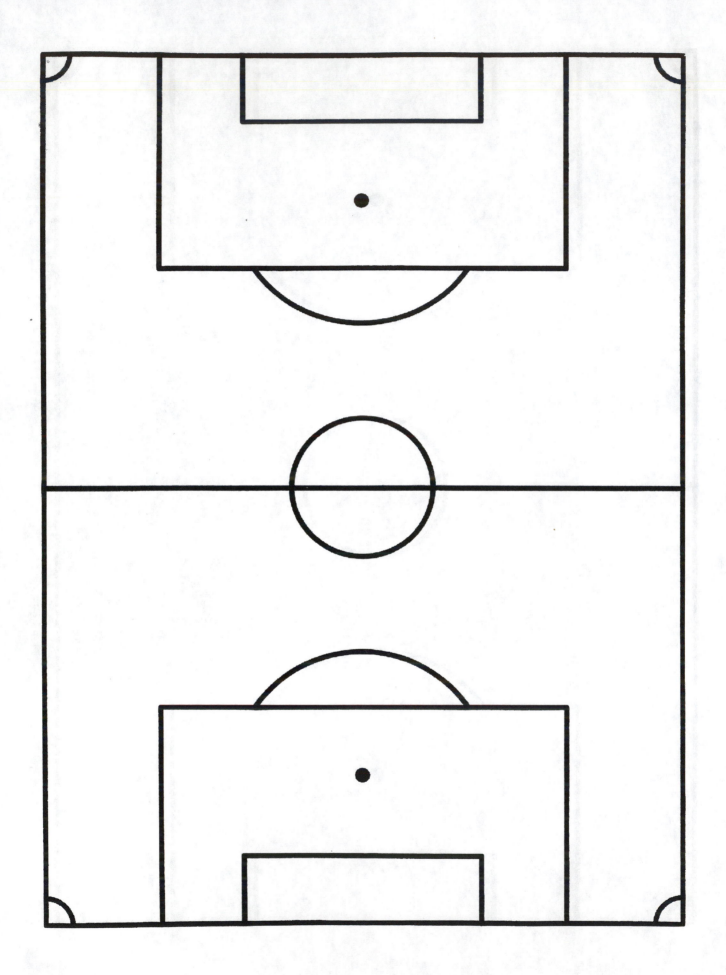

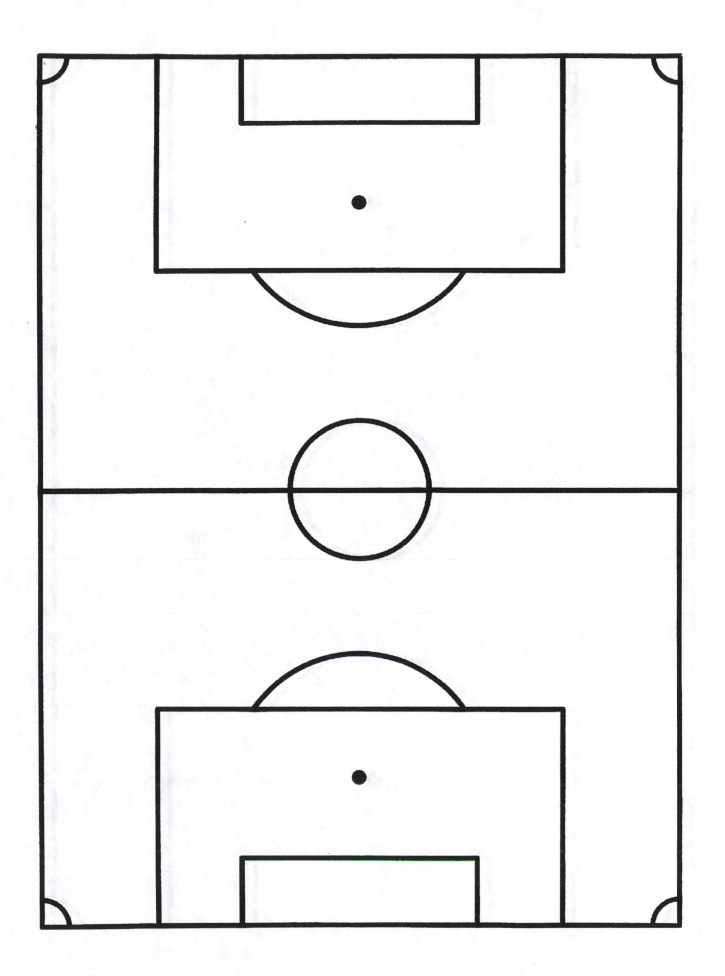

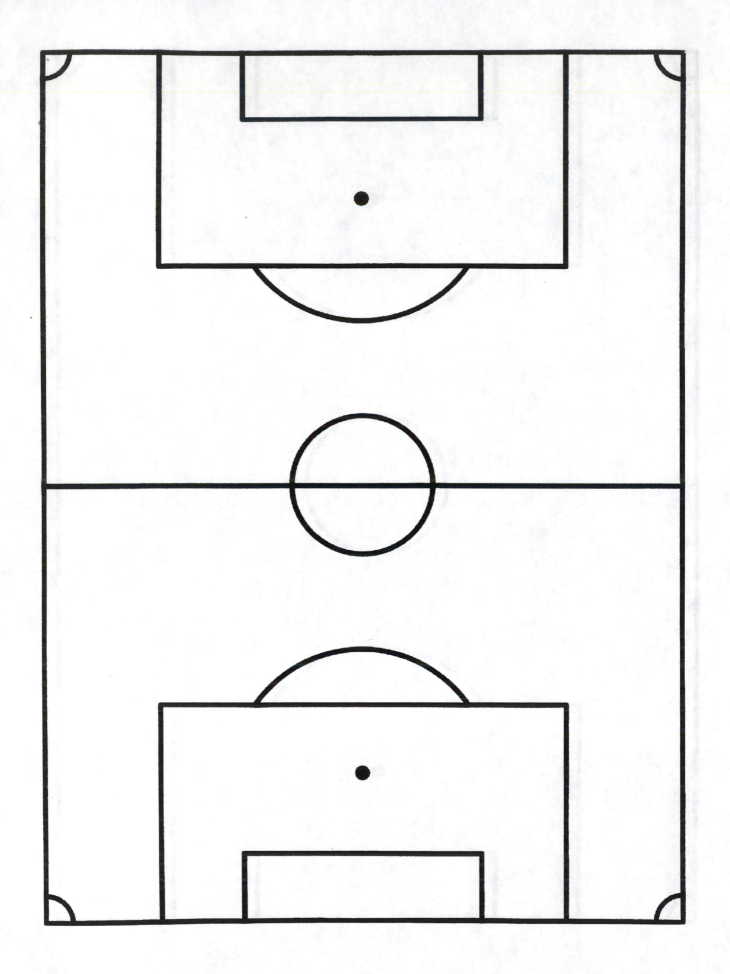

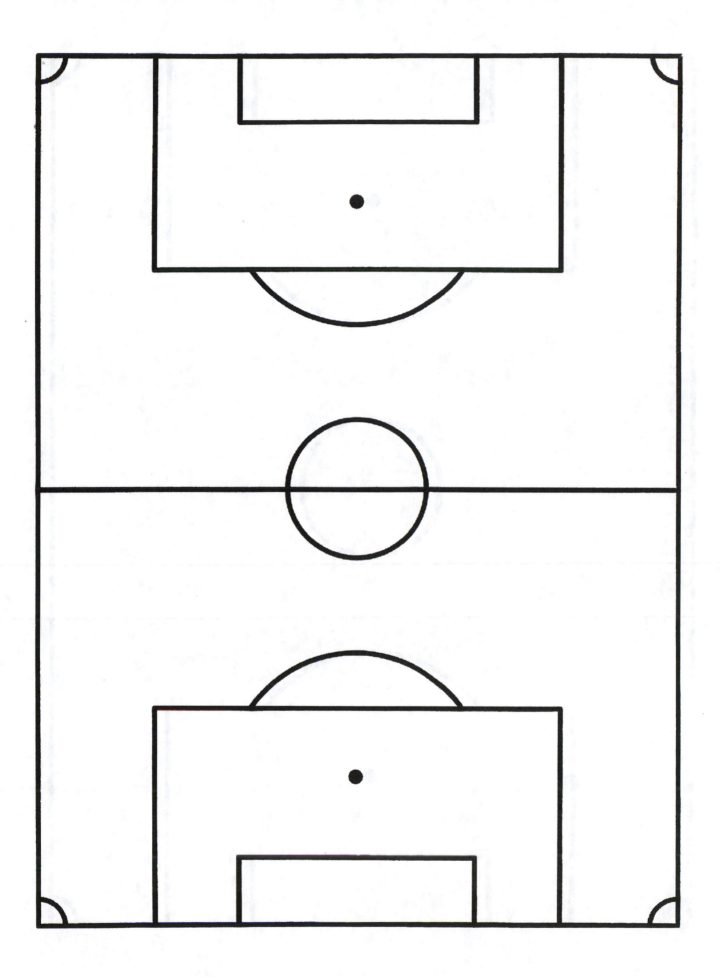

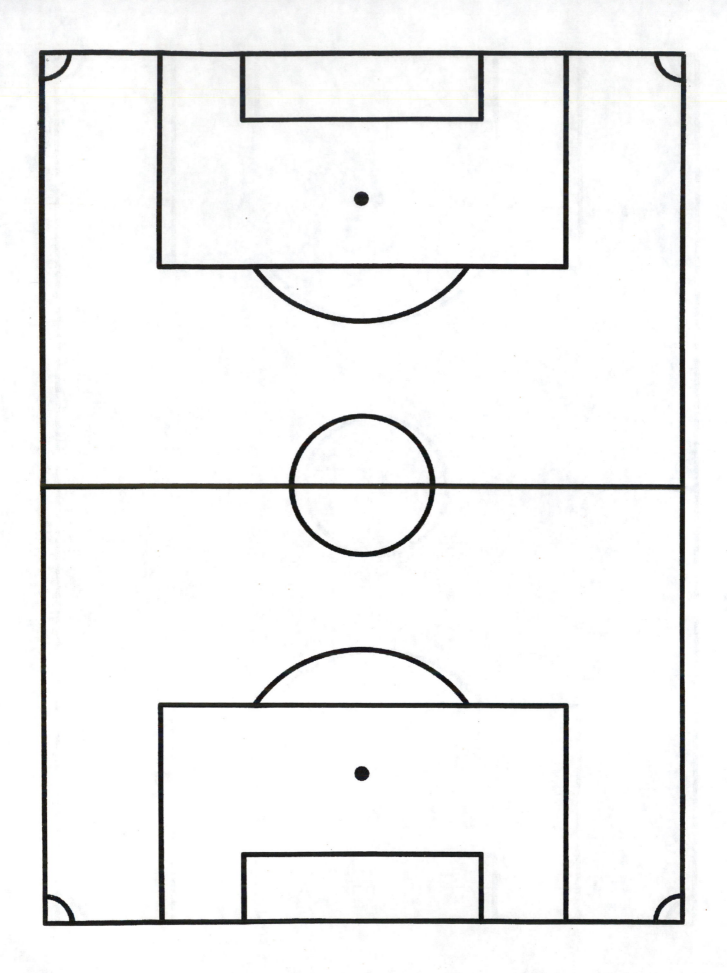